D0856652

DISCARD

EASTERN PHILOSOPHY

EASTERN PHILOSOPHY

Chakravarthi Ram-Prasad

WEIDENFELD & NICOLSON
LONDON

For Judith

First published in Great Britain in 2005
by Weidenfeld & Nicolson

10 9 8 7 6 5 4 3 2 1

A CIP catalogue record for this book is available from the British Library.

ISBN 0 297 84744 9

Design by www.carrstudio.co.uk
Printed and bound in Great Britain by Clays Ltd, St Ives plc

Weidenfeld & Nicolson

The Orion Publishing Group Ltd
Orion House
5 Upper Saint Martin's Lane
London, WC2H 9EA
www.orionbooks.co.uk

Contents

Acknowledgements

This book has benefited from my engagement with many scholars over the years. Roger Ames and Chad Hansen have been generous with their time; my understanding of Chinese philosophy is heavily influenced by them, and their classic works have given me my orientation in that field. Arindam Chakrabarti, Roy Perrett, Mark Siderits, Stephen Phillips and Richard Sorabji continue to discuss Indian philosophy with me, patient in their response to many 'quick' emails and phone calls on the big issues; Frank Clooney, Julius Lipner and Laurie Patton bring in perspectives from the larger questions of Indian thought. Jonardon Ganeri's work has been invaluable in its sharp focus on Indian logic and language.

The Department of Religious Studies, Lancaster University, has been a wonderful environment in which to tackle cross-cultural studies.

Richard Milbank has been very helpful in seeing this book through to publication. Ben Dupré has been a truly wonderful editor. If this book is anywhere near readable, it is because of him; if not, it is my fault.

Finally, of course, I would like to thank my family for their enthusiasm and support; most of all, Judith, to whom I dedicate this book.

Introduction

This book will be somewhat unusual – in the manner, one might suppose, of a rationalist exploration of ghosts – in starting with a denial of the existence of its subject matter. There is no such thing as Eastern philosophy. Well, obviously, as the reader will immediately notice, that statement is artfully vague. There is no *one* such thing as Eastern philosophy.

Although there are many difficulties with the notion of the West, Western philosophy does have a certain historical integrity to it. By historical integrity, I mean the awareness that later thinkers possess of the work, significance and presuppositions of earlier ones. If history had run differently – if the Greek tradition had not been recovered in Christian Europe after the so-called Dark Ages that followed the collapse of the Roman Empire – there might have been no such combination of Judaeo-Christian and Hellenic thought that we now call 'Western philosophy'. Sometimes there is mutual incomprehension between Western traditions, as when 'analytic' and 'Continental' philosophers talk past each other. But they all refer back with familiarity to the same figures, from Plato to Kant. Moreover, modern thinkers like Wittgenstein are incorporated into very different styles and systems of Western philosophy. It is common awareness of tradition, if not common goals and intellectual values, that allows something like Western philosophy to exist, even if its borders are diffuse and its contents diverse.

There is mutual ignorance between the Indian and Chinese thought worlds; there is no cross-fertilization between these civilizations. The interpreters of Confucius and the Upanisads know as little about each other as they do about Plato. In fact, there is intriguing evidence that there might have been historical contact between ancient Indian and Greek thinkers, with parallel developments in their philosophies, but none with China. The evidence of parallel development and the many independent similarities between Greek and Indian thought have even led some experts to think that the great distinction is actually between Chinese and 'Indo-European' philosophical cultures. Certainly, their common linguistic inheritance suggests that these two traditions share a common 'language' that is very different from Chinese. As I hope this book will show, the fundamental concerns, conceptual frameworks and goals of the Indian and Chinese traditions are utterly different; it is only a romantic illusion that there is some common, mystical 'wisdom tradition' that bound these cultures together and differentiated them from the West. All too often, India and China could be made to resemble each other only by imposing on them the alien structures of early modern Western thought!

So, there is no history of mutual discourse and debate between India and China. The one truly pan-Asian tradition is Buddhist religion, but its philosophy does not quite make that transition. Buddhist philosophy emerges in the specific context of the existing intellectual and social culture of the priestly brahmin class that we now see as the source of mainstream Hinduism. Some Buddhist schools are often closer to Hindu schools on a variety of issues than to others of their own religion. Their preoccupations survive the spread to Tibet, but already a change has occurred: the Tibetans are seldom interested in engaging with Hindu philosophies, as there are no Hindus in Tibet. Instead, they compete to interpret the same Buddhist materials. The Buddhism that spreads to China does initially carry native Indian theories and techniques, but soon the basic positions of the transplanted Buddhist schools are re-expressed in Chinese terms, doubtless expanding the

Chinese philosophical vocabulary but nonetheless speaking to concerns that make sense only within China. In Japan, Buddhism accommodates itself to native Shinto concepts. In other words, Buddhism does not make India, China and Japan speak to each other; it speaks to each of them in their own tongue. So, too, Neo-Confucianism is common, but confined, to East Asia, in particular China, Japan and Korea.

The lack of a common 'East', however, should be treated not as a problem but as a wonderful opportunity for creative and novel comparison. The inescapable fact of the cultural preponderance of the West in global communication has naturally meant that efforts to think across cultures have followed the pattern of reacting to the West: comparing and contrasting, arguing across and harmonizing Western philosophy with one or another 'non-Western' philosophy. There is worth to that; but possibly the time has come for global philosophy to move beyond the model where the West is at the centre of radiating spokes of comparison. A different metaphor should come into play, of a skein of friendly introductions and conversations at a buzzing party, where rich and poor, the powerful and the marginal, people of different colours and clothes and experiences, meet and move amongst each other.

This book is an opportunity for an Indian philosopher to politely introduce himself to the East Asian traditions, asking if perhaps they can turn away a moment from Western philosophy themselves, to engage in an all-too-rare conversation between the 'Easts'. Perhaps, once Indian and Chinese philosophies learn to talk to each other on their own terms – as this book tries to make them do – they can then bring their somewhat better-developed knowledge of Western philosophy to bear on the task of doing truly global philosophy. But that is the work of many books still waiting to be written!

General notes

Eschewing references, I have tried to introduce the actual words of the philosophers of the various traditions into the body of the discussion. Furthermore, to draw attention to the philosophy rather than the philosophers, I have sometimes referred to the position of schools in general rather than name specific philosophers. This is often the case with Indian schools. In classical China, texts are often named after single thinkers but are in fact a combination of a core of original writing and an accretion of later material by anonymous followers. I have followed the custom of talking as if the view in question were that of the specific philosopher to whom the corpus is attributed.

There are lacunae even within this relatively modest undertaking: geographical traditions such as the Tibetan and the Korean have been given little or no attention, and many areas that may legitimately be considered philosophy, especially aesthetics, have largely been neglected. Philosophy of religion has been rendered marginal, because of the profound worry that such a category makes no sense in East Asian culture. Many of the exclusions doubtless have to do with my own limitations. Also, this is by no means a comprehensive textbook. I have not sought to state every school's view on every topic that the traditions discuss. In general, I have chosen to write more deeply on fewer topics and thinkers, rather than give a whistle-stop tour of the very crowded landscape of Asian philosophy over 3000 years. The aim has been to give a sense of the range and depth of these philosophical cultures, as well as their sophistication and originality; and when useful, to make comparisons between these cultures to illuminate further their varied yet potentially universal appeal. Also, since recent Asian philosophy is still seeking its own distinctive voice in the contemporary world dominated by modern Western thought, and would in any case make little sense without knowledge of the traditional sources, I have confined this study to the classical, pre-modern period.

For those who are interested in the precise use of terms, by 'India' I mean that broad region now encompassed by the term 'South Asia', with a heartland in the Indo-Gangetic plain, extending east to what is now Bengal and west to Afghanistan, and encompassing the peninsula of what is now South India. The 'Indian philosophy' referred to is the thought of the culture pre-dating and standing outside Indian Islam; it refers to the traditions now identified within the religious categories of Hinduism, Buddhism and Jainism, although the Hindu schools did not think of themselves in any such unified way. 'China' is a less problematic category, although modern China includes many ethnicities that do not have a common past with the demographically and politically dominant Han people. Chinese philosophy is the heritage of the Han.

For Chinese words, the Pinyin system has been followed. Sanskrit has been spelt in the standard academic way but without diacritics. In both cases, admittedly, this makes pronunciations a matter of specialist knowledge, but the apparatus required to clarify them would have either been too elaborate or deviated too much from the matter in hand. I have given the original words for key terms, especially when there is much scholarly debate on them. (It should be noted that many very different Chinese ideographs have the same pronunciation. As a result, very different concepts, such as 'potency' and 'virtuosity', are both *de*; 'ritual' and 'pattern' are both *li*; and so on.)

1

Ultimate Questions and Answers

What are ultimate questions? They are questions of such a kind that philosophers, having once asked them, assume that they have reached the furthest limits of their task of understanding and explanation. They simply do not find anything more fundamental – anything that needs answering in advance of these questions. The answers philosophers give to these questions provide meaning for everything else they have to say. They may not always start with these questions and answers, and they may not always wish to present these answers explicitly as a foundation for their views, but nothing else would make sense unless these questions had some answers in their systems and teachings. If they left these questions unanswered, we would feel there was no point in following them through the rest of what they have to say. Ultimate answers involve ideas that we need to understand in order to see why a philosophy exists and what it aims to achieve. In subsequent chapters, we will look at the purposes of philosophy and the ends it seeks. But before that, we need to explore these ultimate questions, without which we would not see what any philosophy was about.

It has been necessary to give the framework for this chapter in highly abstract and general terms – in terms of questions and answers, rather than something more substantial and direct, like ultimate truths or ultimate reality. If ultimate reality is to do with whatever is really there, or whatever it is that makes the world what it is, then, as we will soon see, Chinese philosophy simply does not concern itself with an ultimate reality; but it does ask questions of the most fundamental significance. It poses ultimate questions without ever concerning itself with ultimate realities.

At this stage, an important concept from Western philosophical terminology needs to be introduced: metaphysics. Metaphysics is the investigation of the structure of reality. It is the study of the most general and necessary characteristics that any particular entity must possess in order to be an entity (or even, that particular entity). The emphasis on the *most* general must be noted. Many branches of science would seek to determine the identity of entities, such as dogs and planets, but metaphysics deals with the fundamental questions that science can only presuppose. For instance, in the case of planets and other objects of science, metaphysics would ask if there are physical objects at all in the first place and what would count as such objects in general. For this reason, in the West metaphysics has traditionally been called the 'first' philosophy.

Metaphysics seeks to understand reality such that we can make sense of the world as we encounter it. These ways of under-standing may only be interpretations of things encountered in the world ('what is time?', 'what are numbers?') or they may be about entities whose existence is supposed to make sense of that world (God, fate, objects-in-themselves that are never experienced yet make experience possible, and many ever more puzzling and abstruse things).

Metaphysics, then, is driven by the need to ask what really makes up the world that we live in. An example of a typical question would be 'Is there really a world of things external to us that we seem to perceive, or is it all in our mind?' The crucial connection between such questions is that they all wonder what things are really, *really* like, what makes them the way they are. The metaphysician is dissatisfied with taking the world just as it is perceived, and asks not only what *makes up* the world but what *makes* it the way it is. What makes up the world is then explored in terms of the most basic constituents of the world, be they physical or non-physical, mental or material, abstract or concrete. The deeper question is what makes the world the way it is. Do things function the way they do because of their own intrinsic nature or because some further power makes them function that way? And is that power internal or external to things? And so on.

Why is the metaphysician dissatisfied with taking the world just as it is met with in experience? Possibly, it is a consequence of the worry that things may not be what they seem. There may be more to reality than appears to be the case. Much of metaphysics really turns on this possible dichotomy between reality and appearance. The most extreme form of this split is in the thought that what is present in experience may be wholly different from what is really there. I take myself to be sitting here and looking at a computer; but am I really sitting here with a computer in front of me, or am I dreaming it? Even if I am not dreaming, is the collection of sensations I have of seeing, touching and hearing anything like what is really outside my senses? These are questions that imply a radical split between what appears to be the case and what might really be there. Of course, this split may be less radical than my worries imply. The metaphysician may just want to ask whether what is experienced is all there is, or whether it is made up of more fundamental entities that explain experience but are not themselves self-evident in experience. It may be true that Judith is standing next to me, but is there just a single, concrete person there, or is there some complex co-presence of form, existence and other essential attributes that together make up that person (even if I do not see those attributes separately)? Another example would be the question of whether the patterns of people's lives – their joy and sorrow, their triumphs and suffering – are all there is to life, or whether there is some further principle that gives meaning to that life.

Such a basic understanding of metaphysics allows us to see that many ultimate questions are likely to be metaphysical. Certainly, the ultimate questions that the brahmanical or Hindu philosophical schools ask are metaphysical. In a more ambiguous way – which we will have to explore carefully – the Buddhist question of the ultimate is also metaphysical. But the classical or early Chinese thinkers we study do not ask metaphysical questions.

To say straightaway how I propose to describe classical Chinese philosophy, I would call it *a*metaphysical. As we look at Confucianism and Daoism in particular, we will see that the ultimate questions they ask are not about reality. They do not seek to determine how things really are. The classical Chinese philosophers reveal no anxiety or dissatisfaction with the existence and structure of the world as they encounter it. Their dissatisfaction – their sense that there is a challenge yet to be met – has to do with how people act in the world. Their attention, then, is on action in this world, not on knowledge of it. Of course, they do set out to gain knowledge of many things, but these are to do with how to *act* in the world.

It would not be helpful to think that Chinese philosophy of the classical period *lacks* metaphysics. It is not as if the Chinese failed in an attempt to ask questions about the structure of reality that they ought to have asked. But it is difficult for those looking at Chinese thought from Western and Indian perspectives to avoid thinking in terms of their own categories and finding these missing in China. A good example would be the issue of the split between reality and appearance. To even say that Chinese philosophers do not distinguish between appearance and reality makes it look as if here was a problem that the Chinese failed to recognize. We might just about say that there is no reality–appearance split in the native Chinese tradition, for that is accurate; but we are still caught in a terminology alien to China. The best thing would be to say that Chinese thought sets out to ask ultimate questions in a way that is an alternative to the metaphysical. The ametaphysical is a different, legitimate and coherent way of asking questions about ultimate value, and it does so in terms that address situations in the world as we encounter it.

There is a positive way of putting it: Chinese thought is based on metaethics, which is the study of the concepts, methods and assumptions of ethical issues such as the nature of goodness and right action. Let us see how ultimate questions in China are metaethical (and ametaphysical), rather than metaphysical.

To start with a simple but major distinction, whereas Indian philosophy (like its Greek and later Western counterpart) tends to be driven initially by the question 'What is there (really)?', Chinese philosophy tends to ask 'What should be done?' The former question is, as we have seen, metaphysical. The latter question is about ethics in all the traditions: what is the good (the best end) that is sought, what is the correct thing to do in its pursuit, and so on. Behind the ethical questions of thinkers in India and the West still lies metaphysics. When they ask at the next level of reflection 'Why should it (whatever 'it' is) be done?', they answer 'Because reality is (ultimately) such that it should be done.' In other words, their goal is an answer to the metaphysical question 'What is really there?' (This is so even when they conclude that there is nothing there, or that whatever is there does not directly determine what we should do; the important point is that they do recognize the metaphysical question in the first place.) Underlying ethical issues is an interest in the structures of reality that give shape to the issues. For example, seeking to help others might be an ethical goal, but why is it so? Because a god commanded it or because of something in the world that makes it so? What are the *facts* about the nature of reality that allow us to attach a *value* to helping others? Or they may ask whether facts are ever relevant to value. Ethical questions, in the end, require some sort of an answer to how things fundamentally are, and such an answer is metaphysical.

In China, on the other hand, the question 'What should be done?' may be answered in diverse ways, drawing on many different and often incompatible considerations, and is followed by an assessment of those answers and the ways in which those answers emerge. The next level of reflection – 'Why should it (whatever 'it' is) be done?' – leads to answers along the lines 'Because we can (ultimately) find guidance for what should be done.' The philosophers generally do not ascend to the metaphysical question, because they still focus on ethics. The important point is that the Chinese tradition assumes that the issue of how to act (in the world as we find it) exhausts the reaches of philosophy. The great challenge is to know how to act. To the Chinese philosophers it would have seemed beside the point to ask whether or not something about the world actually determined how we are to act, for what they were concerned with at all times was action in the world. For them, the ultimate questions have to do with the very idea, motives and goals with which we seek to learn what should be done. That is why I call their 'higher-order' thinking – that is, their thinking about their thinking – 'metaethics'; and because it simply offers an alternative way of thinking about life, I also characterize it as 'ametaphysical'. Whereas in modern Western usage metaethics is an academic examination of ethical doctrines and the grounds for their justification, for classical Chinese thinkers it was a reflection on and assessment of the worth of our ideas of ethical conduct, leading to answers of ultimate value.

With this important idea that Indian thought is basically metaphysical and Chinese metaethical in their respective ultimate concerns, we can turn to looking at some of the important schools within these traditions.

The world: its structure in Indian systems of thought

The earliest attempt to account for reality in a systematic way is found in the school of Sankhya. This speculative system is philosophically interesting in that it posits a basic dualism: reality is made up of two fundamental principles – spirit and matter. It then provides an account of how the two interact to create the things of and in the world, but the intriguing point is that this account can simultaneously be read as the development of either the universe or the human psyche. Spirit acts initially to make inert matter dynamic; thereafter it is passive, purely a witness to the evolution of matter and working only through the things that result. Matter develops through its three constituent natures – the pure, the active and the passive. Intelligence, ego (consciousness of a sense of 'I') and the sensory means of gaining knowledge are all results of the pure nature being dominant in certain evolutionary processes. The gross elements that make up objects, as well as space and time, come from the passive nature of matter. The agency and energy through which intelligence actually interacts with objects is provided by the active nature of primeval matter. Thereafter, spirit is aware of the functioning of intelligence and its grasp on objects, and so is implicated in matter; but it remains fundamentally different from it. One can see how this might be either a general account of how the world and life came to be, or a specific theory of how the consciousness of the individual develops. In either case, this speculative system, despite many elaborations, gradually lost ground. Its basic realism and pluralism – the idea that there is an irreducible and ultimate structure to the material world, and many, again irreducible, individual spirits – were replaced by other systems with similar metaphysical commitments but which deemed its simple account of the world insufficient. We will now turn to the composite Nyaya–Vaisesika school, whose analysis of reality came to be adopted by most philosophers who accepted pluralism and realism.

We have a patient categorizing of reality by the Nyaya and Vaisesika schools, which later came together to form a composite school. Their aim, refined over 12 or 13 centuries, is to develop a commonsensical analysis of things. As has often been noted in both East and West, commonsensical views of reality rarely remain commonsensical, either because they cease being commonsensical when they search for consistency or because common sense is not very consistent anyway. But Nyaya-Vaisesika categories of reality are instructive because they start without any denial of the world as we encounter it. Even while Nyaya-Vaisesika philosophers seek to understand the structures of reality, they are adamant that we already do directly experience that reality. Of course, reality is not exhausted by what we ordinarily experience with our senses, since it is ultimately made up of things beyond the senses. Nevertheless, ordinarily encountered reality is not made up of something hidden from the powers of reasoning. In short, this school puts forward a logical view of reality, claiming that upon reflection its categories are evident to anyone.

Nyaya-Vaisesika makes the general claim that things are more or less (given the mistakes our senses normally make) what we experience them to be, and reality is not, ultimately, so very different from our experience of it. There are substantial objects out there that are independent of us: these have a nature that is essential to them and makes them what they are, and they are continuous and persistent just as our senses take them to be.

Vaisesika ontology (the classification of what there is) is built up of a cascading series of categories and their constituents, and we cannot examine them all in any detail. However, the major classifications are worth noting for their philosophical significance. To start with, we must understand that the classification is not of ordinary objects – trees, cows, tables – as such; it is of entities that render experienced objects intelligible. The attempt is to explore the structure of reality. The starting-point is the object as it is experienced. The issue now is to define the constituents of the object in logical terms (rather than in merely material terms, which would be the task of science). There is a distinction to be made, then, between *objects* (which we experience) and *entities* (which structure them).

These entities come under six basic categories: substance, quality, motion, universal/genus, particular/species, and inherence. A further category, absence, was posited some centuries later.

(1) **Substance** A substance is a thing that exists through possessing qualities and motion and therefore precedes them in existence. It is the substratum of changes. Ordinary objects of experience are impermanent substances, in that they perish after periods of stability; but their constituents (the universals and particulars – see below) remain permanently without decay. Substances are not just material components of objects: earth, water, fire and air. There are also immaterial substances: time, place, self and mind. The immaterial substances, in particular, are philosophically interesting. Take the distinction between the self and the mind, as two different substances. The latter is seen as a separate immaterial substance that is used by the self as the means of perceiving its own states (as opposed to the external senses of the body that the self uses to perceive the material world, including the body itself). The self, on the other hand, is merely the entity that has a mind.

(2) **Quality** Qualities reside (are located) in substances, and never found independently of them. Twenty-four qualities are eventually listed. Some are qualities of the self alone. There are material qualities, like the five external senses; and immaterial ones, like the psychological states of pleasure and pain, desire, effort and aversion. The cognitive ability of judgement that marks the mind (which we will remember is an immaterial substance) is itself an immaterial quality. Other qualities are relational between two different substances, like proximity, distance and contact. Size and shape are, of course, qualities. And there are dispositional qualities, too, which explain why substances behave the way they do: weight, fluidity, viscosity, elasticity, and so on.

A striking feature of this ontology is the inclusion of values in the list of qualities: merit and demerit are qualities that become attached to selves as a consequence of the moral actions they perform, and are manifested in both moral and non-moral consequences. We will return to this inclusion of the moral in metaphysics when we come to consider the Mimamsa school.

(3) **Motion** This is specific to any substance, and brings about contact and separation between substances. It is analysed into various orientations (upwards, downwards, etc.), transformations (expansion, contraction), and locomotion.

(4) **Universal/genus** Universals are generic entities that bring particulars together into a single class. So 'horsehood' is a universal that is common to (and only to) certain particular objects, which for that reason are horses. There can be many levels of universals ('mammalhood' groups particulars at a higher level than 'horsehood'), until the highest universal is reached, namely 'existence'. This is identified by later Nyaya logicians with the notion of 'being': to say that there is a reality made up of things is to say that all things fall under the class defined by the universal 'existence'. Some class concepts, such as 'tablehood' and 'studenthood', are created by us, but there are universals that are independent of us. It is because a universal like 'cowhood' is real that we can have experience of individual things that we identify as 'cows'. (The Nyaya philosophers note that we may *name* the universal, but as an aspect of reality that fixes the commonality of some group of objects, it is real independently of what we call it, whether we call it anything at all or whether we are even around to call it anything. Also, there is some debate over whether a universal is located only in the particulars that come under it or whether the universal itself exists independently.)

(5) **Particular/species** Particulars are indivisible entities that are intrinsically distinguishable from one another, and have no further components: the particularities of material things are 'atoms' – not actual small physical particles but 'ultimate entities, whatever they are' that are required for objects to exist. (They might be compared to points in mathematics, logical requirements rather than actual things that we can experience.)

(6) **Inherence** This is a category that goes well beyond the obvious, and yet starts from a commonsensical question: is there something by virtue of which certain entities are always found together? For example, why are qualities never found independently but only in a substance – why is there no black as such, only being found in and as a black cow or bird or stone? Why can there never be a whole object (like a pot) without constituents (like clay)? The answer is that things that are inseparable are so because of a specific relationship between them, called inherence. Qualities inhere in substances, the whole inheres in its parts. Inherence then becomes a powerful concept to explain why things go together the way they do. The problem is that we are not sure if this is something we actually see, or infer, or just make up as a way to explain the world.

(7) **Absence** An extraordinary aspect of later Nyaya metaphysics is the claim that 'absence' is itself a part of reality. Once embarked on this line of thought, many different kinds of absence come to be seen as part of reality. There is prior absence (the ground before the plant grew), destructional absence (the ground after the tree is cut down), absolute absence (a singing, dancing tree), mutual absence (the tree not being a boulder, and *vice versa*).

This sustained and rigorous effort to say what is ultimately real starts with the observation that it is obvious that the world we experience is real as it is. But that is not sufficient guarantee that our conclusions about what makes up reality will be equally obvious. Indeed, commonsense realism about the world – it is what we encounter – leads to some very uncommon metaphysics indeed.

We will end this section on realist schools of metaphysics – those that take the material, experienced world as having an irreducible and ultimate structure – with a short consideration of the Mimamsa school. Although the Mimamsa philosophers seek to prove that the material world is ultimate, with no further reality (including God) required, they do not set about trying to analyse the components of that world. They are more concerned to defend the need to act – especially to perform rituals laid down in the sacred texts (the Vedas) – so as to uphold order. And this is the interesting aspect of their view of ultimate reality. They argue not only for a material world but also for an order that sustains it. They call this cosmos of ordered functions *dharma*. Narrowly conceived, *dharma* is the injunction to perform rituals. But why are rituals to be performed? Rituals help maintain *dharma*, the order that pervades the cosmos. Order is sustained by the natural functioning of all the elements of the world: the material elements, like the sun and water and wind; living creatures, like cows and tigers; and human beings. The sun shines, the tiger hunts, the human performs religious and social duties. In a profound way, these are natural aspects of reality, since reality is not only things as they are, but also what they do. Furthermore – and this is the challenging aspect of the Mimamsa world-view – the natural functioning of the world that is part of reality includes the actions undertaken by humans. The problem is that humans can choose to perform actions or decide not to do ritual; the sun and the tiger have no such freedom. The Mimamsa philosophers see this and note that humans can choose to realize their capacity to perform natural functions. This school shows that realism can include moral realism – the view that ultimate reality includes not just things and facts about them, but also values that exist independently of human recognition.

Within the world: deconstructing reality

There is no single Buddhist view of what there is, since there are many interpretations of the Buddha's teachings. But the need to relate to these teachings provides a common thread through the many Buddhist schools we will now consider.

The Buddha does have something to say about the fundamental nature of the world, something that explicitly applies to the world *in toto.* It is the insight that lies at the heart of what he teaches and that prompted the birth of Buddhism. That insight certainly asks an ultimate question and gives an answer. What that says about ultimate reality is another issue.

The insight is stated in the form of the famous Four Noble Truths: the world is suffering; desire is the cause of suffering; the cessation of desire is the cessation of suffering; this is achieved by following the eight-fold path. Suffering (*duhkha* in Sanskrit) is interpreted subsequently as general illfare, although it is specifically related to sickness, sorrow, pain, ageing and death. But the concept of suffering includes a more pervasive sense of life being unsatisfactory and limited by so many factors. To find life unsatisfactory is to pursue satisfaction, which is to desire it and the things that provide it. So life is suffering because of desire. 'Desire' here is used in the sense of a pressing quest, rather than merely focusing on a goal, and this psychological urgency is conveyed by translating the relevant Pali/Sanskrit word as 'craving' or 'thirst'. From the first two steps of the teaching, it follows that to cease craving is to cease suffering. The Buddha offers a path that will lead to the cessation of desire: the eight-fold path, which is a combination of ethical, psychological and bodily discipline.

This is the core of what the Buddha taught, and its power to transform lies in the unflinching diagnosis and therapy he offers us. Clearly, he raises a question about ultimate value: how life is to be understood and what to do in response to that understanding. Beyond that, does the Buddha say something about what is ultimate, how things really are? Clearly, yes, he does: life is suffering. It is a truth that does not allow of exceptions, and it is fundamental. Underneath our ordinary experience of suffering there really is just ... suffering. Equally, there is another assertion about life: the cessation of desire will lead to a cessation of suffering. That too is a fundamental truth.

These are truths about the structure of reality to the extent that our lives are embedded in and part of reality. But there are other questions that had already been raised in ancient India and that confronted the Buddha: Is the world eternal or not? Is there a god? Would the Buddha himself exist in some way after his death? Are the self and the body identical? The Buddha has a two-fold response. On the level of logic, he says that these are indeterminate questions, unanswerable because they do not clearly articulate anything meaningful. What do any of the terms (world, eternity, god, self, identical) mean, and how did they come to mean what they do? On the level of psychology, he asks what purpose is served by attempting to answer them. If you are shot by an arrow, do you want to have it taken out or do you want to ask where it came from, what it is made of, and so on? So too, if you are undergoing suffering, do you want it to cease or do you want to investigate the structure of the world in which you suffer? The Buddha therefore says that he will not concern himself with questions of ultimate reality.

But that is not the whole story. The Buddha does make two major, interrelated claims about reality. First, the world and human beings are not ultimately substantial; they lack an intrinsic nature or 'self'. Second, the lack of anything intrinsic to the nature of either the world or human beings means that everything is constituted, not by self-subsisting things that have their own essence, but by fleeting entities that are dependent, for both their being and our understanding of them, on each other. The world is fleeting, there is no self, and all things arise in dependence on each other.

The claim that things arise in mutual dependence (*pratitya-samutpada*) is the core of all subsequent Buddhist metaphysics. It means that nothing in the world is what it is without reference to other things; and that we cannot explain anything without recognizing how it relates to other things. In themselves, it eventually came to be said, things are 'empty' (*sunya*, whose technical meaning is 'zero') of essence. To use a crude illustration with caution, if a thing were a cup and its nature or essence the fluid that filled it, then we could say that each thing is more like a cupped palm than a tumbler: the nature of the thing is never self-sufficient but dependent on something else for it to be what it (always temporarily) is. It is not denied that there is a cup, but the cup is understood in terms of its arising for a while in dependence on something else, the palm. Of course, things are mutually dependent, and this mutuality is not captured in the example. But we are some way to seeing what the Buddha is claiming about reality. Each and every thing is to be understood in terms of every other thing. (This does imply that certain things that have to be self-sufficient by definition do not exist: there is no God, for any proper definition would include the notion that God's existence was self-sufficient.) Something very fundamental about the structure of reality, not self-evident in our experience, has been asserted.

The Buddha does not talk of the dependent co-arising of all things or deny a stable world and an eternal self just to engage in the purely intellectual exercise of providing a theory of reality. He teaches what he does only so that people can be helped on the path to freedom from desire. (What that state of freedom is and how it is construed by different Buddhists will be seen in chapter 4, on the Inward Good.)

To realize that the world is not made up of stable and enduring entities is to realize that we were wrong about what we have hitherto desired. It can then be asked: what is really desired and why it is desired, if it is not what we think it is? Symmetrically, to realize that the person – the individual each of us takes him- or herself to be – is also only a fluid sequence of mental, moral and physical states, without any unifying and eternal self, is to ask of the subject of desire: if there is no persistent self, who desires and for whom? So, what is desired and who desires are both rendered moot. Now, throughout this radical questioning, we may have a persistent worry: if things are really this way (lacking in some eternal and intrinsic nature), how can they appear as they do –

namely, as stable objects and persistent subjects, each with its own intrinsic nature? The doctrine of dependent origination becomes the key concept for subsequent Buddhist thinkers: stability and persistence are mere appearance, not intrinsic to things – they are only an image created by their passing and contingent connection with each other.

This is a finely balanced position. The Buddhist teaching is that we should accept things as we experience them, but at the same time realize that there is nothing to them that is more fundamental or ultimate. Things lack any essential or intrinsic nature. So, to put it in what seem paradoxical terms but on reflection are not: ultimately, there is no ultimate reality.

In subsequent Indian Buddhism, philosophy tried to draw out the full import of the Buddha's teachings about the nature of things as they are. The first attempts were by the schools classified as Abhidharma (which means 'the understanding of *dharma*'). In Buddhism, *dharma* originally meant the teachings and the way of the Buddha, but it also came to mean something very technical: it was the general name for every element of existence, those entities that the Buddha had said were fleeting and interdependent. The category of *dharma* extends beyond the constitution of physical objects and includes all the aspects of existence. The first major Abhidharma school, the Vaibhasika, seeks to list all the elements in the world, but with the purpose of going beyond a mere catalogue to show that they are all interdependent. This leads the school to construct ever more elaborate matrices (*matrika*) of elements.

A matrix is a list of elements categorized under (usually) a dyadic or triadic scheme. Examples of dyadic schemes are pure/impure, visible/invisible, internal/external, homogeneous/heterogeneous, actual/nominal, and so on. One can see how the same things can be classified under different dyadic schemes ('fire', for example, can be pure, visible, external, and so on). Triadic schemes are even more complex; examples include past/present/future, good/bad/neutral, and so on. Indeed, truly complex entities can be classified under many schemes. A famous example is 'feeling', relevant because control of it is vital to the Buddhist path. It can be analysed under a monadic scheme (a single nature): that which is associated with an impression formed through the senses. But it can also be analysed through a succession of more complex schemes – even a ten-fold scheme. The ten-fold analysis of feeling includes the five sense organs (1st–5th); the mind through which it is formed (6th); the specific mental function through which it is manifested (7th); and the three moral forms – wholesome, unwholesome and neutral – that it takes (8th–10th). This kind of analytic listing is meant to demonstrate the interconnectedness of every element. Hence the term 'matrix', which means an environment or situation from which things arise. The world is a matrix, and the lists classify the things of the world to the best ability of the philosophers.

Most later Buddhist schools do the same thing, but the metaphysical dispute comes out of the question of what allows these elements to be connected to each other. The Vaibhasika Buddhists say that the elements (*dharma*s) include some whose function is to hold things together (they are a kind of metaphysical glue). Furthermore, each and every element has to have some special function that makes it what it is. These elements are not ordinary, persistent things, like tables and trees, but more funda-mental elements (rather like the atoms of the Vaisesika ontology we have already looked at), each with its own characteristics. There is some essential nature to them, after all.

The Sautrantika Buddhists perceive the danger that this ontology will violate the anti-essentialist teachings of the Buddha. Their view is that the elements are fleeting in the real sense of being momentary, coming into being only so as to have an effect on another element and then ceasing to exist. So, there are no real categories that exist or persist in themselves. How then do things appear to be stable in our experience? The Sautrantika say that it is a matter of human construction. In our mental grasping of things, we fabricate a sense of persistence and continuity. The elements themselves are just momentary points upon which we apply our concepts and out of which we create our experiences.

The claim that the experienced world is constructed becomes the basis of a major development in Buddhist theories of reality. It is the Yogacara school that fully develops the thought that somehow there is a mental act of putting imagined things together to form the features of our experience. Its most famous proponent, Vasubandhu, sets out to prove that the world that we experience – the world of objects apparently 'outside' – is actually constructed by consciousness. Drawing on the examples of dreaming, hallucinations and errors, where we mistakenly think something is happening outside us, Vasubandhu argues that it is possible for us to have experience of apparently external things without them actually being external. He therefore opens up the possibility that we might be wrong in thinking that there is a world outside us.

A later thinker of this school, Dinnaga, makes the more subtle case that we can describe our experiences without any commitment to an external world: we can simply list all the sights, sounds, feelings, and so on, without having to say that there are objects out there that are seen, heard or felt! What is really there is not a world at all, only mental constructions *as if* of a world. Of course, there is nothing in our experience to indicate that the table is not 'out there'. But that does not matter, say Dinnaga and others: it is part of the very nature of consciousness that it makes things appear to be external when in fact they are only mental constructs.

The upshot of this idealism is that we come to understand that there is no world 'really' there to desire; it is all part of our construction. But, of course, can I not desire my own constructions? In response, the Yogacara philosophers, in common with other Buddhists, argue that there is no 'I' either, no real self, under the collection of mental states, that can truly desire anything. We will look at this denial in the next chapter, on the Self.

Yogacara therefore emphasizes the significance of mental activity as the way to the ultimate state of freedom, *nirvana*. This focus on mental construction as the source of apparent reality finds its most complete expression in Chinese Qan Buddhism, but in a characteristically Chinese, this-worldly manner. Qan Buddhism (says the monk Yong Jia) seeks for each person the attainment of a state in which the mind is not engaged in the 'minor details' of individual phenomena like thoughts and objects. The mind rid of a diversity of concepts is a unitary mind. But whereas in Indian Yogacara this would have looked like a recipe for metaphysical disaster – an idealism that rests on the mistaken idea of a mind – for Qan Buddhists, it is only a psychological attitude of freedom from the bonds of specific desires and objects. With a mind free of internal divisiveness, they believe, a person can act without desire; and that, for them, is *nirvana*. The entire metaphysical dimension of transcending the world that is so important in Indian Buddhism is absent here. The ultimate state that Qan Buddhism envisages is psychological (and, according to some, moral) freedom within this world.

A different way of making the Buddhist case is put forward by Nagarjuna, who founded the Madhyamaka school. He wants to demonstrate that things have no intrinsic nature of their own. But he does not try to do this by denying that objects are external. Instead, he makes a more radical claim: the Buddha, he argues, said nothing about ultimate reality, seeking only to free people from suffering. All he said about reality was that the things that made it up had no essential nature. Any claim purporting to be about the essential nature of things or how things really are – in short, any metaphysics – violates this teaching. Since the Buddha only taught what was necessary for people to attain freedom from suffering, anything that violates his teachings must be unhelpful to the cause of spiritual freedom, and worse, incoherent. The

Madhyamaka philosophers set out to develop rigorous critiques of all the available metaphysical systems, so as to clear the path for the Buddha's teachings.

As for the Madhyamaka themselves, they have no account at all. They merely want to show that no theory of the essence of things is possible. Things are 'empty' of such intrinsic nature and exist only interdependently.

The problem for Nagarjuna and his followers seems to be that he clearly says that no metaphysical position – no claim about ultimate reality – is possible. Is that not itself a metaphysical position? Is that not itself a claim about ultimate reality? If it is, then he is contradicting himself. We have to follow through his argument in defence of himself very carefully to see that this is not so. True, he says, 'nothing can be said about ultimate reality'. But it would be a mistake to read this as 'there is an ultimate reality about which nothing can be said'. His commentator, Candrakirti, gives the example of the man who, told by a merchant that he had nothing to sell, replied that he would buy some of that nothing! The Madhyamaka Buddhist, then, *is* denying exactly what his critic is assuming. His *mention* of the phrase 'ultimate reality' (when saying that nothing can be said about it) does not mean he *uses* it as a reference to something. Of someone who said, 'Don't say "bastard", that's swearing', we would not say that she herself was swearing. As with swearing, so too with metaphysics.

Nagarjuna wishes to prove that all positions are untenable; the importance of his philosophy lies precisely in that demonstration. Any attempt to have a position should be given up. When we realize that things are empty – that there is nothing to say about what they *really* are – the desire to cling to the world vanishes. This entire philosophy is therefore summed up as the emptiness of emptiness. 'Emptiness' – the anti–metaphysical doctrine that things have no independent and essential natures in and of themselves – is not itself a metaphysics. It is itself empty of any such assertion. It is merely the demonstration of emptiness.

Does the Madhyamaka philosopher not prove too much, if his arguments are successful? Can any refutation, however sophisticated, fly in the face of our experience that things appear to have their own nature and qualities? Nagarjuna replies that we should work with 'two truths'. One is the provisional acceptance of the world as we encounter it, where suffering is really felt and where the Buddha really taught. Then there is the ultimate truth – that there is no ultimate reality. We have just seen how that is not a contradiction.

The deconstruction of the world into emptiness, then, is not a simple metaphysical position, denying the reality of the experienced world and replacing it with some set of ultimate entities. The former claim would deny the nature of our experience and the reality of suffering, while the latter would transgress the Buddha's limits on what can be asked. Instead, what we have is a balance between accepting the experienced world and asserting that that world is not what it seems.

In China, Huayen Buddhism marries the Madhyamaka analysis that things are interdependent with the traditional Chinese acceptance of the natural and social worlds as givens, completely altering the Indian Buddhist balance in the process. This leads to the so-called 'positive' interpretation of emptiness: things are empty only to the extent that they are not independent of everything else; but they do exist ultimately in that interdependent state. The famous metaphor for this idea of reality is the jewelled net of the king of the gods that extends infinitely: the facets of every gem that forms the net reflect every other gem. So every element (*dharma*, or *fa* in Chinese) exists in itself, but also somehow contains and is contained by every other element. All elements in the world thus coexist in a harmonious relationship, and that is their nature. This is held to be the teaching of 'the harmonious, unobstructed interpenetration of real and phenomenal things'. In effect, a metaphysical reading of the world alien to the Chinese traditions (as we will see below) nevertheless leads to a search for the patterns of the world's harmony – which is characteristic of Chinese traditions. Emptiness becomes full indeed.

Accepting the world: integrating permanence and change

The great insight of Mahavira, the founder of Jainism, was that reality is 'many-sided', that it is realized in a multiplicity of ways that we cannot always reconcile. The goal of human beings should be to become free from the conditions of life that bring suffering (and in this he was like his probable contemporary, the Buddha). Suffering happens through the accretion of the consequences of actions. Actions bring appropriate consequences to the agent and are driven by the attitudes and values of the agent. It follows that attitudes and values must be changed, so that the agent may act only in such ways as will stop suffering-inducing consequences from accruing. The attitudes and values that Mahavira preaches, such as non-violence and the open-minded acceptance of others, are all seen to be appropriate because of the nature of reality. For the Jains, reality is 'many-sided', and that requires accepting people's variety of beliefs; not attempting to impose one's will on them, but cultivating one's own virtue without interfering with the possibly true different beliefs of others.

There is, therefore, an intimate relationship between the way one should live and the structure of reality. To say that reality is many-sided is to say more than that it is pluralistic. Pluralism is the acceptance that there are many things and principles. The Jain view is that the same thing can be manifested and understood in multiple yet incompatible ways. It might be more helpful to think of this not as 'pluralism' but as 'multiplism'. Jain philosophers demonstrate their recognition of Mahavira's insight by deliberately describing reality in terms that acknowledge opposed metaphysical views. On the one hand, they have a very literal realism about what makes up the world. They say that the world is primarily constituted by substances ('existence is marked by substantiality'); in this, they are even more committed to the literal substantiality of things than the Nyaya and Vaisesika philosophers. The most telling example of this substantialist metaphysics is the Jain view of the soul – the intrinsic self that unifies persons – as a material substance (albeit an extremely subtle and imperceptible one). In any case, things have an essence that makes them what they are.

So far, so substantialist. But, the Jains go on to say, substances also have the three characteristics of origin, (intermediate) persistence, and decay. Naturally, the qualities that give attributes to substances are subject to the same triple-charactered flux as substances themselves. The emphasis on flux is very Buddhistic, in contrast to the assertion of substance. The Jain view is that, while there is an intrinsic nature to things (as Nyaya realists say), intrinsic nature is constantly changing and becoming something else, leaving nothing immutable (and in this, the Buddhists are right when they talk of everything being momentary and provisional). Change is the intrinsic nature of reality! Indeed, the Jains argue, it is meaningless to talk of constant change, as the Buddhists do, without a presupposition that there is something that changes. So there are substantial things, even if their essence is change. But symmetrically, it is to deny experience to say, as Nyaya rigidly does, that there are eternal essences.

Reality is both being (what things are like) and becoming (what happens to things), according to the philosopher Siddhasena. He points out that Mahavira said that both standpoints – 'there is substance' and 'there is change' – are valid. It is only a matter of how and from what perspective one analyses reality. From the perspective of a general theory of things we will say that there is 'being' (there are things, and they have an intrinsic nature to them). From the perspective of a particular study of a thing, we will say that that thing is always 'becoming' (the thing is constantly changing into something else). Note that each view fails to assimilate the other; that is what it means to say that reality is realized in multiple ways. Reality is more than complex – it is more than the bringing together of different truths. It is multiplex, in that it contains separate and incommensurable truths.

The Jain does offer us this comfort: once we have understood that there can be intractable differences in understanding reality, we have grasped the Jain way of behaving, a way that is appropriate to a 'multiplist' reality – a non-assertive, peaceable accommodation of a multiplicity of perspectives about truths. This will form a life that is non-violent because it does not force others to give up their perspectives.

Beyond the world: the (re)attainable ultimate reality

The most famous and most misunderstood account of ultimate reality in Indian philosophy comes from the interpretation by Sankara of the concept of *brahman*, as expounded in the ancient texts, the Upanisads. The school of Advaita (non-duality) founded by him believes that *brahman* 'alone is the truth'. Everything else is modification initiated by language. *Brahman* is real, the rest is unreal. This *brahman* is the sole reality, out of which arises the world of appearances. It is also the 'supreme self' from which no individual self is different. Thus the teachings of the Upanisads – 'all is *brahman*', 'you are that', 'there is no second that is separate' – are interpreted to mean that the diversity of the physical world as well as the plurality of individual beings are all ultimately manifestations of the one *brahman*.

It is clear that, whatever *brahman* is, we can anticipate that the reduction of world and self to it will make for a radical metaphysics. Such an interpretation will quite probably invert our normal expectations about what reality might be. To start with, we may think of *brahman* as simply the term for what is ultimate. The ultimate is that beyond which nothing is. It is irreducible. In investigating anything, there is a point at which ever-finer discrimination of the constituents of things has to come to an end, and a different order of logic has to be applied. (We saw with Nyaya-Vaisesika how one type of reduction was of substances to their ultimate material constituents – the logical atoms or mathematical points of irreducibility – but another type of reduction was to split things up into different categories.) But in any type of reduction to components, at some point there is an end, with some category that affords no further analysis. Pluralist systems will end up with many different irreducibles – many different things that form the ·fundamental or ultimate elements of their metaphysics, as we saw with Nyaya-Vaisesika.

Now, it should be noted that this sense of 'ultimate' is fairly technical. For example, in a system that had a creator god and a world created by God, people might normally think of God alone as ultimate. But according to the terms above, the world is also ultimate if God, having created it as a separate body of things, then allows it to exist independently. God may go back to being the sole ultimate reality at the end of time, when the world ceases to exist, but until then the world is irreducibly different from God. The philosopher Madhva, founder of the theistic Hindu school of Dvaita Vedanta, holds that God is the overseer but not the creator of either the world or individual selves, which are eternal. God, individual selves and the material world are all ultimate. ('Dvaita' means 'duality' and may refer to the difference between either God and the world or God and individual selves.) For the Advaita philosophers, *brahman* alone is ultimate. So far, then, *brahman* is the name for the ultimate – indeed, the *sole* ultimate reality, to which everything else is reducible. Even by this point, we can see that a radical metaphysics is being put forward: despite the appearance of plurality, in fact, ultimately, there is only one being.

What is the nature of this sole ultimate, which we call *brahman*? The famous description of it, going back to the Upanisad texts, is that it is 'existence–awareness–bliss' (*sat-cit-ananda*). The first characterization, that it is existence, amounts to saying that *brahman* 'is' – not only that it exists but that, in some sense, it alone is to be considered existent. Obviously, the idea of 'existence' is used here in a way peculiar to Advaita, since the riotously plural world of experience cannot simply be dismissed out of hand. Indeed, it is the Advaitic theory of the world that has caused so much puzzlement and even charges of philosophical lunacy. But before we turn to that, let us look at the other two characterizations, since they show even more sharply how radical Advaitic metaphysics is.

Brahman is awareness. Fundamentally, reality is not the material world but a singular, universal consciousness, *brahman*. Awareness is non-dual in two ways. First, the apparently separate and limited consciousness of the individual self is not different from limitless, universal consciousness (this identification comes out of a probing analysis of the nature of consciousness, which we will look at in the next chapter, on the Self). Second, non-duality holds between that universal consciousness and the world. Advaita maintains that the proper interpretation of the sayings in the Upanisads – '*brahman* is the truth, the world is false', 'all is *brahman*', and so on – implies that the world is not real in the way *brahman* is. That means that, ultimately, only a universal consciousness exists. This limitless awareness is the foundation of all things. The world comes out of it (the very word *brahman* has the root meaning 'to grow'). This awareness pervades everything that came out of it. Now, *brahman* is both the 'instrumental' and the 'material' cause. It is instrumental in that it brought about the world; and it is material, in that the world came of it or emanated from it. But Advaita says that the resulting world is not real in the same way that *brahman*, its cause, is real. All effects are only virtual transformations of the cause; only the cause continues to exist ultimately, while effects, although having their own structures, are reducible to the cause. The material world of experience, then, is reducible to the universal consciousness out of which it came.

The third characterization, that *brahman* is bliss, is a source of much debate. Other schools, which disagree with Advaita, simply take this to mean that *brahman* is the personal God, whose intrinsic freedom from limitations and suffering is indicated by 'bliss'. The problem for Advaita is that 'bliss' is a word that seems to apply to a person (even the supreme, divine one), whereas *brahman* for them is an impersonal, cosmic principle of existence. There is no satisfactory answer, but one Advaitin, Vacaspati, says that, because the *absence* of bliss (eternal and unchanging happiness) is the mark of *limited* consciousness, the ancient texts use 'bliss' purely as another way of saying that it is limitless consciousness.

Let us now focus on the idea that *brahman* alone is real in some way that nothing else is. For the Advaita philosophers, reality is that which is independent of but which pervades everything that is not. Whatever is not independent is not ultimately real. What, then, is independence? There is a technical definition from Indian logic that will help us define independence. For any two things, *A* and *B*, suppose these conditions hold: (i) Whenever *B* occurs, *A* occurs (or must have occurred). (ii) When *A* does not occur, *B* never occurs. A looser way of stating these conditions together would be to say that *B* occurs only when *A* occurs. Then, we can say, *B* is dependent on *A* for its occurrence. Finally, (iii) *A* can occur without *B* occurring. Then we can say that *A* is independent of *B*. Now, this logical understanding of independence is not at issue; the Advaitins accept it in common with other schools of thought. The striking point is that the Advaitins take the notion of independence further, and say that which is independent is alone real (ultimately real). But the world is not independent of *brahman*. The world subsists in the universal consciousness that is *brahman*, and it occurs (as we encounter it in experience) only because of *brahman*. As *brahman* alone is independent, it alone is real (*sat*); the world is not.

What then is the world? The most famous Advaitic description of it is that it is illusory (*maya*). But we should not take the Advaitin too literally here. Illusion is a suggestive metaphor for the metaphysical status of the world. The Advaitin wants to indicate that it is possible to see something and take it to exist, and yet come to understand later that it does not exist in quite the way we thought it did. In other words, appearance may not be reality. (The philosophers say that appearance and reality have different 'ontological status': they are part of the furniture of reality in two different ways, one that is dependent and one that is not.) In ordinary life, we do not deny that there is an experience of an illusion: there is some kind of 'reality' attached to the experience. But the status we give it is not the same as that which we attach to whatever the illusion is based on. The single most famous analogy in Advaita literature is that of the snake and the rope. We can have the experience of seeing a snake, but it was only a rope that was 'really' there. It would be inadequate – in explaining both the perception (the experience as of seeing something) as well as our psychological response – to dismiss the experience. After all, our fear was real enough! We have to make space in our explanation for the snake, even though it was never there; but in the end, we must say that there was only ever a rope. The snake was an illusion, in that sense.

The Advaitin says that the world is as the snake to *brahman*'s rope. The real point is not that the world is an illusion; this very example, the Advaitin is aware, requires a distinction between illusion and object in the world. It is, rather, that just because we had an experience of something, we should not conclude that that something exists *just as* we experienced it. We should not rule out the possibility that that something is not what we took it to be. The world is 'real' enough, in terms of our experience of it – in terms of our seeing and touching and moving and thinking about it. But from such experience we cannot conclude that it is ultimate. All we can conclude from experience is that we must *assume* that the world is real (for that is how it appears to us); however, it is real only in the immediate sense of being stable, continuous, external to our senses, material and so on. Yet this reality is only empirical (*vyavahara*): it is only to be thought of as real in that it is the object of our transactions (of sensing, moving, using, discussing, knowing and so on). It is not unreal (*asat*) in the way impossible objects – physically impossible, like golden mountains, or logically impossible, like the son of childless parents, to use two favourite examples in the tradition – are unreal. But neither is it real in the sense of being ultimately independent; for *brahman* alone is that.

Advaitins use special terms to explain the world as penultimate: it is only empirically or provisionally real; it is phenomenal (capable of being experienced); it is indeterminate between the real and the unreal. However, the relationship between the world (and our many, present, individualized consciousnesses) and *brahman* is even more complex than that. We are able to say this much about *brahman* only because the seers of the Upanisads had such insights about reality and conveyed them to us. But the ultimacy of *brahman* goes beyond what we can say of it. For, in a profound sense, we cannot say what it is; we cannot even, in our meaning of the term, experience it. We should understand that the ultimate reality being ultimate consists also in its escaping our talk of it. This is so because all our language, our thoughts, our definition of what it is to know anything, our very lives are limited parts of this world – the very world that is not ultimately real. The Advaitin even concedes that the sacred texts themselves, being part of this world, are similarly not real! They are merely indicative, they serve only to guide us away from simplistic assumptions about what we can dare to hope. Everything that is said – not just my words, not just the words of Sankara, but those of the seers themselves – are part of the non-ultimate world. What we call experience is based on the body and its senses, on the activities of the mind located in that body, and on the intellect that guides it; in short, things *in* the world. How then can there be *experience* of *brahman*, when what we mean by 'experience' is something that by definition is not of *brahman* (which is beyond the world)? To attain *brahman* – to attain ultimate reality – is something that we can only discuss in a negative way (as not being this or that, or anything that we can say or know). At most, we can indicate in words that *brahman* is beyond words. We can know that what we know is not *brahman*, for knowledge itself is simply part of this world, while *brahman* transcends it. (It will be instructive to compare this ineffability of *brahman*, its being beyond telling, with the unnameable *dao* of Daoism.)

What is there to aim for, then? It is somehow to have such a transformation of ourselves that the apparent gap between this world and the ultimate is bridged. We will see in chapter 4, on the Inward Good, how the Advaitin thinks this might happen.

In the world: Heaven and the Way of tradition

From this dizzying journey to the very limits of human exploration of the ultimate, let us now turn to the very different and wholly this-worldly challenges that the Chinese philosophies pose for themselves, starting with Confucianism.

There are two ultimate categories of Confucian thought: using the conventional translations, Heaven (*tian*) and the Way (*dao*). How are they ultimate? All the motivation behind the Confucian agenda – of self-cultivation, effective rulership, social harmony and political stability – makes sense only by reference to these two notions. That is to say, it is only by reference to Heaven and the Way that the Confucians can say how any actions that they propose are both required and possible.

Tian is a combination of two ancient Chinese ideas: *Shang-ti*, a personal deity joined by deceased rulers in the realm of *ti*; and *tian*, which is a distant and impersonal force modelled on the sky (which is another meaning of *tian*). Subsequently, Confucians came to refer to *tian* as the source of their ethical agenda in both these senses, and it is this word that is translated as 'Heaven'.

As a disciple of Confucius points out in the compilation called the *Analects*, the initial difficulty is that he and Confucius' other followers never heard the master's words on the way of Heaven. Confucius appears not to want his disciples to bother about theories of Heaven but to concentrate on the actions he wishes to teach them (on which see chapter 3, on the Outward Good). Confucius evokes Heaven in various assertions: it engenders the potency of virtue (*de*) that enables him to be a representative of the exemplary ethical path; Heaven wishes to preserve the style or manner (*wen*) of ritual action in society. It is said of Confucius that Heaven means to employ him as 'a wooden bell', the instrument used by heralds to call people's attention to an important message. Clearly, Heaven gives Confucius the strength to be what he is and to do what he wants to do. Confucius is not interested in spelling out what Heaven is. Instead, he wishes to show that Heaven, being what(ever) it is, manifests itself in his actions. For him, theories of Heaven do not contribute to learning how to act properly in the world.

Having said that, we must acknowledge that there is actually some evidence in Confucius' own words about his understanding of Heaven. It appears to be an entity in the natural order that intervenes in human affairs and gives Confucius the responsibility of transmitting teachings on proper action. This relationship with Heaven is also evident when, acknowledging that 'no one knows me' (which is a Confucian phrase that specifically refers to lack of official preferment), he says that it is Heaven that knows him.

It is clear that Confucius' Heaven is some personalized force that interacts powerfully with him. But this does not mean that it is some principle beyond this world, comparable to the god of major religious traditions. However powerful it is in providing motivation for human action, Heaven is not transcendent. Transcendence is the quality of being of some higher order. We can say that God is transcendent in occupying a different realm or level of being, a level that exists and has its own principles of functioning independently of levels below it. In contrast, Heaven is a dimension – albeit powerful and significant – of the same world that we inhabit. Of course, most conceptions of God in other traditions also include this notion of immanence, which is an intimate and interactive pervasion of this level of being; but if we were to apply this terminology to *tian*, we would say it was *only* immanent. We should think that *tian* is, for all its power, part of the world (in the same sense in which the sky, even if distant, is still of this world). In the *Analects*, *tian* is some sort of personal, fundamental force within this world that motivates ethical action but to which no theory attaches. Its interrelationship with human beings is evident in the phrase 'unity of heaven and human', which is common in China. This conception of a natural realm of things in which all dimensions are unified at the same level is nowadays called the 'anthropocosmic' nature of Chinese thought.

Mencius, Confucius' first and best-known successor, uses the concept of Heaven to strengthen his key claim that human nature is naturally good and given to ethical performance. He does this by claiming that Heaven is what endows human nature with goodness. But we still get no clear idea of what this fundamental force is. In keeping with the Chinese orientation towards metaethics, we must continue to focus on what Heaven does rather than what it is supposed to be. It licenses the Confucian to teach ethical practice. Fundamentally, it works purposefully towards some goal (in short, it has a teleology). Heaven, then, motivates the Confucian pursuit of a society in which proper action can secure a stable and harmonious order.

Xunzi, the third of the classical Confucians, wrote a treatise on Heaven. It is still not so much a consistent and explicit theory as a combination of uses of that concept in defence of Confucian ritual and ethical action. In Xunzi, we have a clearer idea of Heaven, as the total order and collection of things in the world – in short, nature. (So is Heaven actually nature? The need to be very careful with translated words is obvious here.)

Actually, there are two notions of Heaven in Xunzi, the second related in a subtle way to the first. The first notion is of Heaven as nature in its totality, with no purpose and no norms. Ethical significance comes rather from *human* action, where proper ritual performance (*li*) can guide and correct such action. Heaven forms only the constant and natural backdrop for human action.

Xunzi has another reading of Heaven, in which its being Heaven-as-nature relates in a more complex way with the ritual and ethics of human action. Indeed, we can see this as an extension of the first meaning. Heaven is the natural basis of human nature. Heaven is nature, but nature also contains ethical significance because it includes human beings, who naturally possess ethical capacities that are normative and purposive.

In comparison to the number of times *tian* is used in the *Analects*, *dao*, conventionally translated as the 'Way', is used more frequently. (In order to keep in mind the very many complex uses of *dao* and 'way', I shall always use the term '*dao*/way' when talking of this concept.) We will soon see how complex *dao*/way is in Daoism, but its use by the Confucians might at first lead us to think that there is common ground here, pointing to some ultimate reality. *Dao*/way for the Confucians is, in fact, something important but very much rooted in human action.

The best starting-point for Confucius' own view of *dao*/way is his famous statement that it is the human being who is able to extend the *dao*/way, not the *dao*/way that is able to extend the human being. This immediately shows that 'the *dao*/way' is not independent of or prior to human action and so is not some pre-existing metaphysical principle. But what is it and what is its status? Confucius frequently talks of his own *dao*/way, and how it will grow forth – through the cultivation of the roots of humanity in all people (but first, in the exemplary person). He takes the *dao*/way of the exemplary person to be free of error, even though it is a long one. It becomes clear that the *dao*/way for Confucius is in fact the sum total of the norms of his culture. It is the accumulation of the correct texts, rituals, rules and performances that enable order to be achieved – in a word, a tradition.

This could mean that the tradition is some ethical absolute, a body of guidance on how to act, and one that is independent of any person. Although created, it is objective in that it is not subject to the decisions of specific individuals. However, a more liberal interpretation of the Confucian *dao*/way would focus on the nature of tradition: even if it is elaborate and detailed, it is always indeterminate and open to interpretation. Furthermore, tradition is multivalent – people attach different values to the same rules and actions. The *dao*/way is not really an ultimate; it is constructed out of a relationship between the field of cultural wisdom and the individual's particular focus within that field.

How are *tian*/Heaven and *dao*/way related? Quite simply, the human way (*ren dao*), which is the normative cultural tradition (as interpreted by Confucius), is also *tian dao*, the way of Heaven.

Under the impact of Buddhism, later Chinese philosophy was confronted with the idea of some ultimate state of being, and Neo-Confucians sought to recognize this. From the time of Zhou Duni, there is an attempt to integrate some notion of an ultimate state of being into the Confucian world-view. This is articulated as the Great Ultimate (*tai ji*), but one searches in vain for any attempt to say what this might be. The *tai ji* is the name for the source of the elements of the world and all the moral categories of Confucianism, which latter continue to be the focus of attention. The real concern of the Neo-Confucians is the integration of ritual and ethical action into general patterns of conduct (another character with the same name, *li*). The Great Ultimate is an attempt to graft an alien metaphysics onto traditional issues; it is not needed for the fundamental concerns of Confucianism. That is why, despite its presence in Neo-Confucianism, it is not itself the focus of explanation (contrast the study of *brahman* in India). It is a 'place-holder', a sort of empty and formal name for the unknown source from which spring the really relevant things – culture and the codes of conduct.

Ways of and through the world

Whereas other things in the world do what is appropriate to them spontaneously and without reflection, human beings act according to highly reflective, elaborately formulated codes of conduct; this is something the Confucians note and approve of. Despite great differences in style and outward direction, the Daoist philosophers Zhuangzi and Laozi have a similar judgement, which contrasts with that of the Confucians. Spontaneous movement is natural, and each such movement is an expression of a *dao*/way; constructed action is unnatural and alienates humans from their *dao*/way(s). In whatever else Confucians and Daoists overlap, on this the division is clear.

The question to ask now would seem to be: 'What is *dao*?' But that is to make a massive presupposition about the study of Daoism: it misreads how we should go about understanding the idea of *dao*. That question presupposes that there is a reality that has to be sought out, whose structure, now hidden from us, has to be revealed. It requires metaphysics. By contrast, Daoism has a different starting-point: there is a world that we live in, and how we behave is different from how nature is, to our detriment. The question then is 'How is the *dao* to be followed?'

Having said that, let us nevertheless proceed as if we are indeed answering the question 'What is *dao*?', even if the answer is, roughly, 'The *dao* is that which is not to be determined but is to be followed; and to say how it is to be followed says something about what the *dao* is.'

Zhuangzi observes that the social construction of action leads to disagreement between different schools. The other schools think that to assert the way they act ('this is it'/*shi*) is to reject another way ('that is not it'/*fei*), whereas Zhuangzi says that the way to understand the *dao* way is to not to find such opposites at all. 'Where neither this nor that finds its opposite is called the axis of a/the *dao*/way.' At that axis, both what there is and what there is not are limitless. At the axis, there is no opposite, and in that place, free of the constraining opposites that we create, a/the *dao*/way begins.

Where there is natural freedom, there is a *dao*/way. It is made deficient through identifying and limiting the distinctions between what is (what you do) and what is not (what you reject). Following your *dao*/way is to allow for the limitless possibilities of what you do and do not do. The limitless possibilities are everywhere, since all ways of doing anything are *ways* of doing. Humans are in their *dao*/ways, says Zhuangzi, like fish are in water. All life is a context for *dao*/ways of living.

It will be noticed here that Zhuangzi is talking about something that may be quite general but is not a single, universal thing. He is talking about *ways* rather than *the* way – something that is captured in the uninflected and very ordinary way in which 'way' is used in English, but that still suggests a deep insight about living: life is made up of ways of doing – assuming, judging, distinguishing, rejecting, asserting, physically acting. Any way of doing something (say, distinguishing between what to do and what not to do) requires the assumption of some other way (how our community makes choices or how our parents taught us).

Upon reflection, we can see that 'a way' can be understood in two different ways (the pervasive usefulness of the word 'way' in English is a good indicator of the role of *dao* in Daoism). A way is a principle that we take to provide us with guidance ('there is a way to the office'). But the way is also my actual taking of a specific action, my performance ('I make my way to the office'). We can ask: what is the relationship between the way-as-guide and the way-as-performance?

If Zhuangzi had said in a straightforward manner that in each instance of the need to act, there is a *dao*/way that has to be found and acted upon, then we could have attributed a position to him. He would have been asserting that there are *dao*/ways out there that have to be discovered. (The Huang-Lao school of thought in fact held some such position – that there is a pre-formed natural order which, if discovered, guides proper action. We could say that the Huang-Lao are confident of moving from what there *is* to concluding what we *ought* to do.) But Zhuangzi does not do that. He aims to leave us with the feeling that any attempt to assert the right *dao*/way (a result, he says, of Confucian-style adherence to unnatural social rules) is bound to fail, so that all we are left with is the actual doing. The sage *treats* everything as one, but that is not to assert baldly that everything *is* (in a predetermined way) one. As Zhuangzi says, a *dao*/way comes about as we walk it. In short, he does not distinguish between a pre-formed way and a performed way. Over a period of time, a pattern of behaviour emerges that is guided by the way in which we understand ourselves and realize what we have to do in any particular circumstance. The ultimate for Zhuangzi is to realize natural action in oneself. There is nothing else; to coin a phrase, it is *dao*/ways all the way down.

This free-flowing and eternally provisional way of looking at the *dao*/way is somewhat different from what we find in the *Laozi*, the collection attributed to the semi-mythical figure of that name. Laozi too seeks to abandon the unnatural social constructions propounded by the Confucians, but he does not seek to live fearlessly and without any explanation of his *dao*/way in the manner of Zhuangzi. He wants to express what he seeks – even if it cannot be expressed. Laozi's way of proceeding is paradoxical, but it is informative about his richer conception of *dao*/way, compared to Zhuangzi. (It is because it is richer – more complex and appearing to refer to some particular entity – that it has invited metaphysical readings from Western commentators, who have compared it to God, the Absolute, *brahman*, and so on.)

The *Laozi* famously begins (and every translation is fraught with significance), 'The *dao*/way that can be made a *dao*/way Is not the constant *dao*/way.' He says later, 'The *dao*/way is constantly nameless.' This is at least paradoxical, if not outright self-contradictory. Is the very act of denial not also an act of assertion? What is a *dao*/way, if it is not a *dao*/way? If no *dao*/way is constant, what is a constant *dao*/way? And how is the *dao*/way nameless if it is called 'the *dao*/way'? Furthermore, what is the point of saying anything at all about the *dao*/way, if all that can be said about it is that nothing can be said? Are there no *dao*/ways that Laozi wants to talk about? In fact, Laozi is actually saying what the *dao*/way is in terms of what it is not. 'She is not a sister' is a way of saying that she is a singleton. And even when a denial leaves many alternatives, it can still say a lot: 'he is no politician' can be laden with meaning. Laozi's words on *dao*/way are even more subtle, since the characterization of it is that it cannot be characterized.

Clearly, Laozi puts forward specific ways of behaving that he claims are found in a return to a natural practice. His conception of the *dao*/way is more than just a classification of guides to action. He struggles to recognize a sense of wholeness – the constant *dao*/way. The very definition of a *dao*/way is that it is a guide to action. That is perfectly comprehensible and needs to be said if Laozi is to teach rulers (his main audience) how to act. From that, it may seem simple to think of the totality – the Great *Dao*, if you will – as the sum of all the guides to action. But if a *dao*/way is a guide to action, then the sum of all *dao*/ways is no guide at all. Guidance requires a specific *dao*/way, to be followed through the person's interpretation of it. (In this, incidentally, Laozi is different from Zhuangzi, in that the former does distinguish between the norm and its performance.) The metaethical rendering of *dao* – as a kind of 'Way of ways' – has no use for the metaphysical question of what *dao* is (what can be named). As the real question about a *dao*/way is what it does (that is, how it is followed), the sum of *dao*/ways is not itself a *dao*/way. The totality is there, but it is nameless, because what can be named is only a *dao*/way that can be followed – and we have seen that the sum of *dao*/ways is not what is or can be followed. The only constant is the fact that that there are *dao*/ways to be followed.

Here, we may seem to be on the verge of a metaphysical move to identifying ultimate reality, but we should recognize that Laozi understands by '*dao*' something that by its nature is not a metaphysical entity at all. Because he refers to it as the constant *dao*/way, and because he talks of its very nature as being incapable of singular description, commentators have sometimes taken him to be talking of a metaphysical entity that is ineffable – beyond capture in language. But in the end, Laozi's *dao*/way only lends itself to such comparison if we ignore the ametaphysical context of his thinking. All he is saying is that there are natural *dao*/ways to be discovered in the constantly changing flux of the world in which humans find themselves.

The natural, the way in which every *dao*/way is found by us, is defined as everything becoming itself (*zi ran*, strictly, 'it-self-so-ing'). In contrast to the classical Indian metaphysical enterprise of classifying and defining the essence of all being, the concept of *zi ran* is about recognizing that each thing does its own thing (literally and colloquially). This is contrasted with the artificiality of social ritual. The *dao*/way is discovered in the changing, fluid world in which we find ourselves.

We will end this study of *dao*/way with one more development that is virtually metaphysical, but not quite. Wang Bi, in his commentary on the *Laozi*, says that *dao* is *wu*. Now, *wu* is usually translated as 'nothing' or even 'non-being', in contrast to *yu* (being). But 'being', of course, is a word loaded with specific meaning in each philosophical system. If we import the Western (or Indian) idea of being, as a general category based on the *fact* that there are things (without reference to any particular thing and its name and form), then it would seem that Wang Bi is making a significant metaphysical assertion. He would seem to be identifying the *dao*/way with some state of nothingness out of which all being came. But in fact that is not the case. *Yu*, as Wang Bi himself says, is what has name and form, what is differentiated; *wu* is then better translated as 'non-differentiated being' than as 'non-being'. *Dao*, ultimately being *wu*, is no specific thing; but neither is it some mysterious non-being. Only differentiated being – specific things, with name and form – gives guidance on action. Since the differentiated – that is, the specific – alone is accessible as a guide to action, nothing more can be said about the ultimately undifferentiated totality of *dao*/ways, other than to deny that it is anything differentiated. The *dao*/way considered in this general way is, as Laozi puts it, 'an uncarved block'; it is waiting to be given shape by particular, or differentiated, guides and actions. This is the most that can be said about the ultimate.

2
The Self

The self is a fascinating topic. Initially, it seems as if there is little to investigate: we know ourselves, do we not? But as anyone who actually tries this out immediately notes, we may well know several things *about* ourselves (although we are also aware that there are many things we do not know about ourselves, some best left unknown…); but that is not the same as *knowing* ourselves. Still less is it to know what the 'self' in 'ourselves' means. We have an intuitive sense that understanding something about ourselves is of tremendous importance to our lives. Yet we can proceed only a very short distance before having to choose a particular path to explore, with its own questions to formulate and answers to seek. This is because what it is to know ourselves is an issue deeply rooted in the rich soil of intellectual culture and bound up intimately with many ideas and attitudes specific to that culture.

There cannot be a greater cultural difference than that between classical India and China on the philosophical approaches to selfhood. To deal in any depth with these traditions, we have to consider them separately. Interestingly, the spread of Buddhism from India to China allows us to see clearly how the same doctrines and arguments can be transformed utterly when faced by radically different philosophical assumptions.

The many meanings of the self
We must first see that the 'self' can mean different things, which are best captured in English by using different words. These

distinctions are not obvious and are not always based on normal usage. Rather, I wish to use each term for the self in a particular way, so that we can keep in mind how the 'self' is laden with many implications. Three readings of the word given below are key to what follows in this chapter.

The self can mean the 'soul'. A soul is an immaterial and conscious entity (a substance that is not physical), which resides in the physical body of a (human) being; is the truest and deepest identity of that being; makes that being alive at the start; and – being itself immortal – continues to exist after that physical being is dead. All other things about that physical being may change in the course of its life, but the soul is unchanging and lasts beyond that life. Usually, the soul is seen as coming from or having been created by God. This non-material substance animates the body and directs it through the mind; in Western philosophy, the mind is often taken to be the soul itself, or an instrument of the soul. The soul acts through the body, and together with mind and body, constitutes a person. Eventually, whatever happens to the body, the person's deeds are the responsibility of the soul, to which all moral qualities attach and which therefore faces the consequences of those deeds.

The self can mean the 'person'. The person is the single being that brings together the total physical and psychological history normally found associated with a body from birth to death; a being that develops not only a relationship with the world around it (family, relatives, society, the natural world) but also with itself (namely, its psychological and physical states, through thoughts, emotions, desires, feelings and sensations). Such a being is separate from all others by virtue of its particular history. It has its own identity. Many contemporary philosophers from around the world, who do not believe in anything other that the physics and chemistry of material bodies, think that the identity of persons depends entirely on their distinct and separate natures, developed through relationships between themselves and the world. (This has led to interesting discussions about who the person is when their access to psychological states is altered, for instance by implanting someone else's memories in their brain.) By contrast, people in the West who are not materialists – people who feel that there is more to reality than material things – have tended to see the identity of the person as given by the identity of the soul. So, the person known to himself and others as Ram-Prasad is who he is because of Ram-Prasad's soul, which is the real Ram-Prasad. In either case, the important thing about the person is that she is a concrete and specific individual, like no other, and identifiable as such (by herself and others).

Finally, the self can mean the 'subject' of awareness. It seems that when there is a state of awareness (a seeing, a touch, a thought or desire), it is experienced by a particular being. This is what is meant by saying that awareness has a subject. A subject of awareness is that *to which* awareness happens. The contrast is with an object of awareness, that *of which* there is awareness. Awareness needs a subject; part of the definition of awareness is that it is *like* something to be aware. (In recent Western philosophy, this insight has been made famous by the assertion of Thomas Nagel that it is like something to be a bat – the flying mammal, not the implement in the game of cricket. The contrast can be made by saying it is not like anything to be a bat in the latter sense.) It is this quality of awareness – to be aware not only *what* one is aware of but also *that* one is aware – which is captured in the statement that awareness is subjective or always has a subject. So awareness is awareness of it*self*. The Indian philosophers called the subject of awareness the 'self' of awareness. This was because, they all noted, a self is not like anything else. A self is at the very least conscious, capable of grasping the fact and nature of its own existence. A self is not inert, like rocks and other things that have no such intrinsic grasp of their own existence. (Animals are usually thought to have selves, in classical Indian philosophy, although not the fully developed consciousness and individuality that human selves – i.e.

persons – have. Even plants were considered borderline cases.) Of course, such grasp of the fact and nature of one's own existence is nothing other than awareness. All this is combined in the following line of reasoning: awareness has a subject, and the self is aware; therefore, the subject of awareness is the self.

The self can, then, be understood in a variety of ways: as a soul, as a person, and as a subject. To anticipate the course of this chapter, the self as subject of consciousness is the focus of Indian philosophy, as the self as person is of Chinese philosophy.

Rebirth, depersonalization and the inner controller: the self in ancient India

The earliest texts in India centre on human interaction with a complex cosmic order. The sacred Vedas and the texts that are appended to them seek to guide human beings – or at least some qualified, high-status males – towards action that will lead to appropriate reward in the form of material benefits such as personal wealth, family well-being, social order and natural stability. While this vision is cosmic, in that the actions are directed towards maintaining a complex universal order, the primary concern of the Vedas is with human beings as such. The core idea is 'man' (*manusya*, from a root word meaning 'think' or 'minding', or *purusa*, from a root word meaning 'abundant'). Man thinks ahead, plans for the future, has choice in action, seeks immortality (in the literal sense of never dying). The term *manusya* is sometimes applied particularly to the high-born and 'noble' person (*arya*), in contrast to subordinate groups (the Chinese too, as possibly most other civilizations, have a similar initial identification of a general term for human beings with an elite class). At the beginning, then, Indian thought is oriented towards the concrete human being, the high-born person with rational abilities, privileges and responsibilities.

By the time of the last of these early texts, however, a transcendental dimension to the human being has entered the picture.

One such text, the *Aitereya Aranyaka*, says that what is special about man (*purusa*) is that he is intelligent, discerning and has cognitive power; he can not only think of tomorrow's world but – importantly – the world beyond this world; it is in him that the *atman* is most manifest. Now, the basic meaning of *atman* is 'breath' and could initially have indicated life. But in this passage, some deeper meaning has started to emerge. The word *atman* is usually translated as 'self', but that English word, we already know, has many different implications. The 'self' here is obviously something tied closely to the idea of consciousness and knowledge. The prime characterizations of man refer to his thinking – intelligence and cognitive power (even the word translated as 'discernment' – *vijanati* – conveys not some general cultural sophistication but knowing one thing from another). So even early on in Hindu thought, it is implied that the self of man is something tied to cognitive power or consciousness. Sometimes this self or *atman* is identified with life breath or vital force (*prana*), as something immaterial that outlasts this life.

In the next layer of texts, the Upanisads, *atman* comes to be identified in terms of that elusive principle that is the 'seer of the seeing', which is itself not seen; in other words, the consciousness whereby there is grasp of the world. This close association between selfhood and consciousness influences a great deal of later debate about the self in Hindu and Buddhist philosophy in India.

In the Upanisads, the *atman* develops as the focus of inquiry. The Upanisads have many different preoccupations and ideas, and *atman* sometimes appears to be merely a reference to the body. However, the general idea of the *atman* as the essence of the human being gradually gains ground in the tradition. Repeatedly, many Upanisads assert that the most developed and wise are those who have no desires other than 'the desire for the self', which is a desire for understanding. A distinction is made between the human being and the self, for human beings seek to understand what is true or essential to themselves. What is not yet clear is the relationship between the 'man' and his 'self'. That relationship is tied to the emergence of an idea that, amongst civilizations, took root only in classical India – namely, rebirth and the cycle of lives.

In the Vedas, there is little evidence of belief in more than one life (and one afterlife). But gradually the belief begins to take hold that this life is merely one of many, that there is a constant sequence of life and death. Before this life, there were many lives, and after this life, there will be some other life, here or elsewhere; and then another and another, potentially for all eternity. We do not know how or why this idea became influential in ancient India, but since it is an idea about something that we do not experience in this life, it is no more or less arbitrary than the belief in an afterlife in some other world. The idea of a cycle of lives undoubtedly has an impact on the concept of the self. If the belief is that there is only this life followed by just one afterlife, then the self that undergoes life and death is relatively clear: it is the earthly, time-bound, particular person who has this life and then goes into another one. But if there is a round of lives and, furthermore, some of these lives are not even human, it becomes uncertain who or what it is that is reborn each time. It clearly cannot be a *person*, since the person 'I' am is not the reborn cow that your great-grandmother ate (or, indeed, for her sins, your great-grand-mother herself), even if the essential, true *self* (the *atman*) might have passed from an unnamed cow (or, indeed, your great-grand-mother) to Ram-Prasad. There has to be a distinction between the concrete, particular person (or even the particular animal, which has a self but is not a person) who/which lives and dies, and that being's essential self, which was in some other being before now, is in this one now, and will be in another in the future.

We do not know quite which idea – of the cycle of lives or of a depersonalized self/*atman* – came first; possibly they arose at the same time. But by the time the major Upanisads have come into being, the *atman* is something that transcends the body and its experiences. It does animate and provide the foundations for a person through a life; without it, there would be no person. But when that person – that being with parents, personality, character, relationships, and body, which has its own identity – dies, the self does not cease to exist with the person. It passes into another life and becomes the foundation of another person (or an animal, which lacks personhood). This is somewhat paradoxical: the self of the human person is truly and really what that person is, but that is precisely because the true self is more than – and lasts beyond – that person! Given this separation of the true self or the eternal subject of awareness from the concrete human person with a particular identity, it is better not to translate *atman* as 'soul', since the soul in religious Western thought has a specific identity tied to the person it is (and remains, in the afterlife).

The many Upanisad texts do not speak with one voice about the relationship between the self and the concrete, specific person. Indeed, popular Hindu culture also reveals ambiguities. Everyone (apart from a few materialist philosophers of the Lokayata school) agrees that something persists after this life. But whereas the strict philosophical view is that the *atman*, as the pure conscious self free of personality, goes from one life to another, there is an irresistible tendency to think that it is the actual concrete person who goes on to the next life after death in this one. But this latter idea is used for purposes other than philosophical analysis – in an ironic way to teach lessons (the king is born as the prey of a tiger whose mother he killed in a hunt), or to drive narratives (the disappointed lovers are born again to have another chance at romantic union). In philosophical texts, the self takes on an identifiable life – that is, takes on personhood – and engages with the world only within that life; as a person, it does not realize what its true nature is; and it continues from one life to another, before eventually doing something or knowing something about itself, in such a way that it need no more go through the round of birth, death and rebirth. (We explore this goal of liberation from the cycle of lives in chapter 4, on the Inward Good.)

Another important aspect of the Upanisadic conception of the self is that it is the 'inner controller'. The Upanisad texts give the general idea of a self as the essence of living beings, including humans. This essence consists in its consciousness (which many of the Upanisads identify in some way with a universal, foundational principle of being called *brahman*, which is explored in chapter 1). This self, then, is the subject of consciousness; it is what is truly and always aware in a person; and it persists not only through that person's life but existed before and will do so afterwards, in other lives and other forms.

Furthermore, the sages of the Upanisads are impressed by the fact that the inescapable feature of *any* awareness (of the world or of oneself) is that there is always a direction given to it. Our awareness 'points' in some direction and is moved towards something or other. They conclude that there must be an entity directing awareness in this way. And how can such direction be given if there is nothing that can direct? This is the common thread running through all our awareness, including all our efforts to inquire into and understand reality: an entity that gives direction to our thoughts at all times. The self is the inner controller or director of awareness.

Control, philosophically, is just the basic notion of directing awareness. It is evident to us that we *do* make (many of) our thoughts go in certain ways. Consciousness has the intrinsic feature of being willed in certain directions. The Upanisads, however, go far beyond this insight. In some places, they show a much more ambitious interpretation of the idea of control. They suggest that, if the self is essentially the controller, then under-standing it in a complete sense will give complete control over how it works (so that all our awareness goes wherever we want it to). Since the self is also of the nature of the universal consciousness, *brahman*, out of which all things arise, realizing the extended nature of the self should give control over all things! Not all Upanisadic passages on the self have this explicit aim by any means; but there is no doubt that this expansive idea of control, as mastery of all that consciousness can comprehend and control, was influential at the time of the Buddha.

The Buddha and the doctrine of non-self

The Buddha rejects the *atman*, because in general he does not think it is possible to define anything by its essence, where an essence is what makes a thing that very thing without reference to anything else. We saw in the last chapter that the Buddha teaches us that each thing is to be understood or defined in terms of other things, since all things arise only relationally. They are interdependent in the way they arise, and so cannot be characterized through any value, quality or characteristic that is essential to them alone. The human person too is interdependent on many things, and without an essence. As the Upanisads say that the self is the essence of each of us, the Buddha's teaching of the essenceless dependence of things upon each other is consistent with his rejection of the essence of persons. In short, it is a rejection of *atman*. Indeed, the standard Buddhist view is often stated the other way around: things do not have a 'self', they have no essential nature.

The basic reason he gives (in his 'second sermon') turns on the assumption that if this subject-self or *atman* is the 'inner controller', then it must literally control everything that comes within its purview. But no candidate he can find – for instance, the material body, perception or even awareness – has such control. The body, perception, thoughts – all are subject to uncontrolled changes. How then can any of them be a controller? He suggests to his audience that they are mistaken in searching for a controlling self, for none of the things that he can imagine to be the self has such power of control.

Another important argument he puts forward rejects the eternality of the self. The Upanisads take the subject-self or *atman* (especially given its identification with *brahman*) to exist before and after a person's life; indeed, to be eternal. The Upanisads maintain that *atman* exists timelessly, although it enters time when it becomes an embodied person in each life of its cycle. The Buddha says that here, too, whatever candidate he can find – the body, perceptions, awareness, dispositions, and so on – fails the test of eternity. He can find nothing that is eternal, and if the self has to be eternal, there is no self.

But that prompts the question: what of the person? Is there no person? Is it being denied that there is someone here, talking or listening? The Buddha does not want to deny that there are people whom he is teaching. He is as much concerned to deny 'annihilationism' – the doctrine that there is nothing beyond the physical being – as he is to deny 'eternalism' – the doctrine that physical being requires the *atman*. He seeks the Middle Way, in which there is something personal and spiritual that goes beyond the physical body and yet is not eternal. But how can there be someone here if there is no self? The Buddha's view is expressed in the famous analogy of the chariot. What makes the chariot what it is? Surely, its yoke, axle, platform, wheels and so on. Take them apart, and there is no chariot left. There is no such thing as a chariot in itself; there is no essence to a chariot. Thus it is with the person. She is constructed out of body, dispositions, perceptions, etc.; yet when reduced down to these components, she vanishes into nothing. But nobody denies that there is something conventionally called a chariot, which performs in a certain way, is instantly recognizable, and so on. There can be a chariot/person, without some essence-giving chariothood/personhood.

While this has been an influential line of thought, two remarks must be made. One is that the analogy is prey to competing intuitions. Many might agree that there is nothing more to the chariot than its parts, but others will feel that the whole is greater than the sum of its parts and that the chariot is not merely its constituents. So, too, the person may be greater than what makes her up. Secondly, the supporters of the *atman* will protest that the analogy is inappropriate. The subject-self, in their view, does not emerge from any components, but is what makes identity possible (there would be no being with an identity, without the *atman*). The components may go together to give the personality, but what renders that the personality of a person is the metaphysical self. The analogy misses the point: there is nothing comparable to the self in the chariot, and that is because the chariot is reducible in precisely the way the self is not.

At any rate, this line of argument set in motion a great debate in India on whether or not the self, conceived as the unified subject of consciousness, existed. (The larger significance of this topic is explored in chapter 4, on the Inward Good.) All the main Buddhist schools, following the Buddha, argue that the eternal, conscious subject-self of the Upanisads is simply superfluous: everything that needs explaining about the concrete person can be done without resorting to that idea. Instead, the concept of inter-dependent origination (explored in the last chapter) does the job. The Hindu schools, on the other hand, whatever their other differences, are committed to the claim that a unifying subject-self is needed to explain the experience of a continuous, concrete person. They believe that the subject-self gives personhood to the human being. Let us see how their reasoning runs.

Self and person: the debate over the Buddhist denial of *atman*

It will be remembered that a person has a relationship with herself (her psychological and physical states, through thoughts, emotions, desires, feelings and sensations). Such a relationship requires a conception of who she is; and that is possible only if there is some special link between those states (so that they can all be said to belong to *her*). That link will be evident in the fact that she has intimate access to those states and not to others (which belong to other people). A person, then, must have (i) continuity of identity, (ii) potentially, special access to the content of states of awareness (although not necessarily all), and (iii) necessarily, access only to some states of awareness (which are therefore said to belong to that person) and not to those of other persons. These are undeniable features of personhood. Most Hindu schools believe that they can be secured only if there is a subject-self. Being a stable and persistent entity, it explains continuity. Having the nature of consciousness, it gives special access to its own workings. Finally, being found uniquely in each person, it distinguishes and separates one person from another. Of course, the identity of that person also depends on the origin and existence of the body and the mind (the mind being, in Indian thought, merely the internal organ that senses states of consciousness). When that body-mind comes to the end of its existence, so does the person, while the eternal subject-self goes on to become embodied another time, giving rise to someone else.

The Buddha's teaching is that there is no underlying and unifying self, but only a series of states of awareness. Buddhists maintain that, upon reflection, it becomes clear that awareness only finds particular examples of itself – a looking, a touching, a feeling, an emotion, a memory, a thought. Nothing like a single self *apart from* those particular and momentary states is found. The Buddhists argue that we must therefore start with the acknowledgement that only particular states of awareness are apprehended, and not a self. But they agree that there must be some explanation of the relevant characteristics of personhood – namely, continuity, intimate access to states of awareness and separateness from others. The key to their explanation is the doctrine of interdependent origination. All things arise in terms of other things, and so it is with momentary and fleeting states of awareness. Each state of awareness (a looking, a touching, a feeling, a thought, a memory) occurs as an effect of a previous state, and contains within it the potential to be the cause of a succeeding one. Each state of awareness therefore is an effect (of a preceding awareness) and a cause (of a succeeding one). Such a state depends on the occurrence of a preceding awareness to come into being as an effect; and it depends upon the occurrence of a succeeding awareness to realize its potential as a cause.

The Buddhist view, then, is that on analysis only states of awareness are found, and that each state is dependent on others for its occurrence and nature. This, they claim, is sufficient to create the features of personhood. The interdependence of states of awareness links them to each other, thereby delivering continuity. As for the requirement that there must be intimate access to one's own states of awareness, well, *each* state of awareness is aware of itself, because that is what awareness is. There is no need to make a further appeal to a separate self that is aware of each state of awareness. Finally, some states of awareness are simply more closely connected as causes and effects with some other states. There is greater interconnectedness (or interdependence) between some states of awareness than there is between others. So we have states of awareness that: a) link continuously with those before and after them; b) are each aware of their own content, in intimate access; and c) link more closely with some states than others. We conveniently give the name 'person' to such a set of reflexive, continuous and relatively more closely interconnected states of awareness. Another such set of states is another person. True, this is not a 'real' person, in the sense that the Hindu philosophers want a person to be underpinned by a single, stable, unifying self that has access to its own states. Rather, it is merely a convenient fiction, a person in common parlance but without a metaphysical unity. But that is precisely the point. Persons are 'empty' (*sunya*) in that they have no essence to them, such as would be given by a stable, single, metaphysical entity like the *atman*.

Most Buddhist schools argue that ultimately there are only these moments of awareness. The Madhyamaka school, however, takes this one step further and says that even these momentary states should not be granted any ultimate nature; even they are susceptible to analysis, if only we could extend it that far. In either case, Buddhists argue that a concept of a person constructed out of momentary states of awareness is sufficient. It does not fail to explain all the features that persons undeniably have.

Hindu philosophers respond that, as a matter of fact, such a concept does fail to explain all that it must. The features of personhood turn out, on deeper analysis, not to be amenable to the 'selfless' construction of Buddhism. Memory, and what it says about the continuity of the self, is an example. (There are many other debates on the issue, which we cannot consider here.)

Initially, one might think that, since memory is about the same entity's experiences in the past, something must continue to exist between the experience in the past and the memory of that experience in the present. Buddhist philosophers of all stripes reject this consideration. They argue that a suitable link between a series of states of awareness is sufficient to build up continuity between the past experience and the present memory of it. That link, of course, is provided by the dependent origination of each state of awareness. If the original state and the memory of it are connected through intermediate states – with each state being an effect of the one before it and the cause of the one after it – nothing more is needed to tie them together. A rice seed produces rice and not barley because rice seed and plant are appropriately connected; likewise, my experience of a cat produces my memory of the cat and not of a dog.

Hindu philosophers such as the Nyaya thinker Vatsyayana, who advocates the reality of the subject-self, respond that there is more to memory than continuity of awareness through intermediate links. The memory awareness is not just 'cat seen yesterday' – that is, a simple link with a past awareness of the cat. Rather, the memory takes the form '*I* who saw the cat yesterday remember it now.' The memory awareness involves not just the link with the past awareness of the cat but the awareness that the two awarenesses are those of the same subject. How can that be secured without a self that ascribes or attributes the two awarenesses to itself, thereby linking them appropriately?

Buddhists such as the Yogacara philosopher Dinnaga develop the theory that a feature of each state of awareness is its ascription of what it experiences to a subject of experience (they call this 'auto-awareness' or self-knowing, *sva-samvedana*). This is simply the feature of having intimate access to itself. The subject of this auto-awareness, of course, is just each state of awareness; it is not some further, enduring subject like the Hindu *atman*. This theory eventually leads to the Yogacara position enunciated by Santaraksita, that the word *atman* can actually be used by Buddhists to refer to the reflexive access of each momentary state of awareness to itself, so long as it does not imply the reflexivity of a stable, continuous entity behind the series of states. (The Madhyamaka Buddhists find this unacceptable, since they do not grant essential existence even to momentary states of awareness, holding even these to be interdependent and provisional.)

Hindu thinkers respond that such momentary reflexivity fails to explain remembrance. It is not enough that each state of awareness is aware of itself (for instance, 'there is a memory now of a seeing of a cat yesterday'). Awareness of awareness is actually awareness that all these states of awareness belong to one being (for instance, 'the self that saw the cat yesterday remembers now that it saw the cat yesterday').

There we must leave it. These are perennial debates, each side relying on deep intuitions about what is true. Furthermore, each view is driven by what the philosopher enunciating it is searching for. The 'impersonalist' account of the Buddhists is not self-evident, but they mean to challenge us to rethink our ways of analysing experience. The Hindu philosophers, in general, feel that it is necessary to explain satisfactorily the normal understanding of our experience, and not challenge that understanding. The exception is the Advaita school, whose deeply counterintuitive view of the self we will now consider.

The self beyond the 'I': Advaita and consciousness

Although the Hindu schools in general are committed to the doctrine of the self or *atman*, they are very far from agreeing what that doctrine means. The biggest disagreement is between the Advaita Vedanta school and the rest over the proper reference of the self. The Nyaya and Mimamsa schools, which are followed by others in this regard, argue that the self is the individual, immaterial substance that becomes resident in the human body and, through its workings, sustains personhood across a lifetime. As we have seen, the person is not the subject-self, as the latter passes from body to body, and when in a non-human form, is not even a person. But when born in a human form, the self constitutes the person. It acts through the body, and actions are attributed to the person-in-the-body who performs them. The self is temporarily identifiable with the person. The person is what the self is when it is embodied, since the birth, form, relationships and actions of that body (including the mind) constitute and express personhood. The self is dependent on the body, since it can express itself only through the apparatus of the body – its mind, speech, limbs and other organs.

The self manifests its quality of consciousness through the workings of the mind. It picks itself out through the unique use of the concept 'I'. 'I' is the name each self uses to refer to itself, and when called upon to identify that 'I', the self refers to the person it is at that time and in that life. Each of these claims is backed by extensive argument that we do not have space to consider here. The standard Hindu view is that there is a plurality of such *atman*s. Each of these acts through a body, and when in a human life, is manifested as the person. The contrast with Buddhism is clear enough. And apart from the eventual distinction across lifetimes between the self and the person, it is very like the dominant Western, mainly Christian, idea of the soul.

Advaita Vedanta challenges this notion. Going back to the Upanisads, the founder of this school, Sankara, is impressed by the following consideration. What is most striking about the nature of consciousness (*cit*) is that it is undeniable; since the act of denial itself is an act of consciousness, it becomes an affirmation of existence. This undeniability means that consciousness must be the essential or necessary feature of our existence. We can question anything else that might make us who we are, but not the fact of our nature as conscious beings. So, the Advaitins conclude, consciousness is our essence; it is this by virtue of which we are what we are and otherwise would not be. Already we can see an intriguing line of thought developing: it is not that there is in each of us a self that is conscious, but rather that consciousness *is* the self; consciousness is not a quality of the self but the self itself. Of course, this is because 'self' means something different here from what it does with the other Hindu schools. For Advaita, the self is not the individual essence of a person but the universal awareness that is realized in each person.

This analysis has another component. What is undeniable is the general fact of consciousness, and not the existence of a particular subject who is conscious. Equating consciousness and thinking, the Advaitin would deny the legitimacy of Descartes's famous saying in Western philosophy, 'I think, therefore I am.' Rather, we can only say, 'There is thinking going on here, so thinking exists.' The 'I' is not undeniable, only the 'thinking' (that is, consciousness). As soon as we start answering the question, 'So who is the "I" that thinks?', we enter into all sorts of doubtable (and therefore potentially deniable) assumptions: our name, birth, memory, relationships, and so on. In short, the 'I' (*aham*) refers to a person who is constructed and based on assumptions, while the bare fact of consciousness alone is indubitable.

Advaita therefore arrives at a curious conclusion: the self is a general consciousness, but the self is not the 'I' that apparently separates each self from another. The 'I' is the person who is constructed, and it is a fundamental mistake to take that to refer to the self. The self cannot be referred to at all; it is never an object, only the conscious subject of all and any thought. Going back to the Upanisads, the self is the seer that sees, not the seen; it is the thinker, not that which is thought of. Yes, we do assume that we think of our 'self', but we are wrong. What is thought of is only the person, which is referred to through the 'I'. This is not the self. The self is what is always doing the referring. It always escapes being thought of. The very thing that makes the self undeniable – that it is required even for one to deny it – is also what stops it from ever being an object of thought. The fact of its inviolable presence makes it forever absent from its own content.

The Advaitins take very seriously the Upanisads' identification of this ever-present self-as-consciousness with *brahman*, the foundational, universal consciousness. Their belief is that the self is actually this universal consciousness. In each person, this universal consciousness is mistakenly thought to be a separate entity, unique and limited to that person, but it is actually general to all persons and not bound by any of them. Consciousness fails to see that it is not limited to the separate living human body within which it finds itself. In this limited form it is called *jiva*. As such, it functions to give personhood to that living human body. The so-called *atman* of the other Hindu schools is really only the *jiva*. When other schools talk of the *atman*, they are only talking of it in its ignorant state of apparent separateness, when it takes itself to be limited and one of many. In its true and ultimate state, it is infinite, unlimited and universally one.

Advaita therefore accepts all the arguments of the other Hindu schools about *atman*, but says they apply only to the limited self or *jiva*. Yet, in a curious way, Advaita is closer to Buddhism, in that the latter too denies that the self is the conscious being contiguous with the individual person. But whereas Buddhists argue that consciousness is composed of states that are infinitely less in duration and nature than the apparent person, Advaitins argue that consciousness is infinitely more than the apparent person. The denial of the claim that self and person are contiguous led other Hindus to call Advaitins 'crypto-Buddhists'.

Egoity or 'I'-form awareness: its role in Indian analysis

Let us end this survey of Indian views on the self with something that is common to them and yet allows us to see how different they are. In the Upanisad of the Great Forest (the *Brhadaranyaka*), in the course of a famous discussion with his wife Maitreyi, the sage Yajñavalkya says that the true self is an all-pervasive entity which is not found directly but only through such things as the body, through which it manifests itself. Among the many analogies he uses, he mentions the music of the lute, which cannot be caught; one can only catch the lute or the player. Already here we find a subtle notion of the self as present yet ungraspable. The self is both intimate and elusive in this Upanisad.

Some centuries later, the Buddha presents a critique of the self which uses the same analogy. A king hears a lute being played and asks his servants to bring the sound to him. They bring him the lute, but he says he wants the music. They explain to him that the lute is made up of parts, which together 'speak' the music. He breaks the lute into ever-smaller parts without finding the music. Now, Yajñavalkya says the self is like the music: present but not graspable, unlike the lute/body. The Buddha, however, says the opposite: the Upanisads, in his view, are like the king who searches for the music in the materials of the lute; they search for the self, whereas it is simply a temporary phenomenon that emerges from the functioning of the body, mind and dispositions. So, whereas the Upanisadic moral is that the self is present but not an object, the Buddha's conclusion is that there is no self at all. Clearly there are deeply conflicting intuitions here.

The Hindu schools that arise after the Buddha appear to be deeply impressed by his reductive analysis. They agree that the body, mind and dispositions cannot pick out the self, although they are needed for its manifestation (just as the wood and strings of the lute are needed for production of the music). They call these expressions of selfhood 'egoity' (*ahamkara*, literally the 'I'-form; this translation allows us to distinguish the technical concept here from the conventional 'egoism', which refers to the centring of all moral psychology by people on themselves). Egoity is nothing other than the sense of self: it is the expression of 'I am … (this, that or the other)' that people make to identify themselves to both themselves and others. The self, for the Hindu schools, is no more the ego through which it expresses itself than the music is the lute. This, of course, ends up being diametrically opposed to the Buddhist position. The Buddhists say that there is nothing more to the self than egoity. It is a temporary manifestation of interacting factors, just as the music is of the wood and the strings of the lute; take away the collection of physical, mental and emotional factors that people refer to when thinking or talking of themselves, and nothing is left. The burden for the Hindu schools is to explain, in their different ways, what the self is, if not ego; for the Buddhists, it is to explain how there can be an ego without a self.

The metaphysical subject, then, is the focus of classical Hindu and Buddhist discussions of the self. When we turn to China, we find that the focus of thought is the quite different issue of the concrete, social person. It is not that the person does not figure as a category in Indian thought; it does, but merely as a presupposition in social and religious life.

The concrete person, ametaphysical traditions, and models for living

The reader will have anticipated, especially given the previous chapter on ultimate questions, that the strongly metaphysical character of the debates on the self in India is unlikely to be treated with sympathy in China. The main issue about the self in China has to do with the formation and development of the person. But what is the 'person' in classical Chinese thought?

At the beginning of this chapter, we saw how the self could be understood as 'the person'. In Indian philosophy, the person is a relatively unproblematic category, although it is distinguished from the self-as-metaphysical subject, thereby splitting apart what in traditional Western thought has normally been taken together. The Chinese concept of the person is in many ways very different from the Indian one. Most obviously, there is no metaphysical subject in classical Chinese thought (later, under the influence of Buddhism, Neo-Confucianism posited a metaphysical self). It will be useful to refer again to the idea that Chinese philosophy is ametaphysical: it does not reject or fail to recognize the possibility of hidden, deeper and ultimate realities behind appearance as such; it simply proceeds to address only what is available to ordinary experience. The ametaphysical self of classical Chinese thought is the person – the concrete human being whose proper identity is given by a particular family history.

In the Indian tradition (as in the classical West), exploration of the self takes place against a larger vision of reality that may be called 'cosmogonic' (from the Greek *cosmos*, 'universe/order', and *gonia*, 'creation'). In a cosmogony, understanding the world requires an account of the first principles behind its structure; hence the attention paid to the source and nature of the metaphysical subject-self (*atman*) in ancient India and to the soul in the West. The Chinese vision of the world is focused on how to live within it, and its attention to the past is historical (concerning those who passed before) rather than cosmogonic. In such a vision, questions about the self are about the cultivation required to live appropriately in this world. Whereas the Indian project is to discover, define and realize the self as it really is behind life, the Chinese project is to model and guide the self in life.

This person, however, is not merely a material person, as many contemporary Western philosophers would have it. The Chinese do not seek to reduce personhood to the physical/chemical/biological functions of the body. In a passage attributed to a legendary thinker called Zichan, who is supposed to have lived before Confucius, it is said that 'a man's life' is transformed by earthly aspects (*po*) and then by heavenly aspects (*hun*). These aspects become strong if a person has a good life, but haunt the place where he lived if he did not have a good life; and as such, become ghosts. Clearly, these are non-material dimensions of a person. But they are simply part of a larger conception of nature, in which one single realm encompasses the material and non-material things of both human existence and Heaven (as we saw with the concept of Heaven or *tian* in the previous chapter). These dimensions of the person do not transcend the normal conditions of the subject as they do in India; instead, they are part of those very conditions.

The person, then, is an irreducible complex, endowed with these different aspects. However, there is no general theory or unifying concept of the person in Chinese thought. What we have, instead, is a series of concerns – taken immensely seriously by various thinkers – about the self-as-person; and from these we are able to discern what the self means in Chinese thought. So, rather than trying to define the meaning of the self and then exploring the issues connected with it (a characteristic way of proceeding in much Indian and Western thought), with the Chinese we are better off drawing out a meaning from the ways in which the issues are discussed. Let us, then, look at a number of interacting notions at whose meeting point the idea of the person begins to emerge.

The main aim of the Chinese thinkers is to offer models for human life, rather than to argue for a specific conception of the self. These models of the appropriate life for a person are developed indirectly by suggesting how one should live. They are built out of a combination of key themes in Chinese thought.

Humanness and co-humanity

The first idea, which goes back to an early and tentative development in Confucius, is *ren*. There are two ideographs in Chinese for *ren*. The older one simply means 'human', but was initially used by aristocratic clans to refer to themselves in contrast to common people. In Confucius, we find another *ren*, which appears to be a combination of the original character and the sign for 'two'. The relationship between these two ideas, and the concept that arises out of them, is mysterious even in Confucius (his pupils complained that they did not hear him explain what *ren* meant). The conventional translation of the second *ren* is 'benevolence', although that sense emerged only with Mencius, not with Confucius. The ideographic character has persuaded some Sinologists to translate the second *ren* as 'co-humanity', in contrast to the first *ren*, which is rendered as 'human'; others translate it as 'humane'.

In Confucius, *ren*-as-human is still strongly associated with the aristocracy, as people of distinction and cultivation; so *ren*-as-human is quite narrowly understood by him to mean something like 'noble'. This is an interesting pointer, since at the heart of the later understanding of 'human' is the idea of being endowed with special qualities – a quality of nobility that is instilled in some way. When Confucius then juxtaposes this meaning with the second type of *ren*, he is indicating some special quality that people ought to have, even if it is not easily found. A translation of one of his famous sayings in the *Analects* is indicative of this: 'If *ren* (first type) were not *ren* (second type), what would become of ritual conduct (*li*, on which see the next chapter, on the Outward Good)?' We may translate this narrowly, 'if nobles were ignoble…'; or more generally, 'if a human were not humane…' In the end, though, an idea begins to emerge here: there is something of human nature that, brought out properly in human beings, will enable them to become fulfilled expressions of themselves.

The translation of *ren* as 'co-humanity', for all that it sounds artificial, is helpful in indicating the elusive quality involved in Confucius' early use of the idea. Human beings have, in some way, a capacity to go beyond themselves, manifested in the ability to encompass other people in their considerations. Properly brought out, persons are more than themselves; they open up to others and bring them within their own lives. Humans become human in the proper sense through the impingement of others on them (a human becomes a 'co-human', a human only with other humans).

The extension of co-humanity was a part of the history of Confucianism. Soon after Confucius, Mozi criticized Confucians for their inadequate understanding of the need to have universal love that extended beyond family. The idea of later Daoists that there is an ultimate *dao* that encompassed everything, and the Huayen Buddhist claim that all things shared in a Buddha-nature, both mutually influence later Confucian ideas of co-humanity. In the 11th century, the Neo-Confucian Chenghao claims that the person of *ren* (a person of co-humanity or benevolence) regards all things in the universe as one body; his *ren* (feeling of benevolence) extends everywhere, and he feels *ren* (benevolence) for all things, as he considers them part of him. Selfhood reaches its fullest realization in an identification with the physical universe, through a feeling that self and world are coextensive. In the 15th century, Wang Yangming asserts that this sense of a fully extended self is what lies under the compassion (of a great man) for all things. Chenghao's and Wang's expansive identification of self and world is a moral one – the fully cultivated self shares a nature with the world and is therefore deeply engaged with it. This notion of harmony is postulated as lying behind the ideal behaviour of great men. This is not so much a developed metaphysics of selfhood in which a theory is put forward of how self and world are one; rather, it is a metaphorical way of making the point that the cultivated person should take the self to encompass – become co-human with – not just a few people but all, and not just people but nature itself. The contrast with the Indian school of Advaita and its notion of a universal self shows how, even when there is some apparent similarity, a great chasm separates Indian and Chinese philosophers.

It should also be noted that later Neo-Confucians criticized Chenghao's and Wang's spiritual reading of selfhood as oneness with nature, arguing that this transpersonal understanding was a combination of Buddhist notions of a pervasive Buddha-nature and Daoist ideas of a natural *dao*. They argued, instead, for a return to graduated love and careful social practices as the expression of the self's co-humanity.

There are other issues here regarding the influential idea of the human self in Confucius. Notably, even the 'noble' person has to *become* 'noble'; the human has to *become* humane. This means both (i) that *everyone* needs to become more than they are; and (ii) that everyone *becomes* more than they are. The former is a meritocratic point. It is not that Confucius and others in any way rejected social hierarchies; they were not egalitarians. But in principle, anyone can develop the self through proper learning, so the potential for full selfhood is available to all in this life. The latter point (ii) says something about the fluidity and development of the self. An observation in contemporary Chinese philosophy is that there are no human *beings* but rather human *becomings*! The self is something that develops over time, is cultivated in a variety of ways, and eventually, by becoming properly linked to others, improves itself. This never stops. Confucius says that if one has a seed in one's hand as death approaches, one's last act should be to plant it. There is always some scope for one to extend one's humanity.

Another point to note is that there is no simple definition of what constitutes co-humanity. Indeed, it is fundamentally intuitive, and understood only in the concrete actions of model persons. This absorption in the need to guide individual action will seem unsatisfactory to the Indian or Western thinker, who wants a theory first. In Chinese philosophy, the primary goal is rather to act in a certain way, and the classical figures would have thought it misguided to waste time on enunciating the idea instead of cultivating it.

One aspect of co-humanity as an intuitive guide to the development of the self did generate debate, and this concerned its source. Now, Confucius does not say that *ren* is a simple feeling that something is right. Rather, it is an attitude towards action that develops in a person: one must act (or perform social rituals) with a sense of wanting to act for the good of others. The development of benevolence towards others – the development of a sense of co-humanity – must guide action. Then, as action is performed, that sense will develop further. Good social practice should be structured by the cultivation of co-humanity. At the same time, co-humanity should develop further through such practice. But all this leads to a compelling question: where does *ren* come from, such that it can inform social practice? Mencius answers decisively: co-humanity comes from the human being – it is innate in the person. Every person already has the capacity to encompass others and be benevolent towards them. Humans develop this full selfhood because they have the potential to do so.

Other Confucians, called the 'traditionalists', see no such intrinsic quality in the person. They argue that a person is realized only in his integration (his 'co-humanization') with others. There is nothing innate in people that allows for development of co-humanity; it has to come from the society that surrounds and forms each person. Tradition, in which authoritative and cultivated persons are found, is the source of the sense of co-humanity. In starting education, one turns to the exemplary models of the past, the fully developed persons who are sages (*sheng*), and assimilates the lessons of fine literature (*wen*). There one learns what it is to orient social practice towards others in the manner of the sages. The self develops its encompassing of others through learning from the guidelines of tradition. The self is, in this line of Confucian thought, deeply reliant on tradition for its formation.

This reliance on tradition becomes even more pronounced after Zhuangzi's Daoist attacks on innate abilities. If co-humanity is innate in each of us, Zhuangzi asks, why is it that its expression takes many different forms, most of which the Confucians themselves reject? If selfhood is derived from self, why does the self take so many forms that Mencius will reject as unacceptable? The last great classical Confucian, Xunzi, argues in response that co-humanity is indeed developed out of understanding and following tradition. Intriguingly, he adapts the account of the acquisition of morality from the other great classical Daoist, Laozi, and argues that Confucian conceptions of co-humanity are proper for the formation of selfhood because they are better at responding to the cultural and historical reality of the times. The Confucian self is to be developed because that is the best one for the concrete circumstances of China! (The proper social practices that should be cultivated for personhood are dealt with in the discussion of *li* in the next chapter, on the Outward Good.)

The interesting thing is that, regardless of whether the core of humanity is innate or given by tradition, it has to be brought out; the person has to be educated to develop a proper self. How is this education acquired? In the Chinese tradition, it is acquired through the training of the 'heart-mind' (*xin*). This faculty is another fundamental aspect of the social self of Chinese culture.

The ideographic character for *xin* resembles the physical heart, which the ancient Chinese took to be the organ of thought, feelings and judgement. Phonetically, this word is related to *xing* – (human) nature – and therefore implies that this faculty is something special to people. There is no distinction here akin to the Western one between reason and passion, thought and feeling. This one faculty has the special ability to guide the self in its development, and education is both of and through the heart-mind. The heart-mind is the determining quality of the person. (We will recall how, in India, the determining quality of a person is, one way or another, a metaphysical entity that transcends the body. The Chinese account is wholly limited to the psychological reality of this body and its capabilities.)

The great disagreements are over how the heart-mind is educated. In Confucianism, education can be advanced by understanding tradition or by using an intrinsic ability to gain that understanding; the heart-mind is simply what facilitates the cultivation of the self. Mencius develops a full-blown account of the heart-mind: in it must flourish the 'four sprouts' of compassion, shame, modesty and the distinction between right and wrong. It is these that allow the co-humanity and other virtues of a person to ripen. The Neo-Confucian Zhuxi takes the heart-mind to be the agency through which the self becomes integrated with the world, by means of communication and interaction.

In Daoism, Zhuangzi uses the heart-mind in a more radical way. He says that the heart-mind is full of thoughts, inclinations and feelings that clog up the self's relationship with its *dao*/way. (We will remember from the previous chapter that for Zhuangzi all that is social is artificial and gets in the way of the *dao*/way.) In order for it to function so as to let the self become perfectly one with its *dao*/way, the heart-mind must 'fast' – it must rid itself of artifice (thinking, feeling, judging in unnatural, socially constrained – possibly Confucian? – *dao*/ways). This will involve a 'forgetting' of what the self should do, followed by a natural doing of it. A good swimmer, he says, 'forgets' the water and rights an upturned boat as naturally as a man on land would right an upturned cart. In forgetting he is in water, he becomes like a man on land (who never especially thinks that he is on land and so might be said to have 'forgotten' that he is on it). The sage is like this swimmer in contrast to the ordinary person, who cannot free himself from his fearful awareness of being in water. (Or think of an adult walking on land as the sage, in contrast to ordinary people who are like toddlers acutely aware of the challenge of walking on the ground.) The heart-mind wanders free in a perfected person, and in this state of naturalness lets him move in his *dao*/way as a fish in water.

The heart-mind, then, is key to the development of the self, regardless of how it functions and in what that development consists. The self-as-person who emerges from the functioning of the heart-mind is the 'human becoming'.

From this extended discussion of two major concepts – co-humanity and the heart-mind – a picture of the self in Chinese thought emerges. The selfhood of a person forms through the course of life. If the potential to develop is nourished, then the self becomes fuller as it realizes its larger context. This realization depends on extending the sense of self beyond the particular individual and encompassing the way other people and things function. The literal word for the concept of self-cultivation in Confucianism is *xiushen*, which means 'nourishing the body'; Mencius asks for the full realization of the 'bodily form'. Persons are most themselves when they realize the potential of their bodily form in encompassing others and being integrated with their social surroundings.

Now, it might be asked whether such a this-worldly ethical ideal is not limited to Confucianism. What of the free self of Zhuangzi's Daoism? Is not his 'perfected person' a metaphysical entity? The famous story of Zhuangzi's response to his wife's death points to an answer. After her death, his friend found him singing and drumming, and asked him if he was not mourning her death. Zhuangzi replied that he had been just as sad as anyone else would be, but had then reflected that she had emerged out of the *dao*/way before she was his wife, and her life and death were natural and proportionate events within it. This person, his wife, was now sleeping in a vast room, and if he followed her 'bawling and sobbing' into it, he would merely be showing his lack of clarity about life and death. In this story, there is no philosophical account of a person beyond death, no thought of a subject that is immortal, is reborn or goes on to exist elsewhere. There is no rationalization of his wife's death. All that Zhuangzi does is to give up a perspective that places disproportionate weight on his personal experience. Seeing the *dao*/way, he simply accepts his grief and thereby frees himself from it. This is mystical self-therapy which requires a difficult, some would say impossible, shift in thinking; but it is resolutely ametaphysical. His wife's self is finished, but since the nature of the self is to be finished, what is there to mourn? (We may contrast this with the classic teaching of the Hindu text, the *Bhagavad Gita*, in which equanimity towards life and death is taught precisely through the metaphysical consideration that the self exists beyond the person who lives and dies. Same virtue, different world-view.)

Zhuangzi comes closest of the classical Chinese thinkers to making a metaphysical comment about the self: it seems as if 'there is something genuinely in command here', he notes of himself, but goes on to observe that the only trouble is that we cannot find a sign of it. The Indian philosophers would ask: What is the sign that is sought? How do we decide that nothing has been found? What is it that appears to be in command but does not give a sign of itself? If there is nothing, then why does it seem as if there is something in command? But for Zhuangzi, these are meaningless questions, for they appear not to have anything to say about how one should act.

In the end, the picture of the self that emerges in Chinese philosophy is as follows: the self is the bodily person, who is born human and becomes more truly or fully human through the cultivation of virtues instilled by education. This realization of humanness comes through opening up and becoming integrated with what is beyond the person: for Confucians, it is other people in society (especially the family); for the followers of Mozi (called the Mohists), all other humans; for the Zhuangzi type of Daoists, the natural order as a whole; and for Neo-Confucians, the natural order as expressed in human society. There is therefore a fundamental non-individualism in the Chinese understanding of the self-as-person.

Buddhist Non-self and the Chinese conception of personhood

It is in this context that we must locate the disorienting arrival and history of Buddhism in China. We have already seen that the Buddhist theory of the non-self was originally embedded in the ancient Indian context. It was a reaction to the idea in the Upanisads that the true self of each person is a single, persistent, continuous and unified subject of consciousness. The Buddhists consistently deny that there is any *unified* subject of consciousness above and beyond the body and mind of persons. But when Buddhism reached China, it found no metaphysical self to reject! The Chinese simply worked with the concrete person, the human being born of parents into a family, who grows and develops relationships, cultivates his or her abilities, performs a range of roles, and dies. This physically present and perceptible person (with, to be sure, imperceptible thoughts and feelings) on whose self-development the Chinese thinkers placed such value was unquestionably a single entity. Indian thinkers did not focus on the issue of the social cultivation of the person, but in common with the Chinese, they did not question the very existence of the person. The person was simply the unified entity defined by birth, body, communicative roles through life, and death. The real issue for the Indian thinkers was whether or not a deeper and truer consciousness – a single subject-self – explained the unity of the person. The Buddhists thought not, and by the time Buddhism reached China, they had developed many arguments for their view.

Inevitably, the Chinese interpret the Buddhist doctrine of non-self as an attack on the unity of the human person, so leading to one of the most notable pseudo-debates in all philosophy. The Confucians, especially, understand the Buddhists to be denying the existence of the person, which the Buddhists are not. They are saying only that the person is not an ultimately real or metaphysical self but merely an appearance constructed out of a combination of birth, body, thoughts and relationships. The person exists, but 'empirically', or in human transactions, as an effective entity with an impact on the world; but it does not exist 'transcendentally' or at some ultimate level of analysis. But ameta-physical Chinese philosophy has no role for the reality/appearance distinction. The Chinese account of the person includes development, change, fluidity and cultivation through roles, rituals and relationships. In a metaphysical context, this might appear to be a construction or ultimately unreal convention, but in China it is simply an obvious observation.

Despite this crossed line of communication, the Buddhist doctrine of the non-self did have an impact on the general view of the person found in Chinese philosophy, especially in the form of Neo-Confucianism. The Chinese notion of the person was, as we have seen, of a naturally integrated person, whose identity is derived from family history, birth, status and social roles. The ethical challenge to the person is to cultivate the mind-heart through and in proper ritual and social activity, but the fluidity implied by self-development is simply natural to a person. For Buddhism, personhood is constructed by the mind (and it was the Buddhists who introduced the restricted use of *xin* as 'mind', namely the organ of thought), so it is fragile and impure, subject to desire and consequent suffering. The ethical challenge for a person is to move away from the very concept of a person as a separate, self-oriented (that is, literally selfish) entity, through meditation on the emptiness of self and through ethical care for others. Even if the metaphysical motivation of Buddhism was entirely novel to Chinese thought, the critique of the components of personhood was immediately recognizable as worthy of serious consideration. What the Confucian tradition, in particular, thought of as the secure core of the person – the mind-heart as the governor of human thought, feeling and action – the Buddhists criticized for being the generator of illusion (the illusion of a permanent self). Without necessarily having to engage with why the Buddhists criticized the mind and the integrity of the person, the native Chinese tradition could see clearly the consequences of the critique. The person becomes a problematic category; where formerly the fluidity and changing aspects of the person are only signs of development and cultivation in China, the Buddhists see them as confirmation of the unreal nature of personhood.

This crossed line of communication might have made the traditions run in uncomprehending parallel but for the fact that Buddhism became more and more oriented to native Chinese interests. The success of Chinese Buddhism in its six-centuries-long ascendancy lay in the effective way in which it shifted the focus of the doctrine of the non-self from the metaphysical context of classical India to the ametaphysical world of Chinese thought. The doctrine of non-self in India had been the denial of an abstract, impersonal subject as the foundation of the concrete, temporarily continuous person (continuous, that is, between birth and death). In China, the Buddhist doctrine of non-self drives a programme of analysing the components – body, thoughts, feelings and actions – of the person. The significance of these elements to the eventual aspirations of the person may be denigrated, in a way that rejects classical Chinese views of the integrity of the person; this is, of course, because the Buddhists have a different goal in view (as we will see in chapter 4, on the Inward Good). But the 'Sinification' of Buddhism becomes apparent when we see that this reduction of the person is supposed to lead to the attainment of the Buddha-nature – a principle of ethical and mental purity exemplified in and remaining potent through the life of the Buddha. This Buddha-nature is not some ultimate existent like the *brahman* of the Upanisads; rather, it is a way of being that is potential in the nature of all creatures. In that sense, it is the true nature of all beings, including humans. Realizing this principle in one's thoughts, feelings and actions allows the person to lead a proper life of selfless engagement with everything in the world. This doctrine plays little part in Indian Buddhism; in China, it combines the Buddhist doctrine of non-self with a distinctively Chinese orientation towards engagement in the world.

This directing of the analysis of the non-self towards the attainment of the Buddha-nature was systematized by Fazang, the Huayen Buddhist philosopher. When, in the hands of some Buddhists of the Qan school, this doctrine took the form of a search for a spontaneous expression of Buddha-nature through trusting oneself to act freely, it threatened to become an asocial search for inner personhood that was considered dangerous in Chinese thought. A later philosopher, Zongmi, reformulated the doctrine within a moral vision influenced by Confucianism, maintaining that the attainment of Buddha-nature within the person had to come through ritual and socially recognized religious practice. So, once more, the person becomes integrated into Chinese society, even without commitment to the traditional norms of personhood.

A still later Buddhist development of the concept of the non-self is seen in Japanese Buddhism, in the thought of the Zen philosopher Dogen. Dogen makes a distinction between inauthentic and authentic selfhood. Inauthenticity occurs when a person takes himself to be a distinctive, separate and significant entity, whose interests and regard for himself colour his view of the world and who values it only to the extent that it benefits him. The inauthentic self is fearful that it will lose its distinctiveness, through suffering and death. The authentic self is, of course, not a self at all. It is simply the person who is 'made up of the myriad things' of the world, a person who is not separate and isolated from the world but integrated within it. The authentic self is, paradoxically, selfless, if by 'self' we mean a being distinct from the world around it. The authentic self is the person who lives in a way profoundly embedded in the world and who does not make a distinction between what is and what is not the self. This conception of the non-self is characteristic of Japanese approaches to ultimate issues. It is metaphysical in that it seeks to provide a transcendental account of how things really are; but it is ametaphysical in that the account it gives is contained within the ordinary world of experience. The selfless person (the authentic self) of Dogen does transcend the conditions of personhood (namely, its distinctive identity, its separate history, its role and day-to-day existence); but it does not transcend the world. It merely becomes more closely related to it.

Eventually, Neo-Confucianism develops a Chinese theory of the person that incorporates the Buddhist critique of the self into a traditional, this-worldly moral vision. Two crucial ideas mark the Neo-Confucian reworking of the concept of the person. First, there is the introduction by Zhangzai of the idea, unprecedented in classical Chinese thought, of a material, physical nature (*ji zhi zhi xing*) in human beings that harbours selfish desires; this contrasts with the traditional notion of an original nature (*ben xing*) that is pure and good. This idea acknowledges the impact of the severe Buddhist critique of personhood as the locus of impurity and fallibility. At the same time, the deep Confucian idea of human nature as intrinsically good, which goes back to Mencius, is preserved.

Second, and even more importantly, the aim of living comes to be recognized as the 'enlargement of the mind' in order to 'enter into all things in the world'. The fully realized person is one whose mind (*xin*, now used in the strict Buddhist sense of the cognitive apparatus) gains insight into the principles (*li*) of things – that is, the way they function. This appears to be a recognition of the powerful Buddhist ethical ideal of selflessness, and can be seen in the Neo-Confucian Zhuxi's use of 'egoism' or 'self-centredness' as the sense of separation between self and the world. As one might expect, this new Neo-Confucian understanding of the self is quite different from that of the Buddhists. The latter see selflessness in two ways: metaphysically, as the non-existence of a unified entity separate from all others; and ethically, as the giving up of any overriding concern for the interests of that imagined unified entity above those of all others. The result is a situation in which the boundaries between the imagined self and everything else are dissolved, so that only an impersonal compassion for all beings remains. It is reasonable to presume that the Neo-Confucians were impressed by the Buddhist conception of an ethically selfless engagement with the world, and that this had something to do with their novel idea of the expanded self, free of the egotistical sense of separation from others. But Zhangzai's expanded self, whose mind enters into the principle of all things, does not dissolve its 'natural' (or given) boundaries of identity as a consequence. Indeed, the opposite happens. The identity of the person is realized precisely by entering into a productive moral relationship with the world. In other words, the self is affirmed through selflessness. Clearly, the Neo-Confucian ethics of selflessness seeks the same kind of engagement with others as does Buddhist ethics. But there is no metaphysical selflessness in Neo-Confucianism. The Neo-Confucians in fact assert that enlargement of the mind is the very essence of that classical Confucian ideal, co-humanity. It is a matter of some intellectual delicacy here to decide whether, in the Neo-Confucian ideal of the person as a mind realizing its benevolent relationship with all others, we have a native metaphysics, albeit one emerging naturally out of the deeply concrete sociality of classical Chinese thought.

3

The Outward Good

We may broadly divide the worthwhile ends of philosophy – the good things or, as philosophers say, the 'goods' – into those that are attained in the world of the thinker and those that are attained in the thinker herself. I propose to call this distinction one between 'outward' goods and 'inward' goods.

The outward goods that philosophy seeks are to be attained in the world that the thinker inhabits – the human world. A great deal of thought is devoted by philosophers to finding out what will secure a desirable and worthwhile state of affairs amongst people. The philosopher here considers human beings in terms of their relationships with each other and the order that underpins those relationships. The differences in power, status and scope for action between people; the way in which one's identities are determined in reference to others; the impact of larger groupings, such as organizations, on the individual's roles, duties and entitlements – all these are questions about the Outward Good. How should such relationships be ordered? Why should they be ordered in one way rather than another? What will come of that ordering? In short, what is the state of affairs between human beings that should be sought, and how is it to be attained? Generally, outward goods, or the sum of them, which we may call the Outward Good, are also public goods. The public consists of people sharing openly what is common to them all, and the Outward Good is sought in and for a common world.

In contrast, an inward good is that which the philosopher thinks is to be sought by individual people, through their own personal – mental and moral – resources. Strictly speaking, such a good is not private, if by 'private' we mean something that pertains to one particular person alone (as one might say, 'my fantasies are my private affair'). The Inward Good is not private because what the philosophers seek is a good – is truly of worth – precisely because it is a good for *all*. (Not everyone might be able to seek a good, for they might lack in ability or qualification in the view of the philosopher, but that only means that they cannot immediately reach a good. It does not mean that it is not a good at all.) So the Inward/Outward distinction does not map onto the more familiar public/private distinction.

Generally, the Inward Good is the highest good, and the Outward Good is either a means to it or an outcome of the pursuit of it. In most mature formulations of philosophy, the two are not clearly distinguished but form a continuum, with the Outward Good assimilated into a larger account culminating in some Inward Good. Some philosophical systems and traditions make explicit and sharp contrasts between the two, while others remain less concerned about distinctions. We should, in fact, think of the distinction more as a tool of analysis, to help us make our way through dense and diverse philosophical literature.

Let us sum up this short introduction by defining the good as that which motivates philosophy. The Outward Good is something that is sought in the common world, so that the world may be made better. The Inward Good is something that is sought for the sake of the person undertaking that quest, so that she may be transformed in some significant and valuable way.

It is better to confine ourselves to these generalities at this stage. We will deal with different conceptions of the Inward Good in the next chapter. For the time being, this introduction to the concepts of outward and inward goods is sufficient to get us started with looking at the former.

Political order and ceremonial ritual action

The self-image that Confucius, the earliest Chinese philosopher, projects of what he is doing informs the outward purpose of philosophy in much of subsequent Chinese thought. He takes himself to be preserving and restoring a tradition in decline from a high point in the past. Key to this task is the propagation of appropriate social intercourse, made formal and precise in ceremony, or ritual action (*li*). Ceremony is manifested in rituals that govern all manner of interactions, from visiting a temple to talking to one's father, from showing hospitality to a guest to approaching the king.

What exactly are rituals? They are the structured aspects of every kind of social action. Music, dance and clothing are all part of ritual. There is a description of Confucius's own ceremonial performance, when he was in the service of a local lord: when summoned, he would move with brisk step and serious expression, but so smoothly that he seemed to glide; he would bow with clasped hands to colleagues to his left and right, and his movements would be such that his robes were spread evenly in front and behind. This concern for appropriateness in action extended to such precise and specific movements as whether to bow before or after ascending the steps to a temple.

In time, indeed, elaborate ritual texts were composed that prescribed social conduct in minute detail. But it is not the laying down of ritual that is Confucius's main concern. Rather, it is to teach people (especially rulers, as we shall see) about the importance of ceremony in sustaining the right life. Instruction has to come from the very performance of ritual by the Master himself. Ritual performance is to be judged by its aesthetic quality – its beauty as revealed in the skill with which it is performed. Indeed, while Confucius would teach people about the importance of ritual, he would not teach the specifics of what to do, since the aesthetic worth of his own ceremonious behaviour lay precisely in his being unselfconscious about its performance! This unselfconscious personal refinement is to be identified as the quality of style (*wen*), something implicit, beyond the prescriptive rules of ritual. The English saying, 'manners maketh man', is really a Confucian principle.

Confucius is concerned about ritual because it is the performance of what is ethical – conduct that is right (*yi*) and fitting to both oneself and others. The right thing to do, for Confucius, is not given or predetermined, but lies in the tendency of the cultivated person to act in the appropriate way. Rightness – or rather, the urge to act rightly – by itself is not sufficient for harmony amongst people, since ritual is required. But social ritual must certainly be infused with rightness, for ritual is not inherently moral. Ceremony or ritual action is important when tradition has declined. For Confucius, since the time of the exemplary and legendary kings of the past, there has been only chaos in the political scene due to competition over power and legitimacy; and scepticism amongst the people about the efficacy of religion. All this is evident in the decline in the care and attention that people give to status and role in social intercourse. In short, Confucius interprets the crisis of his times in terms of a decline in the ceremonies of ritual action. This leads him to express his belief in what has to be done: if ritual action can be re-established, then surely political and social order will be regained and maintained.

Here we see an interesting move that renders ritual action a philosophical issue. Whereas, historically, ritual had been the *result* of political and social order, Confucianism makes it the *source* of that order. Confucian theory develops the claim that individual ritual performance has the potential to lead to an ordered state of affairs for the people in general.

How can ritual action have such power to create social and political order? Confucian philosophers see that ritual can efficiently convey complex meaning, since each aspect of a ritual is important for what it symbolizes rather than for what it literally does. An example in ancient China was the ritual at a banquet in which guests would select stanzas from a body of well-known poetry and sing them to each other. This was not mere singing but an opportunity for the guests to use the words and cadences to convey their own feelings within a shared world; the ritual went far beyond singing, and became a means of binding those present together. A simple comparison would be the ritual of toasting someone: it is not the act of drinking that is really relevant, but what is conveyed by the collective act of a social ritual.

Increasingly subtle messages can be conveyed as more and more symbols are incorporated through more and more carefully constructed ritual. Social interaction can eventually be controlled by ritual action if the latter has such powerful symbolic value that normal social actions are determined by it. There is a story that a man who had usurped the kingdom wanted to employ Confucius as his advisor and called for him. Confucius did not want to recognize the legitimacy of the usurper, so he did not go, since going voluntarily would have indicated that he acknowledged that his position was legitimate. The usurper, however, had high social status in any case, and he came up with a plan. He sent a pig as a present to Confucius. Now, when a man of the usurper's legitimate rank sent a pig to someone of Confucius's (lower) rank, the latter was obliged to pay a courtesy call, so Confucius had to go. However, there was no specific indication of when he had to go, so he carefully picked a time to pay his call when the usurper was out of the house. But unfortunately the usurper met Confucius on the road! Through the constraints of ritual action, Confucius was defeated. Although the details are strange, the actions look familiar: 'ah, the games people play', we think to ourselves. But, from the Confucian point of view, we dismiss rituals as mere social games precisely because we do not take ritual action seriously; that is why we do not live in a harmonious society (where even differences – like Confucius's dislike of the usurper – are contained through commitment to ritual).

This story introduces an important aspect of the Confucian concern to propagate ritual order: the role of the ruler or the head of state. The decline of traditional order, we will remember, is linked by Confucius to the end of the political rule of ideal kings. The re-establishment of order – the outward, public good of a harmonious society – through ritual has to come through political change. Social order can come only through political order, and political order only through the ruler. Benefiting the people is the aim of the ruler. The pre-Confucian idea that eventually the good of the ruler coincides with the good of the people regains influence in Chinese philosophy through Confucius.

Confucians maintain that every proper ritual act has an impact on those towards whom it is directed. As recipients are influenced, they in turn act properly or at least appreciate the need to learn to act properly; so commitment to ritual action and its propriety spreads through society. Without the moral constraints of ritual action, there will be discord, as people will not agree on how to adjudicate on their desires for different outcomes (compare the different desires of the usurper and Confucius). Such disagreement will lead to disorder. Confucians argue that this did not happen in the past because the exemplary rulers maintained order by establishing proper ritual action in accordance with their sense of rightness. The ritual action of rulers will have the greatest impact in making the people adopt proper ritual in turn.

Confucius concludes that rulership or government is itself a matter of ritual action. If the ruler loves and obeys ritual action, then people will be easy to rule; they will acknowledge the potency (*de*) of the ruler as manifested in the rituals of his government. If the rituals of his government manifest order, then the people will assent to it. So, an efficient government will not be one that punishes wrongdoers but one under which there is no punishment because there are no wrongdoers. Given that ritual is potent because it conveys meaning efficiently, the ideal ruler will be one whose rituals of governance convey the meaning of order with least confusion. This usually means that the ruler will have to weave different rituals into his system of governance: as Confucius tells a ruler, referring to past dynasties and specific regions, use the calendar of the Xia, ride the carriage of the Yin, wear the cap of the Zhou, have the music of the Shao and Wu.

Mastery of ritual action in government need not necessarily show itself only in intricate combinations of ceremonies. Rich symbolism does not always require complex rituals; far from it. Maximum symbolic value can attach to an utterly simple ritual, provided only that the ruler who manifests it has the potency to convey the meaning of his action. The ideal for Confucius was the legendary emperor Shun, who did nothing and yet ruled: he merely sat himself in a respectful posture and faced due south, that was all.

Confucians believe that people can be educated in ritual action through instruction. (Instruction is clearly important for the continued vitality of ritual. Consider the case of toasting the health of someone. Suppose some guests were not instructed in its meaning and protested that they did not want to be forced to drink. Only by becoming familiar with the ritual would they realize that all they needed to do was put a glass to their lips, for the symbolic point at issue in raising a toast is not the actual act of drinking.) Conveying this education to people becomes an important purpose of the philosopher's work.

This is especially the case with the Confucian thinker Xunzi. Confucius's follower Mencius, committed to the idea that human nature is innately good, expresses his concerns about the Outward Good by arguing for the power of people to overthrow a bad ruler. Mencius is more interested in prompting the ruler to take economically wise decisions than in his manifesting the potency for ritualized governance. For him, ritual action is an internal sense of good manners. Xunzi, in contrast, does return to the significance of ritual action, but in a sense rather different from

Confucius. Utterly rejecting Mencius's view of human nature as innately good and capable of right action, Xunzi says that the very fact of disorder and discord shows that human nature is evil. Ritual action is important because it imposes order on naturally disorderly human beings; it is more efficient than punishment in regulating people. Rituals temper our desires and inclinations, which, unchecked, would lead to disorder. Rituals, learnt properly, allow us to express our desires without entirely losing our sense of who we are and what we want. For example, funeral ceremonies are meant to channel grief into proper expression that does not threaten others or endanger us. Furthermore, rituals are given to us appropriate to our role and status in society. They indicate to us, even as we perform them, our entitlements. Ceremonies also vary according to the tastes of different classes and people, a prime example being music. With proper and proportionate expression of desires and inclinations, ritual action constrains people and maintains order.

Ritual action − *li* − is therefore the great objective of Confucian concern for the outward good of gaining social and political order. It is a strikingly complex concept, in that it combines two seemingly incompatible conceptions. It is a universal category of action. It is not just a set of rituals, for it contains the idea of propriety − the appropriateness of action gauged by moral considerations of who one is and towards whom one is acting. In that sense, it is quite generally applicable to all humans. Yet, in its details, it is explicitly constructed through the specifics of the social situation. Rituals vary according to roles, status, conventions and local variations; even kings are advised to combine elements of ritual from different predecessors and regions. So ritual action is intensely local and yet universal. (The comparison with the Hindu idea of *dharma* will be evident later in this chapter.) The need for flexibility constantly fights against the ossification of Confucian ritual. Two thousand years after Confucius, the Japanese Neo-Confucian Nakae Toju explains that ritual action is relative to time, place and rank, which are dimensions, respectively, of heaven, earth and man; in this way, Confucian institutions are melded into the alien setting of Japan.

Regaining the natural order

Although there are many overlaps in concepts between Confucian and Daoist writings, there is little doubt that a sharp contrast can be found when it comes to what public end the Daoist is thinking of. The text we focus on here is the *Laozi*, attributed to the legendary Laozi. It is explicitly directed at a ruler in power (albeit in a small state attempting to survive against larger ones; in this sense, it is contrasted with the ambitions of the ruler to whom the Confucians direct their attention, who aspires to the status of the great emperors of the past). Here, too, the goal is to secure social and political order. Laozi advocates the striking and apparently bizarre notion of Doing Nothing (*wu-wei*) for the attainment of the outward end of order amongst people.

By and large, Daoists focus on individual self-cultivation and take political order as its consequence. Nevertheless, the *Laozi*, being addressed to a ruler, does aim to provide instruction that is for the larger good of the state and society. The heart of the public purpose of the *Laozi* is, of course, the attainment of their natural *dao*/way by ruler and people. People can function naturally – that is to say, in spontaneous harmony with the world – through an integrity in which their very being is expressed. But they can also become 'unnatural', by creating habits of thought and action that alienate them from their natural *dao*/way. The challenge for the *Laozi* is to convince the ruler that he is applying policies which are unnatural in their distortion of human nature, and that he must therefore correct them.

The philosophical task here is first to undermine the plausibility of the ruler's authoritarian – unnatural – policies. Then, Laozi seeks to persuade him of an alternative way of governing, a way that is natural. Here a problem presents itself: the actions of governance are always unnatural, since they are social constructs that deviate from the natural *dao*/way. They are artificial and self-conscious, deliberate in their conception of what to aim for and how to get it, and therefore arbitrary in what they impose on others. They lack the spontaneity that is natural to humans. So, what statecraft can the Daoist possibly preach that will not itself be unnatural?

The answer is given in the apparently contradictory notion of 'Doing Nothing'. This does not mean to be inactive as such, but to do nothing unnatural, nothing that is the cultural construct of government, such as war, punishment, ritual action and the like. Doing Nothing is to take the unnatural construction of government out of people's lives, leaving them to realize their own potential. Paradoxically, a ruler who is without the desire to rule the people frees them, and thereby finds himself ruling a state worth ruling. Of course, this non-governance is itself neither arbitrary not idle, but a carefully cultivated treatment of the people. (Indeed, Heshang Gong, in his commentary on the *Laozi*, interprets Doing Nothing as being primarily concerned with the self-cultivation of the ruler, its impact on the people being secondary.)

A famous and often misunderstood passage presents the features of proper administration: empty the minds and fill the bellies of people, weaken their purpose and strengthen their bones, ensure they are without knowledge and without desires. This cannot possibly mean what it appears to mean, for that would be a prescription for authoritarian rule at odds with the whole thrust of Daoist thought. It is better to think of it as an ironic use of deliberately reversed terms, a parody of authoritarian rulership. The provocative surface meaning (which is authoritarian) should actually be read more subtly. The mind is emptied, yes, but of artificial notions of ritual and status. The purpose that is weakened is only the purpose of attaining power. The knowledge that people are left without is only knowledge of social conventions and political agitation. And the desires that are removed are the desires that keep people locked in unnatural *dao*/ways. People are then left to find their way back to their (natural) *dao*/ways.

An interesting distinction should be made between this prescription and one in Confucius that sounds very similar. Did not Confucius exalt the emperor who ruled by sitting and doing nothing? Is that not the same as Laozi's ideal? As would be expected, Confucius and Laozi mean almost opposite things with their example of the ruler who does nothing. Confucius's emperor exemplifies the purest and most potent ritual action, for he has distilled all the symbolic value of ritual into the act of just being there and facing due south. So his doing nothing is the finest and greatest ritual act, the most focused performance of ceremony possible. By contrast, when Laozi's ideal ruler does nothing, he is certainly performing no ritual, but rather opening up the possibility of returning to those natural actions of the *dao*/way of the ruler that ritual contradicts.

The outward purpose of Daoist philosophy according to Laozi, then, is to give instruction to the ruler in the art of being totally devoted to the natural condition in which people act spontaneously.

Zhuangzi, the other great classical Daoist, on the other hand, is primarily concerned with ways to the Inward Good, as we will see in the next chapter; but he does recognize the pragmatic need for a public politics of harmony. Zhuangzi thinks that harmony comes through seeing beyond the differences that create conflict. A monkey-keeper handed out three nuts every morning and four every evening to each monkey. They were outraged. So he gave them four every morning and three every evening, and they were delighted. Without changing the substance of his decision, he moved with the circumstances (presumably, the monkeys were either blinded by the larger number being given first, or they really preferred more food in the morning than in the evening). His way was for the public good.

Ruthlessly caring for all

Perhaps the sternest philosophy of the Outward Good in classical China is enunciated by Confucius's earliest challenger, Mozi and his followers. The Mohist philosophers argue that nothing is valuable – is a good – that has no use. Usefulness is whatever leads to the material well-being of the people. Having enough food and clothing, being able to make a decent living – these are the goods to be secured for people. This unfanciful idea of what is good leads them to reject ceremonial ritual action of the kind defended by the Confucians. A typical Mohist criticism is directed at the elaborate funerals and prolonged mourning advocated by Confucius. Would these enrich the poor, increase the population, bring security to those in danger, and establish order? Well, if they did, the Mohists would accept them. But since these are neither the purposes nor the outcomes of funerals and mourning, the Mohists reject them.

This dislike of ritual extends to music, whose rejection becomes doctrinaire. Here, Mozi's narrow and very specific sense of usefulness is brought to the fore. He asks a Confucian the reason one makes music and is given the answer that music is deemed a joy. One might think that music therefore has a use, namely to make people happy. But Mozi will not have it. He argues that the Confucian answer amounts simply to saying that music is an end in itself – music, which is entertainment, brings joy, which is the state of being entertained; but this is like saying a house is deemed a house, whereas the use of a house is that it shelters people. Music has no use *beyond* itself, and therefore has no use at all.

Not only does Mozi maintain that all actions, to be good, have to be useful (in the special sense of having a further use in bringing about material benefit), he extends this principle to say that the benefit must be for as many people as possible, ideally all people. This 'concern for everyone' becomes the unifying principle of Mohism. In itself, such a principle does not seem that much of a problem; most ethical thinkers, Confucians included, will agree that ideally we should care for everyone. But the Mohists take this principle to be a guide for all actions.

Furthermore, one must at all times care as much for others as for oneself; and if there is a clash between the good of others and one's own good, then the former must take priority. When the two are opposed, the benefit of all outweighs benefit to oneself; so long as something is useful to everyone else, you should do it, even if it is harmful to you. Mozi defends this claim to selflessness ingeniously. A notional opponent, Wu Mazi, says that it stands to reason that he would rather kill others to benefit himself than kill himself to benefit others. The basic principle is not what benefits others but what benefits oneself. Mozi cleverly argues back that if the whole world agreed with Wu's principle, they would all believe that he could be killed for their benefit; while if the whole world was displeased with the principle, in that case, too, they could all kill him and benefit! Either way, not only is he going to find himself killed, but also have it happen on the basis of a calculation about everyone else's benefit! He will lose his life and his principle.

Even this extension of maximum benefit may seem acceptable if it merely amounts to a call for selflessness; after all, many ethical systems idealize selflessness. The truly telling extension of this principle is that the care should be for *all* others, regardless of who they are. In particular, it should be regardless of their relationship with you. Mohism insists on a rigid moral equality. This appalled the Confucians, who simply could not understand how the carefully ritualized relationship of piety towards one's own family, which they exalted, could be so brutally rejected in favour of caring for people in other societies and regions. Mencius complained that Mozi wanted a man to treat his father as he would a stranger.

Mozi's position is actually more complex than that, and two points have to be made in his defence. First, his view is that one should care as much for a stranger as for one's father, rather than that one should care for one's father as if he were a stranger.

Second – and this is admittedly a difficulty with Mozi – he does not say that one should *treat* a stranger like one's father. One should take special care in one's social actions towards one's kin, since doing so leads to an ordered society in which everyone benefits by having high standards of treatment. In calculating the outcomes of one's actions, one should have as much moral *concern* for strangers as for one's father. There are no differences or degrees of concern regarding people, but the application of concern in how one behaves should start with those who are more closely related. There can be differences in social value, but none in moral value. (When Michael Dukakis was running for the US presidency, his Mohist-style views displeased the public. Dukakis opposed the death penalty because he thought that society as a whole benefited by not having it. A journalist brutally asked him whether, if his wife were raped, he would oppose the death penalty for the rapist. Dukakis clinically answered that he would still oppose it. He lost votes because, although no one questioned his love for his wife, people thought, in an un-Mohist way, that his response was inhumanly consistent in its commitment to the value of moral equality.)

The Mohists want this ruthless extension of concern for all to be encoded in the affairs of state. They want a centralized and meritocratic state. (This does not make them democratic, since kings and princes will still appoint people to high offices.) Their philosophy, then, is oriented to establishing the outward good of a materially prosperous society in which, without exception and without ceremony, everyone has to be concerned for everyone else in the moral calculus of action.

Institutionalizing the Outward Good: amoral legalism
There is a school called Legalism, whose great synthesizer is Han Feizi, which concludes that benefits ultimately come from efficient institutions rather than good intentions and moral worth. On the whole, Legalist thinking appears to be totalitarian in its

inclinations, its main aim being to keep people in their place while securing complete power for the ruler. The Legalists tell the story of Prime Minister Shang Yang, who promulgated harsh laws. When the people criticized the laws, he punished them; and he did so, of course, if they broke the laws. Once, he even punished the prince for violating a law. After this, everyone obeyed the laws and order prevailed. But that is not the end of the story. As the state was orderly, people praised Shang Yang for his laws; whereupon he banished them for daring to comment on the laws! People must obey laws, not comment on them.

The impression of a political philosophy that is concerned simply to keep people suppressed is reinforced by a harsh view of people's ability to think morally. Han Feizi argues, for example, that the practice of female infanticide shows that even the relationship between parent and child can be devoid of love and morality. Baby girls are killed because of the parental calculation that they will not be financially productive to their own family in the future (as they will be married away). If that is the case between parent and child, what is one to say of any other relationship? No social system can possibly work in which people's virtues are assumed.

The Confucian idea that the state is built out of a skein of ritual ceremony starting with harmonious relationships within the family and radiating outwards to harmonize the whole world is utterly rejected by the Legalists. Confucius once told the story of an official who was so committed to the state that he betrayed his own father when the latter broke a law. Confucius condemned the unfilial son. (Indeed, for much of Chinese history it was actually a crime for a son to report a crime committed by his father.) Han Feizi criticizes this attitude. He embroiders the story further, saying that the son was executed for betraying his father, with the result that crimes against the state went unreported. He also contrasts this story with one about Confucius himself. Confucius heard of a man from the kingdom of Lu who thrice went to battle and thrice fled from the field. Questioned, the man said that he had to look after his aged father. Confucius was so impressed by this filial piety that he rewarded the man. Han Feizi adds tartly that, as a result, the people of Lu thought nothing of running away from battle!

Despite the impression that Legalism is concerned with no more than preserving the power of the ruler over the people, Han Feizi's description of the ruler is equivocal: the ruler is also subject to constraints. While he need have no qualms in the pursuit of power, he too is tied to the economy of amoral efficiency. He must rigorously follow a system of reward and punishment towards those who look after the machinery of government; he too must not rely on family and friends but follow strict and formal procedures for preserving his security. Han Feizi reinterprets the *Laozi*'s notion of the ruler 'doing nothing' as meaning that the ruler does nothing that is based on his own thoughts, desires, knowledge, ability, partiality or courage. He merely compares the abilities of officials with the demands of the tasks of government, and then appoints, rewards and punishes them accordingly. His personal presence is, in effect, rendered irrelevant to the functioning of the state. Even in the case of the people, although Legalists usually take them to be stupid or ignorant, there is a contractual obligation (with no hint of sentiment, such as love or admiration) with the ruler. In the end, the sole aim is an efficient state, with the hardly acknowledged good that some public benefit accrues to such a state.

Legalism, then, is a philosophy of political control with a purpose. However, it seems better to say that its concept of the Outward Good has little to do with good at all, and more with an outward end, which is public order.

The consequences of love and empathy

We must take some care in identifying the Outward Good sought by Buddhism. It is not the more general concern for ethical conduct as such, central though that is for the attainment of the ultimate end of *nirvana*, or liberation from life-as-suffering (how that is so will be seen in the next chapter, on the Inward Good). The cultivation of virtues is in fact inward preparation for attaining freedom from desire (and thus from suffering, which is caused by desire). Rather, the outward goods that Buddhism seeks are states of affairs in the world that must be secured on the way to final freedom. These goods are sought by the Buddhist out of compassion (*karuna*) for the suffering of all, borne on an empathy (*anukampa*) with that suffering. This compassion comes out of a love (in the Pali language, *metta*) for all, which is expressed in the wish that all people enjoy contentment (*sukha*).

It is this consideration that leads to Buddhist teachings on the social environment. Following the Buddha's teachings, the Buddhist promotes the well-being (*hita*) of others. There are five basic rules to be observed in the treatment of others, and obviously, the adoption of them by everyone will lead to a good social environment. These rules are: (i) respect life, do no injury and make life pleasant for others; (ii) respect the lawful possessions of others and do not take what is not voluntarily given; (iii) refrain from sensual gratification that causes harm or embarrassment to others; (iv) refrain from lying, slander and harsh words, and always speak well; and (v) refrain from addiction to intoxicants. The Buddha also speaks of the proper conduct that should be observed in a variety of contexts: between spouses, between master and servant, between friends, between ruler and ruled, and between religious virtuosi and lay people.

These rules about sociability have a two-fold benefit. On the one hand, the person who follows them benefits, as they help in the cultivation of her virtues. A person purifies herself of selfishness through such conduct, and thereby prepares for eventual freedom from desire. On the other hand, the people who receive such good treatment also benefit, since they find themselves in an environment in which they are not oppressed by bad behaviour and can therefore find the time to cultivate themselves. It should be noted, however, that good conduct of this sort should not be seen merely as instrumental in attaining *nirvana*. The dissolution of desires for oneself (and the dissolution of the very sense of self that prompts desire) is required for eventual liberation from suffering, since suffering is brought about by desire. To do good only because one desired to benefit spiritually from it would be self-defeating. Rather, one should aim to do good out of one's compassion for others. Of course, those who are free, like the Buddha himself, also practise good conduct as a natural outcome of their enlightened state.

What is secured through such deeply cultivated conduct is a 'skilfully attained good' (*kusala*) that is common to all. The outward good that is thus attained is generally understood to be what makes people happy and does not disturb them. Now, there is an apparent tension between two aspects of Buddhism. One is the insight that freedom from suffering comes through the attainment of a desireless state. The other is the goal of working to make people contented through treating them well (making life pleasant for them, letting them have possessions so long as they are legal, etc.). The tension arises since such contentment is as much a part of life-as-suffering as anything else. Clearly, then, keeping people happy through mutual good behaviour is not an end in itself, but it helps to create an environment in which the qualities that allow people to attain to *nirvana* can be cultivated.

The outward good of a happy social environment is therefore relevant only as a prerequisite for the attainment of the ultimate inward good of liberation from all suffering. The former must be subordinated to the attainment of the latter. Sometimes, happiness may come only through apparent disturbance. Once, the country around the town of Nalanda was suffering from a drought, but the Buddha still took a company of his disciples to beg for alms. An unhappy village headman asked him how this could be an act of compassion. The Buddha replied that in all his previous lives he had never known anyone to be harmed by giving alms, and indeed always to benefit from it. Giving alms is the start of a virtuous sequence that leads to wealth, further giving, the accumulation of spiritual merit as an aid to the development of virtuous qualities, the control of desire, and thence to eventual freedom from suffering.

Indeed, the most persuasive argument for the belief that working towards ordinary happiness for others is merely instrumental to the eventual goal of attaining freedom from suffering is that the Buddha's very teachings are immediately disturbing rather than reassuring. To put to people the truth about suffering is not to make their life pleasant, but to shake them up and make them seek the means to gain freedom from it; that is the important thing. Love for others should take the everyday form of labouring to create a happy society secured through mutual good conduct; that is the outward good that Buddhism seeks. Nevertheless, this is only to help create conditions in which people can cultivate those qualities that will help them to their final achievement of liberation.

The good or the right? The ethical order of society

Almost from the very beginning, Hindu thought has the concept of a cosmic order in which natural and social relationships are properly maintained. Reality itself is conceived as an organic and interrelated whole. The cosmos is the natural world of space, time and matter, as well as the various realms and their inhabitants – superhuman, human, demonic, animal and plant, all functioning in an orderly manner. A striking aspect of this understanding of cosmic order is that human action, no less than nature, is considered to be regulated by what is appropriate. The shining of the sun and the martial prowess of the warrior, the giving of milk by a cow and the performance of sacred ritual by the priest – these are all orderly functions in the cosmos. Everything has an appropriate place in the cosmic order (*rta*, from a word having the connotation of 'apt' or 'proper').

Initially, human participation in this cosmic order is conceived to lie only in highly symbolic ritual action. These rituals are quite different from what we encounter in Chinese civilization. The rituals of the sacred Veda texts are not connected with social intercourse at all. They are formal sequences of actions that by themselves have no meaning: laying out an altar; starting and maintaining a fire; making various offerings, such as fruit, seeds, rice or honey, either directly into the fire or in front of it; the precise chanting both of verses in praise of natural forces and of sequences of set syllables invested with hidden meaning (*mantra*); offering sacrifices (often animals to start with but very quickly becoming symbolic substitutions); and so on. The meaning of these rituals comes from their being models of cosmic forces and events. The ritual space is imagined to be a scaled-down representation of the cosmos, the elements in it mapping onto the elements of the cosmos. In this way, the ritual is invested with supreme significance. When a ritual is performed, its elements stand for elements of the cosmos, and so the cosmos itself is held to be symbolically affected by the ritual. (This relationship, in which one thing 'stands for' another, different thing, is called metonymy; by way of contrast, when a description of one thing stands for the description of another, we have metaphor.) In this way, the ritualists influence the cosmos itself, and by performing their rituals systematically, they uphold the cosmic order itself.

Over time, however, the scope of human action to contribute to order widens in the various Dharma Sutras (Law Texts). (By this time, order is called *dharma*, which comes from a root word meaning 'to bear' or 'uphold'.) Taking an older, Vedic notion of social organization, the Dharma Sutras argue that human responsibility for order is to be expressed in the organization of society into four broad classes (*varna*), with the life path (in particular of high-class males) itself being ordered into four life stages (*asrama*). In this later idea, social and personal activity, appropriately conducted, is held to maintain cosmic order; the mapping of human action onto the universe at large has expanded from ritual to wider, ethical behaviour.

This larger pattern of behaviour is determined by the various duties that one must perform according to one's position in society and one's stage in life. It is in performing these duties correctly that one helps uphold social and personal order; this maps onto the cosmos, and therefore eventually contributes to cosmic order itself. Social duties, determined by class, are assigned according to whether one is a priest/intellectual, a warrior (especially a king), a merchant or a labourer. The priest interprets the sacred texts and performs the rituals they prescribe. The warrior/king rules the land justly and fights to protect it. The merchant sustains commerce, and the labourer serves manually.

Duties according to life stages move successively from that of the student, whose duty is learning; to the householder, who has a life productive of family, wealth and enjoyment; to the retired forest-dweller, who withdraws from productivity to start the contemplation of sacred truths; and finally to the renouncer, who gives up all connection with society to prepare for the mysteries of the afterlife. The high-class male, in particular, has normative expectations placed on him about what he should do as he goes through life. Women, too, have their own, less rigidly prescribed responsibilities, primarily focused on the household (as wife, mother and chatelaine), although some texts also allow them the freedom to live as scholars and experts of ritual; in old age, they are usually expected to move into retirement, living a simple life in the forest with their husbands. The duties of the labouring classes are normally fulfilled by their class-based labour, although, again, there are texts that allow them greater scope for self-expression. When people carry out the duties of their station, then society is preserved; and the preservation of society is the human contribution to the maintenance of cosmic order itself.

Duties are carried out because they are right, even if in their performance some things happen that are not good (for instance, a warrior must kill, even if killing in itself is not good). Once one's duties are clear, one performs them. However, it would seem that it is right to carry out these duties only because they eventually lead to some large good – namely social order (and, ultimately, cosmic order). What is right is to be followed only because it results in the good. The tradition is alive to the fact that the larger good of social and cosmic order requires a complex prioritization of different goods. The correct performance of one's appropriate duty is generally seen as the most effective way of contributing to that order, but the problems that come with duty are well recognized. The following incident from the epic *Mahabharata* illustrates this recognition.

When a great archer is teaching the heroic princes of the epic, a young man (called Ekalavya, meaning 'one-cut', which indicates how the story will end), from a tribal group on the margins of society, asks to be taught too. The master of archery refuses, telling him that as a person from a low-status group, he is not entitled to learn the martial arts reserved for royalty. But Ekalavya hides and watches the master teach. One day, the master finds Ekalavya demonstrating his skill, which is greater than that of the most talented of the princes, Arjuna. He has a clairvoyant sense that the supremacy of Arjuna will be vital for the future of ancient India. So Ekalavya is a challenge on two counts: he has appropriated the duty of another, superior class, and he stands in the way of political events of great import. The master asks Ekalavya whether he accepts him as his teacher. Ekalavya immediately acknowledges him. The master now asks: what of the traditional gift you must give your teacher? Ekalavya promises to give anything he is asked. The master asks for his right thumb, vital for holding the arrow. Ekalavya unhesitatingly cuts it off in offering, and disappears from the story; Arjuna becomes celebrated as the greatest archer of all time, and leads the forces of good to victory in battle. By no means is Ekalavya's sacrifice accepted as normal; indeed, it is the tragic greatness of it that drives home the point that the demands of *dharma*, of duty and order, are formidable, their moral quality elusive.

Incidentally, it should be noted that the outward good in the Dharma texts is expressed primarily in terms of social functions, in such a way that the political order which is the responsibility of the king (from the warrior class) is merely one part of social order. By way of contrast, in Chinese thought the dependence is the other way around: the prime mover is the king; it is the securing of political order that leads to a good society. So, whereas the Chinese philosophers concentrate on the ways and means to gain political order first, the Dharma texts of India, while certainly specifying what the king should do, subordinate his responsibilities to the attainment of social order. A famous incident in the other Hindu epic, the *Ramayana*, shows how royal duty is a vexed issue, especially when contextualized within larger ethical demands.

Prince Rama, the very embodiment of virtue (and occasionally in the narrative, recognized as God come to earth as man), is searching for his abducted wife. He needs assistance, and is promised it by a wandering ape, Sugriva, who turns out to be the deposed king of the monkeys. Sugriva's elder brother, Valin, had once treated him as an equal, but when Valin disappeared in battle, Sugriva took over the kingdom in good faith. But Valin reappeared, accused his brother of betrayal, drove him out, and took his wife. Sugriva says that if Rama helps him regain the kingdom, he will help Rama. Rama gives his word. Sugriva challenges Valin to combat, and when the latter looks like winning, Rama mortally wounds him by shooting an arrow from hiding. Dying, Valin sees Rama and questions the morality of his actions. Why did Rama shoot him from cover, not openly, and while he was engaged in battle (the rules of engagement say that one cannot intervene on one side when two warriors are engaged in personal combat)?

Rama gives a number of responses. He is the representative of royal justice; this obliges him to punish Valin for what is effectively incest. Next, he made a promise to Sugriva and he must keep it.

Finally, he is, as a royal warrior, entitled to hunt and kill a mere animal. Valin's main point, however, is not about why Rama killed him. For one thing, he recognizes the pragmatism of the alliance between his brother and Rama. For another, he is prepared to acknowledge that Rama's justice may be beyond his, Valin's, understanding. His point is the manner in which he was attacked. The following are the considerations to keep in mind when discussing the issue. Rama was hardly hunting in this instance. If Valin is an animal, so is his brother; what is the worth of a promise to an animal (in this instance, Sugriva), if it can also be hunted as one? Does having to keep a promise justify what was promised? In a later play centring on this incident, Rama argues that Valin committed incest. Valin replies in surprise, 'But that is part of our [monkey] social order (*dharma*)!' By placing the exemplar of duty and order at the heart of this complex incident, the tradition amply recognizes that the outward good is not so easily determined.

The outward good in India – namely, social order – comes through an external ethics of performance. Even the stages of life, while they concern the individual, are expressed in terms of a relationship with society. It is true that at each stage certain virtues should be cultivated, because it is the possession of such virtues that motivates the individual to act properly: in the student earnest inquiry after truth and a sense of modesty mark his treatment of the teacher and the teacher's wife (who is the substitute mother at this time); respect for family tradition, love of one's family and an understanding of responsibility for dependants drive the behaviour of the householder; and the search for self-knowledge and equanimity move the forest-dweller and renouncer. But these personal qualities are only the initial qualifications for action. It is proper conduct that upholds order. It is not surprising that the last two life stages are seen as extraordinary and special, with much resistance in the *dharma* texts to granting these stages the same significance as the first two. Clearly, the first two stages are not only primarily concerned with social action, they are located within (and thereby maintain) society. The desire to leave society – physically in the forest and, even more so, mentally in renouncing all ties and roles – may have to be acknowledged so that there is a necessary safety-valve for the expression of individuality outside social norms; but it should not be encouraged too much in case too many choose to renounce society, and social order collapses (thereby even endangering cosmic order).

This ethics of performance – where one is required to act properly for the sake of social order – depends upon the person being properly motivated. What connects the exterior life of performance of duty with the inner life, the thoughts and emotions of the person? Almost in tandem with the idea that, outwardly, social class and life-stage responsibilities are good, there emerges the concept of a set of human goals (*purusa-artha*s) that motivate the person. The earlier version lists three goals that make for human flourishing – goods that people may legitimately seek to secure: pleasure (*kama*), prosperity (*artha*) and ethicality or virtue (*dharma*). These are inward goods, of course, and will be considered in the next chapter.

Over some centuries, the human goals were extended to include a fourth: liberation (*moksa*) from the bonds of worldly existence. Now, whereas the first three goals are of a piece, reconciling the outward good of social order with the inward good of human flourishing in the world, this fourth goal does not fit so easily. It involves a radical break from – indeed, a transcendence of – the world, and is in marked tension with the outward good of social and cosmic order. This is a fundamental feature of classical Indian thought to which we will return in the next chapter.

We have just seen the outline of a complex situation. There is the idea of an outward good – social and cosmic order – towards which human life should be oriented. There is the further idea that the cultivation of the inward good relates the personal motivation of the individual to the attainment of the outward good. Finally, there is another, culminating inward good – liberation from the conditions of the world – which cannot easily be integrated into the earlier conception of outward good. But we will notice in all this that the pursuit of philosophical knowledge is directed to some good, some goal that makes sense of and gives legitimacy to human action. In other words, we do things (or are meant to do them) because they lead to an eventual end whose value is intrinsic and which is worthwhile.

The account of *dharma* that we have just given accords with a definition of it proposed by the founder of the Indian Vaisesika school, Kanada: *dharma* is the performance of what is right, the results of which are prosperity and the highest good. There is, however, a profoundly different conception of the purpose of action which does not say that dutiful actions are right because they lead to some good. It is found in the Mimamsa school. The definition of *dharma* that the Mimamsa philosophers follow (given by Jaimini, the founder of the school) is that it is simply 'of the nature of injunction' – that is, obeying the commands of the sacred texts. *Dharma* is what we are told to do by the Vedas and what we do accordingly. This definition is the start of a stringent account of *dharma* as proper action (especially ritual), nothing more and nothing less. To do *dharma* is to obey the injunctions, without any further appeal to some good result. We must act as we are enjoined by the Vedas (which also give us exhortations that motivate and enthuse us). But why should we act in these ways? The answer is, because those are the right actions to perform; nothing more. The ethical life, the life that is led by doing what we should do, is ethical because of the intrinsic worth – the rightness – of what we should do. Acts have to be carried out, not because they help to promote some eventual good, but because they are simply right; and they are right for no other reason than that the sacred texts command us to perform them. It is in this way that all calculation – which is inescapable when action is directed towards some good – is removed from the realm of performance.

At one point, Jaimini acknowledges that, pragmatically, people act and perform sacred rituals not merely because they are right but because they bring some good to the performer: he speaks vaguely of people desiring a celestial realm (*svarga*, misleadingly translated as 'heaven', with its heavy theistic implications). Already, there is the seed of the idea that action might be for some eventual good, although the brevity of its expression in early Mimamsa suggests a deliberate refusal to make a good the explicit purpose of right action. One subschool, under Kumarila, eventually acknowledges that people perform ritual and ethical action so that they can attain some ultimate good (liberation from the conditions of life). However, another subschool, led by Prabhakara, refuses to reduce right action to merely the means to attain the good. Prabhakara and his followers steadfastly explore the details of ritual and other actions for their own worth, because they are right. For them, the right is more important than the good. (So, looking back at the incident from the *Ramayana* above, they would have to say that Rama should not attempt to justify his killing of Valin in terms of what eventual good ends are attained, but should only examine his actions to see if they are right – that is to say, allowed in the authoritative texts on kingly action.)

The Mimamsa school does not believe in God, only in authorless sacred texts that reveal the structure of reality to the seers of the Vedas. The Mimamsa thinkers do not hold actions to be right because of divine command (something argued for by various Christian and Islamic thinkers over the centuries), but only because it is right to perform those actions. This view bears a strange resemblance to some modern theories that refuse to talk of some eventual good and concentrate on identifiable 'rights' that must be served. (Of course, what modern theories take to be right – justice or equal rights – is very different from the *dharma* of the Mimamsa philosophers; it is just that the structure of these very different theories is startlingly similar.) One venerable idea of what should be done therefore concerns only what is right, entirely without thought of the good. With this challenging thought, we end our consideration of the Outward Good and turn to the Inward.

4

The Inward Good

We encountered in the previous chapter the broad distinction between inward and outward goods. The Inward Good is a state of being or even a process of becoming that a person seeks to attain. Such a good is intuitively sought in one's own nature and is realized in the transformation of oneself (or in 'one's self', however 'self' is defined). It is of such evident value that the attainment of it gives ultimate purpose to the philosopher's work. Some preliminary comments must be made about this quite general idea.

First, to emphasize again the point made in the previous chapter, it is not always possible to make a sharp distinction between inward and outward goods. When selfhood is constituted by a combination of factors – thoughts, emotions, memories and sensations, as well as relationships and roles – that stretch from the innermost recesses of awareness to public engagement with the world, a distinction between goods that are inwardly and outwardly sought is hard to maintain. This is especially the case with Chinese conceptions of the person, but it also applies to some extent to the Indian (Hindu and Buddhist) ideas of the person. In both India and China, as we saw in chapter 2, the 'person' is a category constructed through a combination of what is naturally given and what is socially informed. In the case of China, it is better to use the distinction between inward and outward goods as a device to analyse the different ends that are sought. In Indian systems, including Buddhism, there is a certain tension between inward and outward goods which is not so evident in Chinese philosophy. In the case of the Hindu philosophical schools, especially, there is a trend towards the subordination of outward to inward goods.

Second, there are many different goods; that should be obvious. But it is both possible and necessary to think of some suitable general category under which all inward goods eventually fall. This is relatively explicit in the Indian schools, but with some persistence we may identify a more fuzzy and implicit one in Chinese philosophy as well.

Every school and every philosopher who identifies a very general inward good takes it to be of ultimate value. This good is some form of existence that is the key to explaining all other issues in life; there is nothing beyond it worth seeking, and attaining it is to attain (or render needless) everything else. In that sense, there is no justification for why such a good should be sought; someone who refuses to grant that that good is worth seeking is simply not engaging with the person who thinks it *is* worth seeking. (On the other hand, two people can engage even if each thinks that the other has misconceived the good or is pursuing it wrongly, so long as they are agreed that it is worth seeking in the first place.)

Personal cultivation

Confucius sought to guide people, and Confucianism is about getting people to cultivate themselves to the point where they attain a certain quality of life that is both pleasing and correct. A typical Confucian approach to cultivation focuses on a pair of qualities that have a startlingly apposite sound to them: one must have style (*wen*) and substance (*zhi*). These are complex and elusive concepts, but they carry roughly the same connotations as the English terms. The aesthetic expressiveness of action shows the refinement of the person performing it; the perceptible pleasure of others in seeing that action performed is a mark of style. At the same time, this expressiveness is to be based on a moral seriousness that gives true meaning to the performance. In the *Analects*, it is said that a 'small' man – one without cultivation – attempts to use style to cover up his mistakes. The contrast is with the cultivated man who simply acts stylishly because his cultivation is based on a moral largeness of purpose that gives substance to his being.

The Confucian seeks to follow a life that is directed towards self-cultivation, which we might poetically call person-making – that is to say, becoming what one should ideally be. Naturally, there is much debate on what it is to be a cultivated person; but it is possible to see the cultivated state as being the inward good of Confucianism. (We will see later that the goal of self-cultivation means something very different in Zhuangzi's Daoism.)

The cultivated life is a life that coheres with the *dao*/way; it is a life born of tradition and harmonious social functioning and sustained by the sensible interpretations and proper actions of cultivated people. There are two fundamental sources that guide a life towards cultivated expression. One is ceremonial ritual (*li*), which displays and reinforces the harmonious interrelationships in society (see chapter 3, on the Outward Good). The performance of such ritual manifests the person's cultivation. The other is the ideal sense of co-humanity (*ren*) (see chapter 2, on the Self): an integration of self and others through considering oneself to be indivisible from the situation of others. Hence we have the Confucian notion that co-humanity is found in deference (*shu*) to the needs and circumstances of others, as one likens oneself to others and sees the world in their terms. (In the Confucian context, this does not imply an empathy with people in all their diversity; rather, it is in the relatively strict sense of seeing how they relate to common ethical rules.) The sense of co-humanity forms the psychological well-spring of cultivation. The rules of performance and the possession of a suitable emotional attitude are necessary for seeking and attaining a cultivated life.

Confucius concentrates on specific steps in self-cultivation and does not bother to develop a theoretical account of it. His great successor, Mencius, does: he likens self-cultivation to tending sprouts until they develop into plants. He starts with the claim that human nature is intrinsically good and therefore capable of fulfilling its potential. But the best in human beings is not immediately present; only the potential is available. Our resources – our moral energy – must therefore be concentrated on nurturing every tendency towards appropriate thought and behaviour that we have, until we are properly cultivated. Xunzi takes such cultivation to require a programme of reshaping the self, through practising ritual. This developmental theory of cultivation was dominant in Confucianism until the Neo-Confucian Wang Yangming argued that moral power was *already* present in human beings. The proper challenge of self-cultivation, according to him, is to discover that good, not to develop it. Undoubtedly influenced by Buddhism, he claims that our innate good qualities are lost in a welter of desires, so that self-cultivation is the much more markedly cognitive task of removing such obstructions and finding our good qualities. We need to have 'pure knowing' of our good nature, and self-cultivation is the process of gaining that knowledge.

What is the goal of cultivation? The most pervasive Confucian idea of perfection is the exemplary person (*junzi*), sometimes translated with deliberate quaintness as 'gentleman' (although the literal meaning is 'princeling'). Cultivation should lead to one becoming a gentleman (the whole process is confined to men). The gentleman is exemplary in that he is the model: not only of what he becomes, but of how he comes to be so. He is seen to learn, hear others, study, practise, meditate upon what is important, and question himself; in other words, to show the very process of improvement that others can undergo. Mencius, whose belief in the intrinsic goodness of human beings gave him a fundamentally optimistic view of self-cultivation, uses a metaphor that shows how thorough that process is meant to be: just as water does not progress until it has filled every crevice, an exemplary person does not advance to the next task until he has perfected each lesson.

Ultimately, we come to a technical and important idea in Chinese thought: the sage (*sheng ren*). Sagehood (whatever it is) is rarely attained (although Wang Yangming says the streets are full of sages even in his own decadent times), and in that sense is the highest ideal, compared to the more culturally realistic model of the exemplary person. The sage is one who is able to have understanding of the world as a whole, integrating particular facts and actions into a cosmic order of meaning. His actions are a perfectly appropriate response to any of these particularities. However, we do not find an explicit theory of sagehood in the *Analects*. Instead, we must infer what is common to the various individuals that Confucius names as sages, with their often idiosyncratic and always telling characteristics and behaviour.

The Confucian ideal that is realized in the sage is expressed through ritual mastery; but by this is meant something much more than merely a set of formal actions. Ritual is rich with meaning. It is much more than stylized movements in appropriate social contexts (the narrow and pejorative meaning of 'ritual' in ordinary English usage); it is aesthetic creativity in music and dance, expertise in conveying emotion and significance through speech and conduct, and above all, a sincere engagement with others. The sage expresses these forms of ritual perfectly.

How is this so? The Confucians believe that the sage's perfect cultivation allows him to relate with deference (*shu*) to society; that is to say, to relate to each person by 'likening' himself to that person. (*Shu* can be translated more technically as 'analogical projection' – that is, putting oneself in another's place and thereby coming to conclusions about what should be done in that person's place.) Interpersonal relationships become the focus of the sage's ethical life, and he is therefore able to bring people into a harmonious relationship with each other. This is the 'rule of man' (*ren zhi*) – namely, the sage as perfected man, in contrast to a purely procedural or impersonal 'rule of law' (*fa zhi*). When the Legalist school assert that social order can come precisely through the rule of law alone, they are in effect challenging the very coherence of the notion of sagehood. For them, no inward good exists, the achievement of which secures an outward good; there is only the latter (namely, an ordered society). The Confucian inward good is not individualistic in placing the goal of the individual (in this case, the sage) above others. Indeed, quite the opposite: the perfected person is one who ideally expresses the model that all of society seeks to realize. The inward good is inward in the sense that the sage has cultivated his own attitude, interpretive skill, bearing and the contents of his heart–mind to reach such a state. But that state is deeply non–individualistic, in that it coheres, in style and substance, with the collective ideals of a harmonious society under heaven.

Freedom in the world

Sagehood is certainly the good that the Daoist of the *Zhuangzi* seeks. In a very general way, Zhuangzi's Daoist sage also exemplifies self-cultivation – development of a person towards perfection. And perfection for the Daoist, as for the Confucian, is more a way of constantly living out life (in terms of action, knowledge and attitude) than it is a single, determinate and ultimate state. (Hindu and Buddhist philosophies, as we shall see, regard the good both as a way of life and as an ultimate state.) However, Zhuangzi sees the world in a very different way from the Confucians, and his sage is radically different from the Confucian master of ritual.

Zhuangzi's sage – the perfected person – sees that there are an infinite number of *dao*/ways in which people seek to realize their nature. Each such *dao*/way has its own standards, and there is no further, higher standard to determine their relative worth. Variety in norms of discrimination is natural. In other words, one cannot dismiss all the ways of living but one's own, without recognizing that, equally, one's own way can be dismissed by others. Zhuangzi is not making the relativistic claim that no standards exist and that each way is as good as another. That would be incoherent because the claim itself is not relativistic but universal, since it says something that applies to all things even while claiming that nothing applies to them. Of course, judgements show preference for one way over another. But the pluralistic point he is making is that there are many standards and we can only judge according to our own. Therefore, while we can and do normally decide against some things, we must always allow that others can do likewise and decide against what we have accepted.

This pluralism is made more complex by Zhuangzi's further argument that all things are constantly changing. The standards by which we live life in our way will change, as will those of others. (It is not very clear how swiftly Zhuangzi thinks these changes happen, but they are rapid enough to demand a constant shifting of expectations across our lifetime.)

Infinite ways, pluralistic standards and change, then, are the key elements of Zhuangzi's vision of the world. His sage is one who, in his self-cultivation, responds in attitude and action to such a world. The inward good that Zhuangzi's sage seeks to realize is what is appropriate to the world as Zhuangzi sees it. The attainment of that perfection is the Good that this Daoist seeks. Let us look at these characteristics of perfection.

The sage's awareness of the diversity of ways, plurality of standards and the flux of all things is shown in an acceptance of the conditions of life. Seeing the diversity of the world, the sage does not overestimate the significance of his actions. Acknowledging the limitations of his own standards, he acts as his inclinations move him, and does not try to impose his standards on others (in this decisive rejection of social standards, Zhuangzi clearly opposes Confucianism). And understanding that it is natural for all things to change, the sage clings neither to people and things around him nor to his own judgements. The sage's awareness of diversity of *dao*/ways and the plurality of standards is seen in a story in which Zhuangzi is fishing when a king attempts to make him a gift of a state (in return, one presumes, for becoming a court adviser). Zhuangzi notes that the king has a sacred tortoise, dead some 3000 years, its preserved bones kept in honour. But would the tortoise rather be dead and honoured or alive and dragging its tail in the mud? He asks the king's messengers to go away; he would rather drag his tail in the mud.

As for the sage's acceptance of flux, the best-known story tells how Zhuangzi was found by his friend singing and drumming after his wife's death (the story analysed in some detail in chapter 2). Zhuangzi denies that he did not love his wife. It is just that, after being grief-stricken, he reasoned that there had been a time with her and now there was a time after her; she had changed as the seasons do. He had lived the time with her and now he would live the time after her; for someone departing and someone staying are both natural in this world.

This devastatingly direct equanimity can be understood in two rather different ways. At times, the text of the *Zhuangzi* appears to argue for something quite radical: since each moment is both natural and fleeting, one should engage intensely with it, and when it goes, let it go. Each moment and each experience – even the time after a beloved spouse's death – should have its own aesthetic significance and should be lived through. There is nothing immoral or questionable about this, for to moralize and question is to show that one is befuddled by unnatural social prescriptions that take one away from the natural course of life. This awesome sagacity is elsewhere tempered by a more psychologically accessible, if still demanding, reading of equanimity: one need not embrace each fleeting event and moment with appreciation of their naturalness, but one should always remember that they *are* fleeting. Keeping this in mind, one may act according to social expectations, but within oneself one must treat all things equally. Love and loss, failure and triumph – all may be met with socially appropriate actions but with the same inward detachment. This more conventional reading certainly has a resonance with Indian systems, as indeed with the philosophy of the Greek Stoics. The radical sections of the work, possibly unique to Zhuangzi in world philosophy, present an alternative conception of the inward good that is altogether more unsettling. It certainly explains why Zhuangzi's ideal may be called the 'alien sage'.

This state of being is expressed in a life of becoming: the Daoist sage is seen through his actions. Zhuangzi's fundamental insight is that the expressive life is marked by a knack for doing the appropriate thing. Such a knack or skill – a display of virtuosity (*de*) – has a curious relationship with reasoning and logic. On the one hand, skill is marked by a fluency that shows none of the slowness of thinking things through at the time of performance. At the time of doing something, the virtuoso does not weigh alternatives and make choices. On the other hand, this spontaneity is not irrational. To have attained a level of skill, one must have made certain decisions, discarded some possibilities and embraced certain others. Zhuangzi talks of the skill of the old man who caught cicadas, unhesitatingly plucking the insects off their perches; but, we may add, at some stage he must have learnt to disregard grasshoppers.

The classic tale of skill in Zhuangzi is that of Cook Ding, who butchers an ox in perfect rhythm. Zhuangzi talks of how he follows a *dao* which advances his skill: when he first started, he saw nothing that was not ox; later, he did not see the whole ox but only the specific parts he was cutting. Now he does not even use his eyes, his every action simply following how things actually are; his knife follows creases and fissures, never touching ligament or bone. The passage continues lyrically to express Ding's skill in butchery: at one and the same time unthinking and deeply thought out, fluent and precise, bloody and clean.

At this point, one might wonder whether Zhuangzi, in exalting such skill, is not rejecting his own precious pluralism. Is he not simply making a Confucian point about the sage's mastery, only he talks of butchery instead of ritual? Is he not in fact saying that skill obeys certain objective givens (like following the anatomy of an ox) and not its own free *dao*s? That is not quite true. What Zhuangzi brings out is the *fact* of skill, not any particular expression of it. Ding has mastered a form or style of butchery, not butchery itself. Indeed, some forms of skill might even incorporate clumsiness, like the antics of a clown or the so-called 'drunken' style in *gongfu* martial arts. Of course, in the end, there is an end towards which a way wends: even the clown seeks laughter, not booing; the martial artist seeks victory, not a thrashing. That is why Zhuangzi is not an incoherent relativist who says anything goes. His argument is that a skill makes sense within each way, and there are many ways.

We may sum up by saying that the hallmarks of Zhuangzi's perfected person are a certain wariness about knowledge, a sophisticated and disorienting approach to life, together with dizzyingly strange metaphors for inner being, and an all-encompassing demand for the endless cultivation of skill.

The skill of the Daoist sage may reside in many things, but the most extraordinary is in simply *being*. Laozi says that the sage knows the world without going out of his door and sees the *dao*/way of Heaven without looking out of his window. Zhuangzi likewise talks of the man from Ying who, when he got a smear of plaster on his nose, would stand perfectly still and get Carpenter Shi to slice it off with a whirl of his hatchet. A king asked Shi to show him his skill. Shi acknowledged that he had indeed been able to perform his part of the act, but since the man of Ying had died, he no longer had a partner (one who could be perfectly still). The man of Ying was a Daoist master.

Liberation: insight, ethics and compassion

Buddhism shares with the other classical Indian systems (Jainism and the many schools that we now call Hindu) the very general concept of freedom from the conditions of life as the highest Good. The technical word for this in Buddhism is, of course, *nirvana* (or *nibbana* in the Pali language in which the Buddha taught), and it specifically means 'extinction' – of suffering, which the Buddha identified as forming the conditions of life. This strictly negative translation is often interchangeably used with the freer, more positive word 'liberation' (from the conditions of life). 'Liberation' is also the translation of *moksa*, which is commonly used by the Hindu schools, together with 'freedom' (*mukti*); some Buddhists occasionally use these terms to amplify the meaning of *nirvana*. 'Liberation', then, is a good translation for both *nirvana* and *moksa*, since Hindus, Jains and Buddhists all agree that the key concept is liberation from the conditions of life, especially suffering.

The Four Noble Truths that the Buddha realized and taught give us our understanding of what the Buddhist seeks. The First Truth is that life is suffering; the Second is that simple desire for either existence or non-existence is the cause of suffering; the Third is that the cessation of desire is the cessation of suffering; and the Fourth is that the path to the cessation of suffering is eight-fold. This eight-fold path comprises right view, resolve, speech, action, livelihood, effort, mindfulness and concentration.

If we ask what the goods are that the Buddhist seeks, the answer appears to be that they are, first, the elements of the eight-fold path, and ultimately, the cessation of suffering. Obviously, it is through the attainment of a good life (a life lived according to the eight-fold path) that the ultimate goal will be obtained. A study of the Good in Buddhism should look at both the eight-fold path and *nirvana* itself.

The Buddha wants to teach the ways in which people might restrain and conquer desire ('thirst' and 'clinging' are the telling words normally used) so that suffering can cease. He is less concerned to identify the exact content of the state of freedom from suffering, being content to talk of it indirectly and negatively in terms of what it is not. In a famous passage in which the concept of *nirvana* as extinction is identified as the Buddhist goal, the Buddha compares the sage who has gone beyond the names and forms of worldly engagement to a flame put out by a gust of wind; both are beyond 'reckoning', measurement or discussion.

The eight-fold path contains one broad distinction: some of the elements – resolve, speech, action, livelihood and effort – represent ethics (*sila*), while the others represent insightful knowledge (*pañña* in Pali). (The attainment of knowledge also depends on the discipline of meditation – *samadhi*.)

Clearly, the cultivation and attainment of these eight virtues are important in the Buddhist life, the goal of which is *nirvana*. There are certain things we must *do* in order to rein back and end suffering-inducing desire; but there are also certain things we must *know* in order to do this. However, this apparently obvious balance between action and knowledge is complicated by the fact that the state of *nirvana* itself sounds like a state of knowledge. After all, the seminal event was when Gautama Siddhartha became the Buddha – the 'enlightened one' – and enlightenment, like such terms as 'awakening' and 'insight', which are also applied to that event, implies some change in his cognition. In other words, the ethical and epistemic (knowledge-related) aspects of the eight-fold path, while they may in fact be equally important, appear not to be, since the insightful knowledge itself has the nature of *nirvana*. No amount of ethical behaviour in itself will bring about *nirvana*, while insight into the nature of things is what gave the Buddha *nirvana*. Insight is something that should be cultivated in order to attain liberation; but the attainment of insight is itself liberation. Ethics, on the other hand, is only a means to liberation.

These considerations have led many to maintain that there is a radical disjunction between the ethical life and *nirvana*; ethics is a mundane (*lokiya*) good, while the attainment of insight is 'supra-mundane' (*lokuttara*). The Buddha's parable of the raft addresses this issue. A man who is caught on a flooded riverbank constructs a raft and manages to reach the safety of the other, higher bank. So grateful is he to the raft that he carries it around everywhere thereafter! The Buddha warns that the ethics he has taught is like the raft: it is a means of 'crossing over' to *nirvana*, not something that should be misguidedly clung to because of its original usefulness. The Buddha is, in fact, drawing attention to the possibility that, because of the worth of ethics, one may attach disproportionate importance to it and concentrate on it at the stage when one should be seeking insight. The mistake lies in taking ethics in isolation, out of context (like the raft on dry land). But this is not the same as denying its significance. After all, it is the raft that takes the man to the further shore, and it will be ethics that will take him to insight.

The form of Buddhism that evolved after the early period – Theravada – structures ethics around elaborate modes of self-control and personal development. Ethics is largely a matter of moral discipline, expressed in lists such as the Five Precepts and the Ten Good Paths of Action, which talk of not killing, not stealing, avoiding sexual misconduct, abstaining from slander, lies and gossip, and so on. The cultivation of these moral virtues is the focus of Theravada Buddhist life, since it is recognized that these are the more readily accessible and immediate steps to that insightful knowledge (*pañña* in Pali, *prajña* in Sanskrit) that secures *nirvana*. The cultivation of the inward good of morality finds obvious expression in the outward good of social ethics. The focus on personal development is also of a piece with the general Theravada conception of the Buddhist path as one undertaken by every person for himself or herself. Only a strict shaping of one's mental, moral and social life can possibly lead to transformative, liberating discernment of the nature of the world. The model of early Buddhism and Theravada is the *arahat*, the person who has perfected a life of insight. (There is much debate over whether such a person has transcended the bounds of ethical conduct after having mastered them, or if he continues to exemplify them even after gaining insight.) The *arahat* no doubt teaches out of compassion for others, but what is important about him is the model he presents of personal cultivation, leading to perfect understanding of things (and therefore freedom from personal suffering).

The later development of Buddhism – Mahayana – has a fundamentally different view of the ethical task. While the Theravada tradition also recognizes that the Buddha came back from his enlightenment to teach the world, the Mahayana schools take this to signify the greatest quality of all the teachers: compassion (*karuna*). Inward Good should prompt Outward Good – which is itself the realization of the Inward Good by all. The model for Mahayana Buddhism is the *bodhisattva*, the being who has repeatedly turned away from ultimate liberation in order to help the rest of the world. Such a person may have reached the stage of realization that could liberate him, but he keeps returning to the world so that he can achieve liberation for all. The emphasis in Mahayana therefore shifts from the model of impeccable personal cultivation found in Theravada to that of compassionate engagement with other beings. While retaining the concept of insight, Mahayana extends its ethical focus beyond the codes of conduct and formulae for cultivation found in Theravada to another category, called means (*upaya*). The ethics of Mahayana includes not only the cultivation of personal restraint and the fostering of insightful knowledge, but also altruism (literally, 'the ethics of favouring beings'). Such altruism may even require ingenuity: humans are resistant to knowledge and do not even know that they are bound by suffering, let alone how to become free. The good that the proper Buddhist must develop is the skilful means by which others can be taken on the path to enlightenment. Some texts even suggest that such means may be conventionally immoral: for the love of all beings, one may have to lie, steal, or worse! Of course, very few skilful means are even apparently immoral, but the ability to know what to do and how to care selflessly for all is the greatest instrument for the attainment of *nirvana*. It may require finely judged transgressions of ordinary precepts.

There are two uses of the word *nirvana*. One refers to the insight that reality is suffering, which Gautama Siddhartha experienced under the tree. This was when he became the Buddha, the 'enlightened one'. Whatever happened in that event, it transformed the person who experienced it and led him eventually to teach the world about suffering, its causes and their extinction. In that event, he became free of the human condition and attained *nirvana* by having the causes of suffering due to that condition extinguished. But, obviously, not all the conditions of life ended at that time, and neither, therefore, did all the suffering. The Buddha finds the noise and disruptions of an undisciplined group of monks and nuns impossible to bear, and goes away to find peace and quiet; so even the liberated one is not quite liberated from suffering! Complete liberation cannot have happened at the moment of enlightenment. It must have come later. In Theravada, it happens with the death of the Buddha; in most versions of Mahayana, he is still not completely liberated at death, and will wait for the whole world to join him. Sometimes, this complete state is called *parinirvana* or 'final liberation'. An analogy for the distinction is a pot taken off the fire, which is left on the cool earth and takes a while to lose all its heat. The enlightenment event is like being taken off the fire, while the final freedom is like the eventual loss of all the heat.

While supreme transformation is naturally the focus of Buddhist thought, the early texts also recognize lesser attainments (which also become, in our terms, inward goods). There are several stages of lucid meditation that one may attain on the way to *nirvana*. But a monk who has attained such stages says that he is like a man who has found a well without a bucket and rope, and can see the water but has not yet been able to drink it.

The central challenge to our understanding of what happens in *nirvana* is that the negative account rules out all the normal inner life we are familiar with, such as thoughts and feelings, but nevertheless insists that it is *something* that a person undergoes. In a beautiful and frustratingly oblique image, the liberated person's discerning yet liberated consciousness is compared to a beam of sunlight: it settles on whatever is in its path, but in the absence of any such thing it is without a resting place. It shines but is unsupported by anything. (We could take this analogy further. Think of light in a vacuum: it exists, as it eventually shines on whatever it meets, but when there is nothing to interfere with it, it is not seen. It is there and yet not there. So, too, with the consciousness of the liberated person – it is in a metaphysical vacuum, with neither self nor object to 'shine' on.)

Now, what can be said by the teacher and understood by the student about an attainment whose very nature is such that it is free of whatever can be said about it?

A radical answer is given by Nagarjuna, the founder of Madhyamaka. He takes the 'unsayability' of *nirvana* not as a problem to be solved but as the very answer to the question above. *Nirvana* comes through the realization that the sense of self and the objects of the world are constructed from one another and are not real in themselves; thus *nirvana* is seeing things for what they are and ceasing to desire them in consequence. Nothing about the world changes; it continues to be what it was – something that is dependent on us for its nature and existence. But *we* change in our coming to understand that this is so. Nagarjuna drives home the point by saying that nothing differentiates *nirvana* and the condition of bondage (*samsara*) to the world. There is no place such as *nirvana*, no content to it. It is simply (!) a switch in our perspective on ourselves and the world. That is why we cannot say what *nirvana* is; it is empty, it is not some special thing that we obtain, it is merely the name for seeing the same world in a different way.

Japanese Zen Buddhism, more than a thousand years later and many thousand miles away, sought to preserve this attitude to *nirvana* and to focus on the methods that would bring about understanding. The key to the Zen method of gaining insight (*satori*) is expressed by Dogen, who seeks to see through to the interdependence and impermanence of all things by paying intense attention to every little thing in the world around, from rain and wind to pine and bamboo. Using the characteristic Japanese aesthetic appreciation of nature for Buddhist meditative purposes, he says that in reality there is nothing to be attained: there is just the practice of seeing the world with openness and attention. This living engagement with the world expresses our understanding that it is as the Buddha taught us; we are enlightened even as we perfectly contemplate the world.

Another Mahayana school, the Yogacara, was never comfortable with what appeared to be evasions by the Madhyamaka philosophers. The Yogacara philosophers argue that, if consciousness constructs both the sense of self and the experience of external objects, then liberation from desire for the sake of an imaginary self and for an imaginary world must involve a liberation of consciousness from its constructions. (The yoga of the Yogacara school is meant to control consciousness and bring about the cessation of constructive activity.) *Nirvana*, then, must be the freeing of consciousness from construction. Now, the Yogacara philosophers contend, we can say what *nirvana* is: it is the attainment of consciousness that is free of subject (the self that desires) and object (the things of the world that are desired). This 'pure' consciousness, without constructive activity, is the supreme good that the Buddhist must seek.

Both Madhyamaka and Yogacara agree that the Buddha must have both become free from the concepts of the world *and* returned to use those very concepts in order to teach the world about the freedom he had attained. This is because teaching calls for an engagement with people, their suffering, their sense of self, and their assumption that the world of things is essential. Does the Buddha cease to be liberated when he returns to teach? Will a person who attains insight find it impossible to teach others? Is the supreme inward good of liberation from concepts intrinsically selfish? The Mahayana solution common to both Madhyamaka and Yogacara is that, purely in terms of mental life (in terms of language and ideas), the enlightened and liberated person truly does give up some element of freedom in returning to teach. The state of consciousness that follows enlightenment cannot remain; it must revert to the state characteristic of ordinary life. At the same time, the enlightenment event does have a lasting impact on the consciousness of the person who has had it. Once the event has happened, its true consequence is freedom from desire. Even when the person reverts to ordinary language and ideas, there is permanent freedom from the earlier clinging to selfhood and the world. Psychologically, the enlightened person remains free from desire for the world; but conceptually, that same person is bound to use the very concepts of the world that prompt desire in unenlightened people. It is only ultimately (at death or perhaps only when all other beings have reached the same stage) that all conceptual activity ends. In this way, *nirvana* is selfless in both senses of the term: the person is freed from the false sense of selfhood, and with compassion, cares only for others.

Order in this world and freedom from it: the dialectic of Hindu philosophy

It is relatively clear that, over time, classical Indian philosophy comes to acknowledge *moksa* – liberation from the conditions of life in the world – as the supreme good (*nihsreyas*). Starting from a position of agreement that *moksa* is liberation, various schools offer their own account of the content of liberation. This is no accident. A theory of liberation is intimately connected to a general theory of the nature of reality: how things are and how one may gain freedom from them are indeed inseparable.

However, liberation is neither the first nor the only conception of the highest good in Indian thought. We saw in the last chapter that, going back to the Veda texts, the notion of order – cosmic and social – through ritual maintenance was the first major conceptual development in Indian thought. In other words, Outward Good was the primary goal of the early texts. For the individual (ritually qualified) person, the proper performance of ritual action guaranteed material prosperity – cows that brought wealth, sons who preserved the lineage.

By the time of the early Upanisad texts, a radically different concern has developed within the older paradigm of cosmic order and human benefit. In a famous passage, the sage Yajñavalkya proposes that he renounce the world and leave his property to his wife, Maitreyi. This is the appropriate action in Vedic society. But Maitreyi asks him if she would gain immortality if she possessed the whole world. He admits that she would not, and she asks him what would then be the point in her getting his wealth. This leads to a dialogue between them in which he redirects the Vedic notion of cosmic order inwards, towards the metaphysical self that remains the centre of the Hindu philosophical universe thereafter. He continues to make the complex mappings of the cosmos onto the ritual, human domain that characterize the Vedas: earth and body, wind and breath, sun and sight, moon and mind, thunder and sound, and so on; the world can still be ordered for human good through manipulation of the ritual body. But a new idea has developed: the macrocosmic and the microcosmic – the world and the body – are both aspects of the impersonal self (*atman*), which is also the immortal, universal principle of reality (*brahman*). The metaphysical self, identified in some way with all reality, becomes the key to all existence. Understanding it brings immortality. The human goal is not wealth in this world, but immortality beyond it.

Strictly speaking, understanding the self does not bring immortality, in the sense of making the individual person who gains such knowledge live forever. Rather, the person realizes that what is essential is by its nature beyond death, for it is eternal. What dies is not that essence at all. So, in a sense, nothing changes; the world goes on, with its cycle of births and deaths, its trials and its rewards. But the seer has seen through to what pervades and underlies all these things: a principle of being that is none other than the self of the seer. Whereas in the Vedas there is barely the concept of Inward Good in a world-view dominated by the Outward Good, in the Upanisads (for all their superficial accommodation of cosmic order), the inversion is complete: the Inward Good is identified with cosmic reality.

The original prompt for the Upanisadic search for understanding is immortality, a desire driven by the fear of death (or repeated death in a cycle of lives). The end of that search, as we have seen in the story above, is not some obvious magical power to stop death but a profoundly metaphysical re-reading of reality as one in which the self is *already* and constitutively immortal. To realize this truth is to be liberated not from death as such (for the body will always die and the self never dies anyway) but from the fear of death. To that extent, the search for the supreme inward good is prompted by a dissatisfaction with the conditions of life. But the dominant mood of the Upanisads is not dissatisfaction with life and death as such, more with our understanding of their true nature. This understanding may well remove fear, but more importantly it will give power to the person, who, freed from ignorance of the world, will be able to live well in it and to prepare the *atman*/self for what lies beyond.

The motivation to seek inward good in order to gain such power as knowledge will bring is decisively qualified by the coming of Buddhism. As we have seen, the Buddha not only gives a very different answer about the nature of the self (it does not exist), but he seeks that answer for a very different reason, namely to assuage suffering. In that sense, the Buddha focuses on the dissatisfaction that is marginal in the Upanisads. Not just fear of death, but also all other conditions of life, such as disease, loss, infirmity and senility, should prompt the search for liberation from those conditions. The Buddha nonetheless continues the thinking of the Upaniṣads in one way: an understanding of how things are is meant to transform the way we think of ourselves and the way we live. Of course, he differs in the specific answers he gives about the nature of such understanding; but what is psychologically interesting is the way in which he complements the Upaniṣadic account of *why* one seeks understanding. Whereas the Upaniṣads seek the inward good of understanding in order to gain the power of knowledge, the Buddha goes back to the original prompt for such power – to rid oneself of the suffering that fear and the like bring. Thereafter Indian thought, of whichever school, sees liberating knowledge as the Inward Good.

The Vedic ideal is not banished from the scene after the Upaniṣads and the Buddha. However, it is psychologically enriched by taking much greater account of the 'interiorization' of the Good seen in the Upaniṣads and early Buddhism. The evolution of a fuller yet this–worldly account of the Good is marked by a clearer recognition of the inner life. It is no longer sufficient to say that material benefits like progeny and cows will accrue to the one who works for the outward good of cosmic order. People seek a much more complex range of goods. The challenge is to contextualize personal aims within the ancient idea of an orderly world. This challenge is met through the concept of the three-fold (*trivarga*) human ends (*puruṣa-artha*). These ends are: virtue (*dharma*), material benefits (also *artha*) and pleasure (*kama*). The concept of the three-fold ends is meant to frame the ideal life. It therefore includes both a description of how things are (people seek pleasure and benefit) and a prescription for how things should be (people should seek pleasure and benefit in a virtuous manner).

As we saw in the chapter on the Outward Good, *dharma* has outward dimensions. Ideally (and we must always remember that this is a philosophical model, not historical fact), society is organized into classes, and the individual's life course is divided into functional sections. To display *dharma* is to perform *dharma* and dutifully enact its requirements according to one's place in society and one's stage in life. Initially, it may seem that the ordered exterior life is dominant in the conception of the three-fold human goal. People's pursuit of benefits such as prosperity and political power and of pleasures including sex are to be ordered appropriately within the framework of class and life stages. Each class has its own scope for material well-being, through its work and duties; it is improper for one belonging to the priestly class to create wealth through trade or for one belonging to the labouring class to establish status through ritual mastery. Likewise, each life stage has its own constraints: the student must be celibate, the forest-dweller cannot engage in creating wealth, and so on.

On deeper analysis, it becomes clear that *dharma*'s structuring of *artha* and *kama* is not just a matter of exterior ordering of a person's activities. The interior dimensions of *dharma* are recognized too. *Dharma* is clearly identifiable as a range of virtues that people must possess in their very being and through their every action. The authoritative Textbook of Manu (the *Manu Smrti*) stipulates that non-violence, truth-telling, not stealing and controlling sensuality are the *dharma* of all classes. The Chronicles of Vikrama (*Vikrama Carita*) state simply that the *dharma* of a million sacred texts may be summed up thus: helping others is good, hurting others is bad. The great epic, the *Mahabharata*, points variously to forgiveness, compassion, non-violence, truth and other virtues each as the supreme *dharma*; and most importantly, appears to use *dharma* itself as the word for 'virtue'. An even more pointedly inward conception of *dharma*, according to a medieval commentator on Manu, is that it is the following of one's knowledgeable inclinations; and it is work characterized by choice, even according to the otherwise socially conservative philosopher Sankara. In this context, *dharma* is best understood as

cultivated conscience (although all these thinkers take such cultivation to be strictly constrained by qualifications of social status
and education). In that case, the human goals are the cultivation
of virtues guided by one's conscience, and the pursuit of material
objectives (wealth, political power) and sensory enjoyment (sex,
aesthetic appreciation) within the guidelines of the virtues. The
inward and the outward are married in this conception of the
ideal human life. A life of sound judgement and inclinations
expressed in valuable actions restrains and yet directs the natural
human desire for well-being. These are the goods of life. Some
are expressed outwardly, but at heart they are realized inwardly.

In classical Hindu thought, two broad notions of the good
emerge: the good of this life, which is a virtuous existence that
offers scope for the ethical fulfilment of natural human desires; and
the good beyond life, which is a state in which the nature of reality
is understood and the inviolable limitations of life transcended.
The former model treats life as intrinsically worthwhile, its
problems specific and potentially solvable. The latter treats life as
problematic, with the problem lying at the core of its very nature
– the problem of limited knowledge and unlimited suffering. The
tradition seeks to reconcile these two conceptions of existence by
making liberation from life itself the fourth and culminating
human objective; the three-fold goal becomes four-fold.

This move involves a creative equivocation over the nature of
life. In the course of life, many specific problems can be
overcome, and happiness (or at least the temporary cessation of
some sorrows) can be sought. Life is therefore worth leading
for the attainment of certain this–worldly goods. However, the
problematic nature of life itself cannot be denied: the fact
of sorrow and suffering must be acknowledged as intrinsic to
life. Eventually, in this life or some other, one reaches the point
at which one is ready to forsake the minor joys that are
available amidst suffering, for ultimate freedom from *all* suffering
(including the inevitable transience of the minor joys). At that

stage of intellectual, ethical and emotional preparedness, one leaves behind the first three objectives of life and seeks liberation from it. Creative though this is, it is still an equivocation: is this-worldly good worth seeking at all? There are different answers.

In general, the Mimamsa school is reluctant to concede that there is anything more to life than the order that the Vedas had conceived. Its early thinkers, who must be aware of the developments outlined above, resolutely refuse to consider anything more than the proper performance of ritual and the attainment of material benefit (perhaps in a celestial world after this one). But one Mimamsa subschool, led by Kumarila, acknowledges that liberation is the ultimate good, beyond this-worldly good. However, this subschool echoes the commitment to the concrete wonders of this world found in Hindu narratives like the *Mahabharata*: it insists on the need to lead a virtuous life even in the pursuit of liberation. According to this line of thought, liberation is the direct outcome of a virtuous life. The fourth objective is realized simply as the consequence of leading a life oriented towards the first three. To be more precise, when benefit and pleasure have been secured according to virtue, the continued performance of virtuous deeds is precisely what leads the person to freedom from the conditions of life. Freedom from life-as-suffering is the reward for virtue in that life. Of course, understanding the nature of the self and reality is required, but that is only an intellectual task. Such understanding merely shows that the self is eternal and does not die, and that the world is a place of persistent suffering even in the midst of joy. Such understanding prepares the person to treat the world philosophically and without confusion, but it does not directly lead to liberation.

Liberation, on this Mimamsa account, comes only because a knowledgeable person continues to live according to this-worldly goodness (that is, *dharma*) while being purified of continued suffering. Since life is suffering, when suffering stops as the reward for virtuous living, the continued round of lives stops. (This is explained through the assumption of the cosmic working of *karma*, which dictates that all actions have consequences, meritorious actions leading to good consequences and unmeritorious ones leading to bad. Virtuous actions are meritorious, and while some bring good rebirths, the truly meritorious ones simply bring no further consequences, thereby freeing the person from the need for lives in which to experience such consequences.) In a strange way – strange in that Mimamsa is the great opponent of the Buddhists who reject the Vedas – this school echoes the older Buddhist interpretations of *nirvana*, such as Theravada, in describing liberation purely negatively, as the cessation of sorrow.

The Mimamsa conception of liberation *from* this life and world is of a piece with its insistence that while liberation is the ultimate good, it comes only through and because of the attainment of good *in* this life and world. *Dharma* leads to *moksa*. Sankara and his Advaita school, by contrast, reject the need to seek this-worldly good in order to attain liberation. Their core argument is that, if liberation is the ultimate good, why seek anything else?

This argument gets its momentum from their view of the Upanisadic teachings. Liberation comes from an insight into the nature of self and reality. With that insight, it is understood that the individual self is actually a limited expression of the universal reality that is *brahman*. Once this transcendence of limitedness is attained, all ignorance and suffering are seen for what they are, the afflictions of limited existence. Suffering and ignorance continue for a while because that is life; but once the body dies, the free consciousness is no longer afflicted, because it has realized that there is no suffering and ignorance in its universality and limitlessness. (Here, as in Mahayana Buddhism, albeit for a different reason, there is an argument over whether each individual must wait until all others are in a position to gain freedom from ignorance and suffering.) The Advaitins ask why, since liberation is the attainment of freedom from the suffering and ignorance of limited existence in ordinary life, one should spend any time and energy seeking anything within that life. Of course, one should not blatantly violate ordinary requirements – like not killing or lying – but once set on the course of seeking liberation, one should renounce this-worldly goods altogether.

This radical rejection of all goods other than liberation is tempered in places. The story goes that Sankara was once arguing with a philosopher-couple who believed in the need to live according to *dharma* even while seeking spiritual knowledge. He urged renunciation of all this-worldly life and hence of the marriage that the couple had entered into, saying that there was no need to be bound by lesser goods when seeking liberation. The wife pointed out that Sankara, as one who had renounced the social world as a teenager, could not possibly have had the experience to claim with authority that this-worldly good was of lesser value than liberation. Acknowledging the point, Sankara took himself into a supernatural trance and entered the body of a king who had recently died. To the world, it was as if the king had been revived. Thus did Sankara spend some time in a worldly life of benefit, pleasure and socially oriented virtue. Then he quit the body again, returned to his own, and resumed his debate with the couple. Now he had the authority of experience and could maintain even more strongly that nothing he had encountered in that kingly life was worth choosing in preference to the inquiry into liberating knowledge. But we can see that the story is not a simple triumph of the world-transcending good. Sankara appears to legitimate the need to go through a this-worldly life of virtue before coming to a conclusion about the ultimate value of liberation, and that is concession enough to those who would reconcile the good of *dharma* with the good of *moksa*.

The possibility of reconciling different goods was sketched many centuries before these philosophical debates, in that great if enigmatic source of Hindu ideas, the *Bhagavad Gita*. Located within the *Mahabharata*, the *Gita* is a composition that reports events and a dialogue that occur as two armies face each other at the climax of the epic. The warrior Arjuna looks across at the enemy. They are his own cousins, and also teachers and elders who have reluctantly taken it as their duty to fight against him and his brothers. Even though his cause is rightful, Arjuna loses heart at the thought of the violence and destruction to follow.

Arjuna's charioteer, his relative Krishna, now talks to him and shows him why he should fight. The first teaching he offers is that Arjuna should understand that in reality nothing that is going to happen is ultimate; what kills and is killed is not the self, which lies behind and beyond the world (as the Upanisads have taught). Seeing through to this mystery of existence will allow Arjuna to act in this world with a sense of his immediate duty rather than indulge in existential agony over the true consequences of his actions. Gaining a metaphysical perspective on himself and the world, Arjuna should treat the world accordingly. Triumph and disaster, happiness and sorrow − all will happen as they will, but knowing that they are only of this world and that the self that appears to undergo them is ultimately untouched, Arjuna should preserve equanimity at all times.

The need and possibility of equanimity (*sthitha-prajña*) is the next key teaching. Arjuna should neither despair at the prospect of the war that must be fought nor exult in its material possibilities. This equanimity, born of insight into the nature of reality, will allow him to perform his duties in this world − duties to his brothers, his wife and his followers and to a just cause. So, the call of social good can be followed, even if one requires metaphysical knowledge in order to be able to do it. Krishna then goes on to provide Arjuna with a psychological procedure that will allow him to secure equanimity: he should sacrifice the fruit of his actions and act without desire for that fruit. Then he will be performing pure duty, for its own sake. Whatever happens to him, he will not have sought it; he will act only out of the moral obligation to act for others. He will thus be discharging his duties and yet transcending their constraints. With insight into the self and with his purified conduct, he will be moving towards liberation from the bonds of the world, even as he acts within it. He will understand reality, he will suffer but treat suffering with detachment, he will cleave to the worldly good and yet will attain to the ultimate good.

This is necessarily a simplistic précis of the main teachings of the *Gita*. I have presented only the points that are germane to our discussion. The tension between the this-worldly good (both outward and inward) of *dharma* and the world-transcendent good of liberation is ingeniously resolved by the suggestion that the former be sought, but with such a psychological approach as to prime oneself to attain the latter. The connecting thread through this resolution is the quality of equanimity. As in the utterly different case of Zhuangzi, this equanimity can be read in two different ways. The conservative, less radical reading is that one should undergo all the emotions of experience as they happen, but at some higher level of awareness remember that they are not of ultimate significance. Demanding though this would be, the second, radical reading is even more so: understanding the nature of experience, one should always keep a distance from the consequences of its impingement on us, thereby never allowing the normal emotions to arise in us. Detachment may therefore be from the consequences of emotion or it may be from emotion itself. In any case, equanimity is a key accomplishment, a prerequisite good for all else.

Krishna does not stop there. He goes on to explain why a sacrifice of the fruit of our actions − the psychological act that prompts equanimity − is possible. A person who gives up thought of how he will benefit from actions is able to do so because the fruit of his actions will be absorbed by God. Krishna reveals himself as the Supreme Being, from and into whom all things flow. He assures Arjuna that if he surrenders himself to Krishna, Krishna will liberate him from all bondage. It is divine love that sets a person free.

Eventually, many centuries later, this strand of the *Gita* comes to dominate Hindu thinking. Such seminal Hindu theologians as Ramanuja and Madhva argue that liberation from the world can only be attained through divine grace. The content of liberation itself continues to be a matter of debate. Both take the *brahman* of the Upanisads to be the personal God rather than an impersonal principle of reality, and they understand the identification of the self with *brahman* as a relationship between humanity and divinity. Ramanuja takes liberation to be the reunion of self and God, as the self is seen as a limited spark of the divine. Madhva simply takes the Upanisadic talk of identity as a rhetorical device to indicate the eternal intimacy that will come when the liberated self attains the presence of God in heaven. The ultimate good is still liberation, but it is very different from the ideas of the non-theistic schools. (Strangely, this kind of pattern can be seen even in Buddhism. The traditional belief in one's own progression to *nirvana* is sometimes replaced by a quasi-theistic belief in the power of the Buddha or a *bodhisattva* to take people to *nirvana*. This is the case, for example, with the Japanese Pure Land sect founded by Honen, where the demand is for surrender or a turning of one's mind (*eshin*) towards a form of the Buddha called Amida (Amitabha in Sanskrit). Obviously, in such a case, faith replaces striving as the penultimate good.)

In such theism lay a final, radical development in Hindu conceptions of the good. In contrast to the measured love of the divine found in the work of the theologians, the aim of the mystics, saints and poets who advocate devotion (*bhakti*) is simply to immerse themselves in love of God. The devotional compositions (in many languages, stretching over many centuries) often explicitly castigate the philosophically articulated love of God that leads to liberation as a mean and calculating love, a love that is merely an instrument for some other end. The devotional poets care for nothing beyond the love itself. The overwhelming, oceanic love is itself the supreme good, although they care not a whit that it is so. In one way, we are far from the emotional balance of the equanimity encouraged by the *Bhagavad Gita*, as the mystics and poets sing and dance through the streets in a spiritual madness. Yet, looking deeper, there is true equanimity of attitude here, for they are free. The philosophers themselves recognize the supremacy of this devotional life, for they say that, regardless of whether the mystics seek liberation or not, God gives it to them.

A parable captures the feeling that the mystical devotee who rejects the instrumental pursuit of liberation attains it more effectively than the thinker who toils for it on the path of knowledge. A respected scholar of music went to the gates of the palace and asked for an audience with the king. He was allowed to walk up the path to the royal court, and told that the king would wait for him to come. But then, a carefree musician wandered past the gates, singing aloud, with no thought of whom he would impress. The king came rushing down the path to hail him and listen to his songs.

5

Language

For our purpose of gaining an overview of the place of language in Asian philosophies, we should start by recognizing two ways of thinking of the function and importance of language. One is that language is the representation in our consciousness of the world and the things in it. On this conception, language is taken to somehow 'capture' (or, to use a different metaphor, 'map') the structure of the world. Language refers to the world by picking out things in it. In short, linguistic expressions (words, phrases or sentences) designate one or more things or states of affairs in the world. Or rather, they seek to do so, such that they can express the 'truth' of the matter. This conception of language is based on a theory of reference: language somehow refers to the world (truthfully – that is, as it really is). This view of language can be designated *language-as-reference*.

The other way of treating language is to take it as the means by which we make our way through the world. Here, the purpose of language is not to grasp the world as it is, but to grasp how to act in it. Language is important because it is the medium through which commands and guidance can be conveyed and accepted. In such a conception of language, the important thing is that it articulates human action, rather than that it conveys truths. This is the view of *language-as-guide*.

Of course, both these conceptions are part of any account of the evolution of language. But in different philosophical cultures different stresses are placed upon these conceptions. Chinese philosophy almost entirely interests itself with the efficacy of language in organizing and moderating human society; language-as-guide dominates Chinese thinking, although there are interesting challenges to this domination in the classical period. Indian philosophy eventually comes to be wholeheartedly engaged in the search for semantic truth – the way in which linguistic expressions are used accurately about the world. But there is also a line of thought that asserts the importance of language-as-guide (albeit in a very different way from how we find it presupposed in China).

Language as guiding force: the doctrine of the rectification of names

The concept of the 'rectification of names' eventually becomes the single most significant issue in Chinese philosophy of language. Although he mentions the concept only once, Confucius, as ever, sets the discussion in motion. His disciple Zilu asks him what he would do if he were asked to administer or govern (*zheng*) a state. Confucius says, much to the other's puzzlement, that he would rectify (*zheng*, with a different character-graph) names (*ming*). Without names being rectified, Confucius goes on to say, a series of unravellings will occur: language will not function smoothly, social actions will be unsuccessful, ritual and music will not last, punishments will be wrongly meted out, and people will not know what to do with themselves. Clearly, names have to be used correctly, and the role of the ruler is to rectify their misuse; otherwise, chaos will follow. But what does the rectification of names involve? Confucius tells the ruler that he must rectify names, but he does not say how. In another famous passage, the duke Qing of Qi asks him again how to govern. Confucius says that 'the ruler' ought to be the ruler, 'the minister' minister, 'the father' father, 'the son' son. Clearly, what is going on here is that Confucius holds that there are standards to which everyone must conform. 'Son' signifies certain attitudes and values, as does every other name.

Now, one way of reading this is to say that the task of the ruler is to ensure that people come up to the standards expected of them, so that a son acts as he should, and so on. But this is more a rectification of people than a rectification of names! Such an undertaking would not have anything to do with language. Instead, we should understand Confucius as saying that the task of the ruler is to find a person who does personify the values of being a son and *name* him as such, so that he becomes the model for others. This is where the ruler shows his leadership: in providing concrete examples of things and people that exemplify what their names signify. By doing this, he directs the whole of his society towards models; to follow them is for everyone and everything to become ordered. This power of naming is evidenced by the fact that originally the character *ming* for 'name' is explained through another character *ming*, which means 'commanded', 'mandated' or 'cause to be realized'. Names are linguistic expressions that realize or model meanings (*yi*). To *name* a thing or person (which we would conceive of as a purely linguistic act) is, therefore, to *show* people the meaning of that expression (which is a substantive moral project). The notion that language is a guide to people's behaviour is brought out well in this traditional lexical explanation.

From Confucius onwards, the rectification or ordering of names is a linguistic *act*, a performance akin to any other ritual or ceremony (*li*). Confucius says that names are used to generate credibility (for the social order that the ruler seeks by identifying appropriate models). Those named are able to look after the instruments and means of ritual (anything ranging from the appropriate music through clothing, vessels, the performance of duties, and even gestures in their interactions). They thereby enable the rituals to be carried out properly; and, of course, through such ritual, socio-political order is eventually created (on ritual and order, see chapter 3). Language here is understood primarily in terms of what is *done* when it is used. On the side of the speaker (normatively, the ruler), language has illocutionary force: when he names, he is bringing about something in the world through that linguistic act. (An ordinary example is when someone promises or confesses; they *do* something with their speech.) Equally, language has perlocutionary force, on the side of the hearers: those named are made models, everyone else responds to the command to model themselves. (An ordinary example is when someone is cheered up or frightened upon hearing something; something is *done* to them through hearing speech.) In focusing on the rectification of names as the first significant step in governance, Confucius takes language to structure society, with the rectifier of names guiding society and the rectified – those named (and those hearing the naming) – responding appropriately.

The rectification of names would appear to turn on the conviction that language provides standards because those standards are inherent in names. The thing or person named is a *model* of those standards. In modelling, the one who rectifies *interprets* the standards in terms of the context, and that interpretation is taken up by the one who is rectified. These standards, in turn, guide action in the world: once the name is rectified, people can be rectified, as others who are sons see that they must act in accordance with the model son who has been 'named' as such, because of his correct and sincere performance of filial duty.

This notion of linguistic function implies a deeply conservative view of culture. Where do the standards signified by a name come from, such that a model can be identified? Confucians normally look back to the way things were in the near-legendary times of the Zhou dynasty. In that sense, the power of language is traced back to an ideal past, whose standards, interpreted by Confucian rulers, can be imposed on the present. Later Confucians did the same with Confucius himself, elevating him as the person who in fact rectified names. This is not to say that there is no scope for creativity. Confucius makes a point about a ritual vessel: a vessel that is not named is not a ritual vessel. Even a pot that *has* been named a ritual vessel will cease to be one if not continually designated as such; and any pot can become a ritual vessel if so designated. The moral of this observation is that naming is an interpretation specific to a context. The governor who rectifies names can see afresh who is a son and 'name' him as a model, and the son will perform accordingly, so that social order may be maintained.

Mencius, however, sees language as potentially misleading, because it may be used by those skilled in argument to lead people into paths that are not ideal. He asserts that moral guidance lies in the innate goodness of the heart-mind, beyond language. The skill in determining the right way to act is not reducible to skill in using language. If anything, that skill is destroyed by the hasty application of rules of linguistic guidance, like the crop that was destroyed by the foolish man of Song, who tried to speed up its growth by pulling at the ears of corn.

Later classical Confucianism, however, rejected this anti-language attitude. Xunzi decisively reasserts the value and function of rectifying names. He starts with the assumption that the ruler and the ruling class face a world of chaos. Two basic distinctions are seen as lacking in society: the first social, between noble and base; the second natural, between similar and different. Once the ruling class is able to fix the names according to the distinction between noble and base, the functions of people – determining who can use language to guide action and who is to be guided by such action – are clarified. Thereafter, things in the natural world can be fixed according to the same-difference distinction: whether certain creatures are counted as being like domestic animals or different because they are wild will have an impact on whether they are treated as someone's property or hunted for food.

Now, Xunzi operates in a culture in which the original Confucian ideal of traditional standards for the rectification of names has been challenged by the Mohists and the Daoists (see below). Where is he to seek the standards for fixing the models for names? Xunzi is thoroughly reactionary in his response. He insists that the standards must come from the historical tradition as interpreted by contemporary Confucian gentlemen. He makes no attempt whatsoever to go beyond the conventions in finding standards for fixing names. The guidance for language is given by nothing except the usages of the past. This is not only reactionary but also highly elitist. The purpose of rectifying names is to secure the best possible order from the perspective of the aristocrats. Language in Xunzi is thoroughly prescriptive and conventional. At the same time, given his ambition to organize society, Xunzi is acutely aware of the need for activities to 'fit' (*dang*) the world. It is not as if he lacks understanding of the relationship between language and the world; it is just that his dominant concern is how that relationship can help organize action *in* that world.

The Legalist school as represented by Han Feizi takes this even further. He wants to use language as an instrument of state control. The rectification of names is not even the duty of aristocrats. It is a political technique to help the ruler maintain his grip on power. The ruler alone rectifies names, for his own purposes.

What we must note in the doctrine of the rectification of names is that the power of tradition does not mean that language is given and fixed. It is fluid and socially constructed, even if that construction is a matter of elite control. We should bear this point in mind when looking at the deeply contrasting Hindu idea of sacred language later in this chapter.

Utility touches upon truth: the pragmatic standard for making language constant

Mozi, an early opponent of Confucius, shares with him the conviction that linguistic expressions – in particular, 'names' – have the power to influence and structure society. Language guides the actions of leaders when they use it properly, and it guides the rest of society in consequence of that proper usage. But Mozi has two interrelated objections to Confucius. First, he is suspicious of the traditional aristocratic elite (from whose ranks come the Confucian 'gentlemen' or exemplary men) and wants leaders to be drawn from a wider social range of craftsmen. Consequently, he is less willing to think that the standards to which one must appeal should come from tradition. Second, he is unhappy that the Confucian goal in reforming names is a ritually ordered society, which is naturally elitist in whose good it elevates.

For these reasons, Mozi proposes a utilitarian standard for reforming language: whenever words tend to promote good behaviour, he says, they must be kept or made constant. By good behaviour, he means whatever gives benefit (yet another *li*) and avoids harm (*hai*). When benefit is made the standard to which names must conform, tradition is set aside, weakening the grasp of the aristocracy on the interpretation of names. Equally, when the reformation of names is directed towards the attainment of benefit, the Confucian ritually ordered society no longer remains the common goal.

Mozi gives an elaborate account of how linguistic reform should take place and what it will achieve. Taking what constitutes 'benefit' as obvious (presumably some sort of life free of starvation and continuous suffering), he says social leaders discriminate (*bian*) between what is right/should be asserted as 'this' (*shi*) and what is wrong/should be asserted as 'not-this' (*fei*). (Note how *shi* and *fei* associate right and wrong with the linguistic acts of asserting 'this' and 'not-this' respectively. This is common to all Chinese philosophy. Right and wrong are not primarily descriptions of things in the world but acts of assertion in language. Moral judgement in classical Chinese is primarily a performance in and through language. Of course, it is not enough for someone just to say 'this is…' in order to make it 'right'; but what is ultimately agreed to be right and wrong in classical Chinese culture is recognized only through some authoritative source – be it gentlemen or the ruler or some other leaders – making the assertions 'this' and 'not-this'.) Then, to understand the meaning of a name is to know how to apply 'this' and 'not-this' to it. If a guiding discourse is beneficial, then its assertions and usages must be kept constant by asserting what it asserts. If it is not beneficial, reform must take place. Reform of names is effected when, for the names in a guiding discourse, leaders change from asserting 'this' (i.e., it is right) to asserting 'not-this' (i.e., it is wrong), because social benefit is harmed.

Mozi illustrates these procedures when talking about spirits and fate. He says that, according to his 'Three Tests of Language', it must be accepted that there are spirits, but it must be rejected that there is such a thing as fate. The tests are to help decide which discourses and the names that occur in them are to be constant and which are to be reformed. The first test concerns the origins of any discourse and involves a comparison with the usages of the legendary sage-kings. The second looks at the evidence for such a discourse in what the eyes and ears of people take to be real. The third appeals to whether a discourse will, when put into the practice of governance, benefit the people. On these grounds, Mozi says we must acknowledge that it is right to have a discourse in which we have spirits but not fate. A discourse must be reformed if it includes the use of the name 'fate' as applying to some force of inevitability in life. The sage-kings appear not to have resorted to the concept of fate, the people are not agreed on it, and accepting it would hinder administration. But the name 'spirit', as applying to people who live on after bodily death or to personalized forces that guard mountains and rivers, passes the tests. The sage-kings accepted spirits, people have experienced them, and the literature is full of stories about them that offer ethical guidance to people. The concept of 'spirit' should be held constant in language.

Mozi offers here a view of language that has a powerful impact on guiding action in the world. By 'names', he means the terms for things, people and forces that are active in a language. These terms structure how people behave. His three tests are meant to help use and reform language in such ways as to guide people effectively.

At this point, we may ask whether there is at least a hint that Mozi is thinking of language not only as guide but also as reference to the way the world is in reality. In the end, when utility is appealed to as the standard, there has also to be an appeal to the way things are in the world; after all, if language is meant to make people behave in such a way as to avert hunger, it is a fact about the world whether there is hunger or not. In order to conduct the three tests successfully, one must look at the world to check whether a discourse works. The discourse itself is about guidance, since Mozi agrees with Confucius that names such as 'ruler', 'son' and the like (even 'spirit', which Confucians tend to deny) describe how entities act; so the discourse is not really factual. For Mozi, talk of spirits is about whether the practice of people in using the term/concept 'spirit' is admissible or not; he does not engage with the question of whether spirits themselves exist or not. Still, one may wonder whether both Mozi and the people themselves could at all times have taken themselves to be merely 'talking' about spirits without asking whether there are spirits in truth and whether we should believe in them.

Mozi appears at no point to use language to refer to things in the world, and confines himself to using it for guidance alone. In this, too, he is no different from Confucius. (In contrast, language-as-reference is very important in Indian philosophy.)

Later followers of Mozi (sometimes called the Neo-Mohists) show relatively greater readiness to use language referentially. They never became influential because of the very different developments of Confucian conventionalism with regard to the constancy of language and Daoist disregard for such constancy. Mohists, throughout their brief history (of barely two or three centuries), seek to find a way of making guiding discourse constant in its use of names and standards. This constancy must, of course, have the outcome of producing benefit for society, but how is to be secured? They reject the Confucian claim that it must come from the conventions of tradition and gentlemen, for these are not constant. No, what fixes the continued applicability of a name, once it has been applied to a thing or person, is that thing or person itself.

A key concept in Later Mohism is 'fitting the fact' or 'adequacy' (*dang*) (we saw that Xunzi uses it too). When there is a dispute over names, only one will fit or be adequate. When two people argue over whether a young animal is a whelp or a dog, it is no dispute, as both are right; and it is no dispute when both are wrong, as when they argue whether it is a horse or a cow, and it is neither. The Later Mohists argue that the Daoist denial of the need to settle the linguistic fact of the matter (which we explore below) is perverse and impermissible, while Confucian conventions do not settle the matter at all. (Xunzi's response is that this does not matter, provided the rulers can make the people follow a convention!) There is a world, and in that world one naming is applicable and others are not; it is undeniable that some names fit or map onto the world, while others do not, showing that the Daoist is wrong and the Confucian inadequate.

The Later Mohists' conception of language as being rendered constant through fitting the world does appear to involve reference. However, they never develop any systematic account of how language does map onto the world – they merely take it for granted. In other words, language-as-reference is not theorized but assumed. This is because the Chinese philosophers approach language pragmatically: how can language act as a guide to action? They recognize the metaphysical possibility of things having an inherent or unalterable nature (*gu*), a nature of which we have certainty. There can be little doubt here that they are working with an acute awareness of objectivity, or the independent fact of the matter to which language refers. This *would* be a doctrine of realism in a metaphysical tradition, if developed self-consciously, but the Chinese philosophers are not working in a philosophical environment in which this even requires debate. The description of the world therefore is significant only because it points to the possibility of a guiding discourse. This is no failure to develop a theory of semantic truth; it is a matter of identifying and defending a position relevant to their culture.

The limits of language: artificiality and anarchy

Daoism expresses reservations about the efforts of Confucians and Mohists to control and stabilize society through performative language use. Daoists argue that names and discourses cannot be controlled and directed towards social ordering; language has intrinsic limitations that will not allow it to function as a guide. Beyond that, however, Laozi and Zhuangzi have somewhat different views of the way in which language is limited.

Laozi's position is expressed in the famous opening verse of the *Laozi*, the first line of which we examined in chapter 1. Let us return to that verse in its full form, translated in the following manner: 'The way (*dao*) that can be made a way is not a constant way/ The name (*ming*) that can be named is not a constant name.'

Here, a way − a way of living, a way of becoming − is also a discourse or a spoken way, a way of using language to do things. Since names are parts of discourses in classical Chinese thought, the second line is a specific case of the general claim made in the first line. A name that is named is, of course, what *every* name is; otherwise, it would not be a name! Laozi is pointing to the nature of all names: they do model things and people (he does not contest that), but as all things and their functions are always in flux, the names too change. As ways of speaking and doing change, we have no reliable way of making them constant. By the time we attempt to rectify a name, what that name signifies has changed. (For a relatively simple example, the model son may be less respectful and more friendly towards his parents from one generation to another; so what it is for the son to be a son will keep changing.) The lack of constancy means that no name and no way is constant.

This might seem a pedestrian reading of what has often been taken to be a mystical text. The mystical reading would say that there is, in some profound if contradictory way, a constant name that cannot be named, a constant way cannot be spoken of. But the ametaphysical context of Chinese thought indicates that Laozi simply does not think in those terms. And although not a mystical reading, the point that names lack constancy is significant enough, in the context of Confucius and Mozi. Laozi, who is now going to go on to teach a ruler how to rule, sets off by denying that the guiding force of language can secure the constancy sought by the Confucians and Mohists. The ruler has to do something very different, according to him (on which see chapter 3 on the Outward Good).

This suspicion towards the illocutionary and perlocutionary power of language is part of Laozi's larger claim about the artificiality of all social ways (and language as a whole is, of course, the supreme social way). If there is a mysticism in him, it lies in a commitment to natural ways of life that people can grow into, untrammelled by the constraints of social convention. Language's limits are set by the way nature itself guides life.

Zhuangzi, too, is resistant to the Confucian and Mohist attempts to make language order life; he comments that naming and saying are never fixed. But whereas Laozi expresses that resistance by denying that language can take people to a natural way of life, Zhuangzi says virtually the opposite. He takes language to be like other natural noises, such as the twittering of birds. He entirely allows that language is natural to life; indeed, he grants that the *dao*/way of language is a *dao*/way under heaven (*tian*, the natural order). But it is a *dao*/way just like other *dao*/ways; wherever we walk, he says, a *dao*/way is never absent. By granting a place in nature to every *dao*/way, every discourse and every attempt to fix names, Zhuangzi undercuts the claims of *any* of them to be correct or authoritative.

Zhuangzi understands that people have their own favoured discourses, whereby they seek success according to their own predispositions. This is, technically, prejudice (*cheng*) – 'prejudice', meaning to judge beforehand what should be deemed correct. So discourses always proliferate in language and will be incompatible with one another, the Mohist holding 'this is not' of something of which the Confucian says 'this is', and vice versa. At the same time, Zhuangzi does indicate that the sage resists the tendency to proliferate ways: take no step towards saying of something that 'it is' or 'it is not', he says, and the rifts between people will come to an end. So, we are left with two unstable points between which Zhuangzi's view of language oscillates. One is a simple, almost anarchic acknowledgement that every discourse will have its own plan of reforming and stabilizing something that is never constant. The other is the hint, somewhat mystical, that the sage makes no attempt to use language to guide the world. The guiding conventions of language divide, whereas the sage treats everything in nature as one (heaven and earth are born together with me, and the myriad things and I are one, he says, although going on to acknowledge that this is insufficient to grant harmony).

The Chinese philosophers take the limits of language to be reached when natural *dao*/ways show themselves to be free from linguistic regulation (especially naming). As we will see below, Indian notions of the limits of language are explicitly metaphysical, pointing to the deeper and hidden structures of reality itself.

Reference and guidance: the basic debate in Indian conceptions of language

Language is important for Indian philosophers because many claim it to be an instrument of knowledge. More specifically, some maintain that as testimony – the utterance of structured word-sounds (*sabda*, which has the meaning of both the word itself and the sound of its utterance) – language creates knowledge in the recipient. This means of attaining knowledge, they say, is quite different from perception and inference, the other main ways through which knowledge is gained. So, the possession of language should include the capacity to transmit and receive knowledge-bearing testimony. Only some of the schools accept that testimony is a source of knowledge; others, especially the Buddhists, think that testimony can be reduced to inference and perception. (This debate is touched upon again in chapter 6.) Nevertheless, the very fact that language is posited as a means of gaining knowledge is sufficient to give a direction to its philosophical study. But while the philosophical concern of understanding how knowledge is gained eventually came to dominate the study of language, the initial study of language in Indian thought was focused on grammar.

The study of grammar in fact pre-dates the full development of the philosophical schools in the brahminical (that is, Hindu) traditions. Much of the work of the early grammarians is confined to technical description of the way language works and should work, but some of their framework is of philosophical importance. The language in question is, of course, Sanskrit, the language of the sacred Hindu texts. Even by the time of the grammarians, it is not the language of the populace, but that of high culture. Being sacred, the status of Sanskrit does not depend on its usage.

Panini, the founder of grammatical analysis, aims to explain not only how rules of language usage work, but also how language conveys meaning. This interest in the communication of meaning is significant. Panini and the grammarians who follow him puzzle over how language relates to the world, for they take it that meaning comes from some relationship between language and things in the world. For them, meaning is the linguistic capture of the way the world is. Grammatical analysis already carries with it the conception of language as referential (that is, as picking out things). Much subsequent Indian philosophy works with the referential view of language.

In their historical context, however, we must assume that the early grammarians were exceptional, for the dominant brahminical philosophical objective in their time would have been the correct interpretation of the sacred Vedas. The slightly later texts of the Mimamsa school amply demonstrate this very different view of language.

To understand the Mimamsa view of language, we must understand how the Vedas are interpreted. For the philosophers of this school, the Vedas are important because they alone provide guidance on how human action can sustain cosmic order. Cosmic order depends on all things functioning in set ways, and human actions are a part of that order. Although later Indian philosophy comes to think that the maintenance of cosmic order requires a whole range of ethical and other social actions, the original Mimamsa philosophers take it to require highly symbolic, elaborately structured, and tightly regulated ritual actions alone. These ritual actions have no social or political value; unlike Confucian ritual, they are not intended to be vehicles for personal presentation and social interaction. Instead, they are sets of actions that are in themselves literally without meaning: pouring clarified butter into a carefully constructed fire altar; putting drops of water to one's mouth with a hand cupped in a certain way; chanting certain combinations of sounds; and so on. Ritual elements symbolically resemble the real elements of the cosmos (as we saw in chapter 3), and have a virtual relationship with them. When the ritualists manipulate the ritual elements, they use the abstract connections that these elements have with the real cosmic elements. The preservation of order between the ritual elements therefore sustains in a hidden way the order of the cosmos itself.

The information about the structures of the universe is encoded in the knowledge of the elements and actions of the ritual. To perform the ritual properly is to sustain the workings of the universe. (Gradually, as other actions come to be accepted as having a role in the maintenance of order, ethical conduct and social duties are taken to contribute directly to social order, which in turn affects cosmic order.)

Given this belief system, the significance of the sacred Vedic texts clearly lies in the guidance they give on how to act; specifically, on how to perform the appropriate, cosmically significant ritual actions. The philosophical task at hand, according to Mimamsa, is to do a close exegesis of the sacred texts, so that the injunctions (*vidhi*) and prohibitions (*nisedha*) given by the texts may be understood. Then the ritualists can perform actions accordingly.

The early grammarians and most of the philosophical schools (including Nyaya and the various Vedanta systems) take language to be primarily about what 'is (already) established' (*siddha*). In contrast, the Mimamsa school holds that the analysis of language should concentrate on what 'is to be established' (*sadhya*). The distinction between what is already established and what is to be established can sometimes be used uncontroversially to distinguish between past and future states of affairs. However, the distinction is also emblematic of the two different views of language that were introduced at the beginning of the chapter. That which is already established is that which exists, namely the world. If language is about what is already established (as found in the *siddha* view of language), then its function must be to pick out – refer meaningfully to – things that exist. By contrast, if language is concerned with what is to be established (as claimed by the *sadhya* view), it is clearly meant to be a guide towards what should be done. The first formulation makes language referential, while the second takes it to be about guidance.

It is true that the 'guidance', *sadhya* view of language originally relates specifically to sacred language, whereas the 'referential', *siddha* view has wider scope. However, this is not enough to stop a debate from developing between the two views of language, as each side seeks to extend the applicability of its own view. This difference between the conceptions of language-as-referential and language-as-guidance is clearly understood in the Indian traditions.

When traditional Mimamsa thinkers take the interpretation of sacred injunctions − what is to be established (in other words, ritually realized cosmic order) − as the primary task of the philosopher, they highlight the use of language as guidance to action. The most rigorous interpretation of this view is given by Prabhakara, who founded one of the Mimamsa subschools. He seeks to widen the applicability of his theory of language from sacred language to general usage. According to him, indicative sentences, which appear to refer to things in the world, are actually imperatives. On his interpretation, indicative or descriptive sentences, like 'there is a snake in the garden' or 'it is raining', actually contain prescriptions − 'do not go outside' or 'go outside with a stick/umbrella'. Even referential language is ultimately for guidance.

However, other schools, including Nyaya and Advaita Vedanta, assert that language is about what is already established: language is primarily a means of gaining knowledge *that* things are the way they are, not knowledge of *how* to do things. These schools tend not to deny that language has a guiding dimension but they make it dependent on the referential. The Advaita Vedanta school, especially in the works of its founder Sankara, identifies the Upanisad texts, which contain statements about the nature of reality ('*brahman* is all'; 'I am *brahman*'; etc. − see chapter 1), as being of supreme significance. Clearly, these statements are referential, being about the way things (really) are. According to Advaita, the Vedic injunctions to ritual action are merely secondary texts, meant for correct action performed *before* one attains the knowledge of reality that is available in the Upanisads. Their general argument is that one cannot act unless one knows what there is to act on. (For example, unless language refers to ritual implements, how can ritual be performed with those implements?)

Sentences and words: guidance and reference

A highly technical debate in Indian philosophy of language focuses on the unit of meaning: where does meaning lie, in words (*pada*) or sentences (*vakya*)? But even this narrow debate has a bearing on larger issues concerning the nature of language, as we will see.

One view holds that meaning lies in words – the meaning of sentences depends on the meaning of words. The name of the theory may be translated as 'connection of designata', where the designata are individual words or names. Sentences are merely connections of words. The main argument of this view is that such an account better explains the way language works. Only if we know the meaning of the word 'cow' in the sentence 'the cow gives milk' can we understand the meaning of different sentences that we (and certainly the classical Indian philosophers!) may have never encountered before, such as 'the cow jumped over the moon'. The word is constant in different sentential contexts and must therefore be understood prior to sentences; ultimately, each word of a sentence must be understood before sentences can be.

The other theory, which may be called the theory of 'the designation of connections', says that the sentence designates the whole set of connections between words, and thereby gives meaning to them. Prabhakara argues for the Mimamsa view that words convey no meaning except in the context of a sentence. A word like 'milk' by itself is incomplete in guiding action, until the whole sentence, 'milk the goat', is formulated. The word's meaning requires the sentence, and so the sentence meaning is prior to that of the word. When we do understand words, it is either because we have encountered them previously in other sentences ('Milk is got from cows, goats, etc.') or because the word itself is actually a whole sentence that we understand from the context (for example, 'Milk!' uttered by the farmer to the assistant in front of a cow).

A striking feature of this debate is that it appears to have a direct link with the contrasting conceptions of language that we discussed previously. The theory of the designation of connections, which takes meaning to lie in sentences, accords with the view of language-as-guide. If language is primarily about following injunctions, then sentences must be the bearers of meaning, since it is sentences and not words that guide action. (See how even 'Milk!', as uttered by the farmer, is actually a sentence guiding the assistant towards action.) The theory of the connection of designata, in which meaning lies in words, accords with the referential view of language, for words gain meaning by designating or referring to things. (If a sentence refers to a fact, which is made up of several elements, it must depend upon words that refer to the individual elements that make up that fact.) Since Indian philosophy is dominated by a study of how we come to know reality and what that reality consists in, the theory that language is first about word-meaning – the theory that accords with the view that language is primarily referential – is far more influential than the other. Despite their fundamental differences over practically every metaphysical and epistemological point, Nyaya and Advaita, for example, hold this theory of language in common.

In an interesting rapprochement, the other main subschool of Mimamsa, founded by Kumarila, accepts that meaning lies in words, although it still wants to take language to be a guide to action. Meaning does lie in words, but nevertheless, once sentences are constituted out of words, they primarily enjoin action. Knowledge of things through words is necessary, but only as a prerequisite for knowledge of how to act, and this second kind of knowledge is given only through sentences. What comes first (word-meaning and knowledge of things) is not for that reason more important than what comes later (sentence meaning and guidance for action).

One important point that should be noted here is that, for all their disagreements, none of these Hindu schools takes language to be a human construct, subject to change over time. Their metaphysical view of language contrasts with that of Chinese culture. For those who take meaning to lie in words, the act of designation is eternal. Nyaya holds that the designation was done by God, the creator of both world and language. The Mimamsa philosophers, notwithstanding their intense disagreement over whether sentences or words have primary meaning, take language to be part of the very structure of an eternal reality. Indeed, actions to sustain the cosmos by following the guidance of the Vedic language are possible precisely because the language is innate to the cosmos and therefore invariably effective (provided we interpret it properly). Naturally, they all grant that there are secondary languages, but these are seen as derivatives of Sanskrit, the eternal, sacred language; these other languages allow some human creativity but are irrelevant for the purposes of philosophical investigation. (The Buddhists start with a decisive rejection of the sacred status of Sanskrit and the possibility of eternal language; but over time they come to engage with the Hindu thinkers in Sanskrit. The Jains are somewhat more stringent in continuing to write in demotic languages.)

Kinds of meaning

As the theory that primary meaning lies in words comes to dominate, the philosophers pay much attention to exploring different kinds of word-meaning. The simplest type is the determinate word that designates a determinate thing. 'Cow' means cow. Of course, this is only the beginning of the analysis. How does this designation happen? The Mimamsa philosophers (of Kumarila's subschool) say that 'cow' refers to or picks out that which makes all cows cows and nothing else – namely, an abstract entity called a universal, in this case 'cowhood'. They argue that a word must pick out the general idea of what it is to be a cow, for otherwise the meaning of 'cow' will change from one particular cow to the next. The Nyaya philosophers retort that it cannot be the universal 'cowhood' alone, because then it would not be possible to pick out particular cows! They argue that 'cow' must refer to a particular thing (an individual cow) qualified or marked out by the universal 'cowhood'. In this way, the general idea and the individual entity are both accommodated in the use of the word 'cow'.

This leads to a different issue. In whatever way 'cow' comes to mean cow, how did that relationship of meaning come about? Given their view that language is eternal and an expression of the structure of reality, Mimamsa philosophers say that the relationship between word and object is natural and eternal. In contrast, Nyaya philosophers do not think that language is a natural part of reality. They wish to distinguish between things and words. Yet they do not wish to assert that language is purely a human construct. They reconcile these two positions by saying that language is originally a separate creation by God. So, in a sense, the relationship between 'cow' and cow is not natural but a result of a convention to name the latter with the former; but that convention was originally fixed by God. This allows them to say that the ordinary experience of naming is simply the human extension of the divine mandate.

While these debates relate to the primary meaning of determinate words, the philosophers recognize that language actually shows a rich range of other forms of meaning. Over the centuries, different thinkers develop ever more nuanced accounts of secondary meaning (*laksana*). Secondary meaning involves the *transfer* of meaning: in the standard Sanskrit example, 'the village on the Ganges' does not refer to a community on stilts but to a settlement on the banks of the river. Through the bridging notion of proximity, the meaning is transferred from the primary or literal meaning 'on the river' to the secondary 'on the bank of the river'. This relatively simple example is the starting-point for much more complex instances. Other bridging notions include prominence ('he is the family' points to his importance in the family); behaviour ('the king is the god of Death' indicates that he is stern, not that he is divine); purpose ('he is making a mat' is said of a person gathering reeds, because he intends to make one); and so on. Secondary meanings, then, are given by a variety of metaphors. A later development in the notion of secondary meaning is that of 'suggestive power': there are meanings that can be grasped only by someone with a developed capacity to understand language. This applies particularly to the appreciation of poetry, but it might also be relevant to technical subjects, where words that have an ordinary meaning also have a weightier sense that can only be grasped after training.

This is only a sample of the issues in the philosophy of language tackled in Indian traditions. Others include the question of how language is acquired, the connection between sound and word, the relationship between conventional and etymological derivations of meaning, and the basis of the difference between properly formed, syntactically correct sentences and nonsensical strings of words.

Reality as language

The ultimate extension of language's power to capture reality is seen in the awesome theory of the grammarian Bhartrhari: the world is a manifestation of an ultimate principle (*brahman*) whose essence is language. While his monumental treatise *On Words and Sentences* is largely given over to detailed linguistic and grammatical analysis that is neutral between different schools of thought, Bhartrhari also expounds his own metaphysics: the entire world is an outpouring of the transcendental language-principle. Everything in the world has an identity because it has been given its own intrinsic name and form, with its source in a single, unified, supreme Word (*sabda brahman*). Creation itself is a linguistic enterprise! This emphatically does not mean that language is the only reality. Quite the opposite: reality is itself language. This is not the view that all we take to be the world is only a construction out of our language, argued for by some of the Buddhists we consider below (it is also found in some forms of post-modern Western metaphysics). Bhartrhari says there is a reality: both a supreme consciousness and a world that comes out of it. But that reality is itself of the nature of language. Such language is certainly no human construction. Rather, it has an independent and eternal being. We discover a pre-existing language through our innate capacities. It is a language that is bound to be about the world, for we and the world are born from that very language, which is the principle of reality. Bhartrhari conceives of the supreme being – the impersonal, divine absolute (*brahman*) – as the essence of language.

The supreme level of reality is the universal consciousness of *brahman*, which is the infinite potential for all thought and speech. The next level of reality is the articulation of all entities into separate existence. This level contains both the physical structure of the world of names and forms, and the psychological structures of human awareness in which the capacity for language is found. The transcendental language-principle of *brahman* therefore devolves into the things of the world and the human capacity to comprehend them in thought and speech. The final level is the actual production and reception of linguistic expressions by individual human beings, and it is in this exchange that meaning is transmitted.

For Bhartrhari, the ultimately real linguistic expression is the undivided sentence, but he puts it within the context of his unique metaphysics. It is in these whole sentences that the essence of language – which is the manifestation of the supreme principle of reality – is found. Phonemes, words and other units are grammatical constructions, particular and provisional human formulations that lack ultimate reality.

It is fair to say that no more metaphysically sweeping conception of language is possible or has ever been articulated in philosophy. Yet Bhartrhari also treats the linguistic reflex in us as entirely natural (as, of course, it would have to be, given his metaphysics). The instinct that drives speech, he says, is the same as that which prompts the cuckoo to sing in spring, the spider to weave its web, and the birds to build their nests.

The limits of language: the literal ineffability of the ultimate

We have seen that some Chinese philosophers cast doubt over language's range, and set about exploring its limits. That doubt shapes the Daoist view that natural ways of acting and thinking cannot be captured in any systematic way by language; it therefore leads Daoism to challenge the Confucian and Mohist assumption that language provides constant guidance for making one's way through this world. In India, the limits of language are explored, not through doubts about the constancy of its guidance through the natural world, but through the doubt that language can ultimately refer to reality at all. The possibility that reality in some way escapes capture in language is expressed in the notion of the ineffable. There are two broad expressions of this notion of linguistic limits: one is in Advaita Vedanta, the other in Mahayana Buddhism (including some of its East Asian forms, like Zen). Let us consider them in turn.

According to Advaita, there is ultimately only a single, singular, whole, creative consciousness (namely *brahman*) to which all individual consciousness as well as all material existence can be reduced. It is not that there are no individuals and no world; but the way they exist is not ultimate. At some point, the individual consciousness is transformed by the realization that it is not, as it had hitherto thought, a separate being in an external world. At that point, that individual consciousness regains its awareness as the universal consciousness – whole, indivisible and without anything external to it. Until then, all life must proceed on the assumption (although *only* the assumption) that there are individual beings, plurality of things and an external world. (Some of these claims have already been explored in chapters 1 and 2.) Advaita has a radical view of ultimate reality that raises awkward questions about language.

Simply put, Advaitins maintain that language cannot touch *brahman*; it is ineffable. Grant that *brahman* is the single, universal and ultimate reality. Now, words denote things only through name, form, action, their difference from other things, the type of thing they are, and the qualities they possess. Sankara, the founder of Advaita, argues that none of the ways in which words refer to things succeeds with *brahman*. He invokes the famous articulation of the transcendence of *brahman* found in various Upanisads: all that can be said of *brahman* is 'not that, not that' (*neti neti*). Dating back to around the 10th century BCE, this is possibly the earliest expression of the realization that language might be limited in the face of truth.

There is a philosophically subtle argument for why words fail when it comes to *brahman* (as an Upanisad passage puts it, *brahman* is that from which words turn back). Language is part of the world. Even the sacred texts are part of the world as we normally encounter it. However, when consciousness is transformed in the realization that it is *brahman*, everything that had hitherto made up the ordinary world falls away – the sense of being a separate individual, the experience of an external world, and the modes of operating in that world. All the categories of our experience, including logic, theories of knowledge and, above all, language, are part of that hitherto working world that we assumed to be ultimately real. They are all transcended in the realization of its universality by the apparently separate consciousness. So, how can language possibly capture that which, by definition, transcends the world of language?

We can, of course, see the problem straightaway. Bhartrhari, who shares with Advaita the idea of an ultimate consciousness called *brahman*, nevertheless puts the matter succinctly: that which is spoken of as beyond speech, as soon as it is spoken of as being beyond speech, is spoken of! (For him, *brahman* is not literally beyond speech or ineffable; since all language is *brahman*, *brahman* is always spoken of.) Furthermore, the Advaitins cannot simply lapse into silence. For one thing, they follow the injunctions of the Vedas in the matter of ordinary ritual activities. For another, they do wish to convey their teachings to others.

Advaitins therefore develop a theory of the relationship between primary and secondary meaning that gives them scope to talk of *brahman* and yet say that language turns back from it. In some cases, secondary meaning completely excludes the primary meaning. The village is not in any way on top of the Ganges, in the statement 'the village is on the Ganges'; the meaning is wholly secondary – to wit, that it is on the bank of the river. In other cases, the primary meaning is included in the secondary use. 'The lances came into the hall' has not only the secondary meaning that the warriors bearing the lances came into the hall, but also the primary meaning that the lances themselves were brought into the hall. Advaitins posit a third type of secondary meaning, in which the primary meaning is partly included and partly excluded in a statement. In the statement 'the village is burnt', the secondary meaning of a disaster partly includes the primary meaning of actual buildings in the village being burnt. But it does not have the whole primary meaning that literally everything in the village has been burnt.

The Advaitins argue that statements on *brahman* are of the third type. In the key statement 'I am *brahman*', which for them is a teaching about the ultimate non-duality ('*a-dvaita*') between individual and universal consciousness, the primary meaning partly holds. Something of what constitutes the 'I', namely the pure consciousness, is indeed referred to. At the same time, the rest of the 'I', namely the specific person who realizes this (in the original Upanisadic story, the boy-sage Svetaketu), is not referred to, since it is precisely the limited, bodily existence that is excluded and transcended in *brahman*-realization.

Likewise, statements in the Upanisads on *brahman* are partly indicative of its primary meaning. After all, when they assert that *brahman* is consciousness, that it exists, that it is ultimate, that it transcends all language, the texts are not saying anything false. It is the case that *brahman is* all these things. So the primary meaning is partly preserved in statements on *brahman*. But only partly.

These statements exhaust all that can be said of *brahman* through reference to it. But since, to have the quality of being beyond language, *brahman* literally (that is, in a primary sense) has to be beyond language, the statements do not exhaust all there is to *brahman*. Such statements are sufficient to teach people and to express the Advaitic view, and yet they do not lapse into the simple self-contradiction of speaking of the unspeakable. Here is a case where a linguistic theory is key to a metaphysical argument. It is not incoherent to talk of the ineffable (i.e., *brahman*), since something – partial and indirect, yet indicative – can indeed be said about it.

The limits of language: the provisionality of linguistic constructions

A rather different conception of ineffability and the limits – or more precisely, the limitations – of language is developed in Mahayana Buddhist schools. While brahminical/Hindu schools believe that language – Sanskrit – is eternal (either divine or an ultimate part of the universe), the Buddhists take language to be constructed through the conceptual activity of human beings who are entangled in desire. The Buddhists too work with a referential theory of language. They conceive of language as designating things in the world. But the question they ask is whether the things that language appears to pick out really are things in the way language takes them to be. Does language refer to ultimately real things in the way language users assume?

Nagarjuna, the founder of the Madhyamaka school, some of whose ideas appear to have had an influence on the later Advaita philosophers, argues that language cannot capture or refer to reality: he says that what language expresses is non-existent, since no object of thought is ultimate. This claim looks very like what the Advaitins would later say about the *brahman* of the Upanisads. But actually, Nagarjuna is saying something rather different. Language fails, in his view, because it tries to refer to the nature of things, but things are ultimately 'empty' (*sunya*). The remarks of Candrakirti, Nagarjuna's commentator, on emptiness show that this is not a Buddhist version of *brahman*. That language does not refer to the ultimate because emptiness is ultimate simply means that there *is nothing* ultimate. The problem with language is that it does not capture the truth that things are empty. We encountered in chapter 1 the famous analogy for someone who seeks emptiness beyond language and thought. A person asked a merchant for cloth, and when the merchant replied that he had nothing, he asked for some of that! The ultimate truth is that there is no ultimate truth. The limit of language is not due to there being some reality – called *sunya*, like *brahman* – beyond it. Rather, the Madhyamaka point is that, while language appears to be about real things – things with their own independent, intrinsic nature – they are not ultimately like that. They are interdependent, only provisionally true, and lacking any intrinsic existence. This is what language fails to represent. There is no object of thought that is ultimate to which language can refer – because there is nothing ultimate. The mistake of the philosophers lies in imagining that language can refer to something that is ultimate.

But surely, we may protest, language has just done exactly that, in the preceding paragraph? Not quite. The emptiness of things lies in their lacking any nature, in their lacking any separate existence with name and form and characteristic properties. Saying that things lack these properties is indeed to say something, but by definition, it is not to say what they are ultimately. Ultimately, to lack all those properties is precisely to lack any nature that can be captured by language, since language works by picking out the nature of things. Of course, language has the ability to capture certain kinds of lack: a mouse lacks size, a worm lacks mathematical ability, ice lacks heat. But we should not be beguiled by this ability of language into believing that it can capture the lack of ultimate nature. Emptiness *has* nothing (no intrinsic nature, and so on); having nothing is not to have something called nothing. That is the point of the parable of the merchant and the foolish customer.

So what is there? Just the conventional world constructed and captured in language. The insight of the Madhyamaka Buddhist is that there is just the ordinary world of thought and language but that we can see that world from two different perspectives. From one perspective, we treat the world as if it were ultimately real, as if language picked out things that had an intrinsic nature. It is in this perspective that we suffer through our desire for things that language has represented to us. It is also the perspective from within which we begin our inquiry into the nature of things. We end that inquiry with the realization of the other perspective. From this new perspective, things are seen as not having an ultimate nature. They are still there as we experience them, but we now know that they are empty of the nature that language accords them. (How we attain that realization, independently of language, is another matter.) It is at this point that desire ceases (for there is the realization that there are no such things to desire as language led us to think) and liberation is attained. At this point, we cease to use language, for language is coexistent with the world of apparently intrinsic (linguistically characterizable), apparently desirable, yet non-ultimate things. Nagarjuna says of the Buddha that not a word did he utter and yet his disciples were enlightened. But we must use language to get us to this point. As the celebrated Madhyamaka metaphor has it, language and philosophy are like the finger pointing to the moon. Necessary but limited.

Yogacara, another school of Mahayana Buddhism, is not happy with Madhyamaka's radical anti-metaphysical view of the world. Yogacara philosophers feel that Madhyamaka does not offer an adequate account of the state of *nirvana*, liberation. They agree with the Madhyamaka philosophers that language constructs, designates and represents a non-ultimate reality, but go on to add that there is indeed a reality beyond language. That reality is pure consciousness, free of the constructions of language. In such consciousness, there is neither a world of characterizable things nor a sense of self. World and self are the object and subject of desire, and since in pure consciousness there is freedom from desire, pure consciousness is *nirvana*. This conception does sound somewhat like *brahman*. Indeed, Santaraksita, who took Yogacara (and Buddhism itself) to Tibet, says explicitly that his view differs in only one respect from the Upanisadic doctrine. Whereas the *brahman* of the Upanisads is a single, eternal consciousness, the pure *nirvana* of Yogacara is an infinite number of fleeting states of consciousness. Language's limits lie in its constructing a world of experience. When consciousness ceases to construct, language and world cease, thereby leaving consciousness free. By definition, this ultimate state cannot be captured in language, except, once again, in a limited, partial and indicative way, by saying it is a pure consciousness beyond language.

The difference between Yogacara and Advaita, however, goes further than Santaraksita would have it. For Advaita, the world of ordinary experience arises from *brahman*. Although the individual consciousness of persons and other beings is ultimately not different from *brahman*, the individual consciousness does not construct the world; it is consciousness-as-*brahman* that does so. But in Yogacara, there is no such single, ultimate consciousness. All consciousness is found in individual beings, and if the world is constructed in consciousness, it is done in the minds of such beings. So, whereas Advaitins can argue vigorously that as far as we (individual beings with apparently separate consciousness) are concerned, the world is usefully taken to exist independently of us, Yogacarins cannot do likewise. They must – and do – argue that the world is not independent of our consciousness. The things that constitute it exist only as mental entities. Advaitins can say that the world exists as a place of separate and independent things, as far as it goes (until reattainment of *brahman* consciousness). Yogacarins say that the world exists only in minds;

things are not separate from and independent of mental activity at any level.

This leads to a pressing challenge for Yogacara. If the world is not separate and independent, then how does language appear to refer to separate things? After all, language has the word 'cow', which is effective in picking out something in our experience. Even if that thing is really some sort of construction in our consciousness – even if the word ultimately refers to a mental construct – they must nevertheless explain how language can apparently function *as if* there were specific things like cows. Not a problem, say the Yogacara logicians Dinnaga and Dharmakirti: 'cow' is the picking out of what is not non-cow. More precisely, 'cow' is given meaning by temporarily excluding what is not cow in our consciousness. This theory is called the exclusion (*apoha*) theory of meaning.

This claim has an initial charm to it. If I did not exclude non-cows from my grasp of the meaning of 'cow', I might tie up a horse when asked to tie up a cow. Dinnaga asks what 'blue lotus' can mean if it is not an exclusion of what is not blue and what is not lotus. The immediate objection, of course, draws on a rule of logic that has intuitive appeal: double negation. 'Not non-cow' surely just comes down to 'cow', since the two negations cancel each other out? Is the Yogacarin not ultimately referring back to the cow after all? The Yogacarins resort to a theory in logic which holds that, in some cases, to deny something is not to affirm its opposite. This idea is explored in chapter 7 on Logic.

Granting for the moment that there is a form of logic in which 'not non-cow' does not collapse back to 'cow', the Yogacara position is that there need be no commitment to such a thing as a cow to allow us to use the word 'cow'. All we need, at the moment of using a word like 'cow', is the practical ability to exclude everything else. Since everything else is also mental construction, we must be able to keep all other concepts out of our attention when using the concept 'cow'. When we move on to another term, like 'horse', we exclude all *other* concepts; and so on. The result is that language becomes like shadow boxing: we pick out something but understand it merely in terms of what it is not. It is effective (we do punch, shuffle and so on), but it is not real. 'Cow' is just a word to mark a temporary focus in our experience.

The limits of language are ever present in its workings. It never does what we think it does — namely, designate objects in the world. It merely slips from one temporary exclusion to another, apparently picking out something while in fact merely leaving out other terms. (Of course, language also severely misrepresents what it does, since it *seems* to designate external objects while in reality only shuffling between different mental constructs.) In a way typical of Indian philosophy, Yogacara develops a full-blown theory of linguistic meaning in accordance with its metaphysical and spiritual commitments.

6

Knowledge

In a relatively trivial way, knowledge is at the heart of all philosophy, even when we conceive of philosophy much more broadly than the Greek 'love of wisdom'. All systematic thought about the large issues of the human condition after all rests on knowing something or wishing to know something about that condition. There is one major distinction, however, that can be made with regard to what constitutes knowledge: there is *knowledge that* things are such and such ('knowledge-that', or knowledge of things); and *knowledge how* one must act ('knowledge-how', or knowledge of what one must do).

The former conception of knowledge as knowledge of things usually includes knowledge that things are the way they are: regarding the human body or mind, physical objects, numbers, and so on. It is a matter of possessing information about what is the case (the statement of which is the truth), gained in a non-accidental and systematic manner (a child may keep yelling 'cow!' at every animal she sees, but just because one of them is a cow, it does not mean that she knows *that* it is a cow). Such a conception requires an account of non-accidental and systematic methods of gaining knowledge. One also needs to identify and employ certain instruments or means of attaining knowledge (certain putative modes, like guessing or dreaming, will not do; but we will have to explain why not). We need to deal with the possibility that the claims we make may be mistaken, our statements mere errors; are some of our claims wrong or all of them wrong? Usually, knowledge of something, when expressible as knowledge that something is the case, is called propositional or discursive knowledge, indicating that such knowledge is expressed through language. However, Indian philosophy also entertains the possibility that there may be knowledge free of concepts and language; so there is a class of knowledge of reality that is not expressed in terms of knowledge that reality is such and such. There is, in Indian thought, a general conception of knowledge of reality, much of which is discursive but some of which transcends language. Let us call this very general conception *alethic knowledge*, from the Greek word *aletheia*, meaning 'truth', since this is knowledge of how things truly are (whether we can express that grasp in language or not). The contrast is with knowledge-how described below, which is *pragmatic knowledge*.

We can, then, have another type of knowledge: of how to ride a bicycle, cook a meal, lead masterfully, counsel sensitively. This is knowledge of how to do something. It is a matter of possessing skill, an ability to act in a way appropriate to the situation. This knowledge-how has several components. We need to know how to act in a context and to have (or develop) the ability to act in that context. There is the issue of who expects what outcome, and which expectation is significant to the knowledgeable actor. Of course, one may act and yet not bring about an outcome – through not having the knowledge of how to act, not having the ability to act, or not knowing what outcome to direct action towards. (It should be noted that 'know-how' is used here differently from the colloquial English sense, which refers to technology. The latter, from the Greek *techne*, concerns knowledge of how to do something, which requires knowledge that things work in a certain way. The ordinary use, as in 'Japanese know-how' referring to, say, automobile technology, contains within it the implication of knowledge-that pistons, fluids, circuits, and so on, work in certain ways. *Techne* refers to knowledge-how to do something that requires knowledge-that

that thing works in certain ways. This usage is quite different from the 'purely' pragmatic sense in which 'know-how' is used in this chapter.) Pragmatic knowledge tends to concentrate on the variety of things that we actually have the knowledge-how for, since there is no single, general theory to fit all the different knowledge-hows we have, except in so far as we have the very flexible notion of skill.

Any philosophical tradition will in some measure seek both knowledge-that and knowledge-how; and that is indeed the case with the Indian and Chinese traditions. But there are differences in emphasis and in their attitude to the need to produce *theories* of knowledge. To put the matter simply, Indian philosophy is primarily concerned with alethic knowledge; furthermore, it takes the development of theories of knowledge to be absolutely vital to the larger task of securing some ultimate end. It does recognize the need to have knowledge-how (and one school clearly values it above knowledge-that) but generally gives pragmatic knowledge much less attention. Chinese philosophy clearly does recognize discursive knowledge-that, but apart from occasional mention, pays little or no attention to presenting any systematic account of it. Furthermore, while pragmatic knowledge is of vital importance to the Chinese tradition, the search to determine knowledge-how to do things excludes any motivation to develop general theories of knowledge. Despite these deep-rooted differences between the traditions, considered together they help us understand these very different conceptions of knowledge. Interestingly, in both traditions, there are challenges to the assumption that knowledge of any sort is possible; and these very challenges help us clarify what knowledge means.

The significance of alethic knowledge in Indian philosophy

From very early in the history of Indian thought, alethic knowledge is central to the philosophical enterprise. This is closely tied to the emergence of metaphysical views of reality. The Upanisads treat the world of experience as somehow not being all there is to reality; they view the world as an appearance that requires some deeper understanding to explain its features. That ultimate reality may reside in something more, or even other, than the world we experience is a crucial consideration in Indian thought, while the Chinese never even recognize it.

Now, if there is more to the world than we ordinarily see in it – if, that is, reality outstrips appearance – then it is important that we gain knowledge of it. The importance of the knowledge of reality (knowledge that things are *really* such and such) is believed to lie in the power it has to transform the knower in some way. The transformation may come through an accretion of the knower's capacity to influence and change the world of experience, or it may come through the attainment of an insight that frees the knower from the constraints imposed by that world. While the former notion is present in many strands of Indian culture, from mathematics through statecraft and certain religious practices, the philosophical schools in the main have the latter transformation in view. The Upanisads appear to seek knowledge in order to gain both power in and freedom from the world, but a decisive influence on Indian philosophical thought comes from the Buddha and Mahavira (the founder of Jainism), who both make liberation from the conditions of the world the purpose of their teachings.

Classical Indian schools, which come after these developments, tend to put greater or lesser emphasis on the capacity of knowledge to liberate. But more fundamentally, all schools share the conviction that knowledge that things are really such and such actually transforms the knower, altering consciousness and the very conditions of existence. Consequently, the development of a theory of knowledge becomes necessary. If knowledge is the crucial vehicle for the attainment of some ultimate end, then there must be utter clarity about its nature and the means of attaining it.

Epistemology – the theory of knowledge – is thus vital to Indian philosophy.

Knowledge that things are (really) such and such is expressed discursively in language. So alethic knowledge is generally discursive knowledge. However, an obvious worry is that a great deal of discursive knowledge appears not to have transformative value, especially when it comes to matters of spiritual freedom. Knowledge that freedom from desire is freedom from suffering does not make us all Buddhas. There are two lines of response to this worry. One holds that knowledge must be accompanied by mental and moral virtues, such as tranquillity and compassion, in order for the alethic discovery to be truly transformative. The other is that certain truly transformative states, while alethic in that they convey truths about reality to the knower, are not discursive. They lie beyond the conceptual grasp of language; indeed, their status as liberating knowledge comes precisely from their lying beyond language (see the chapter on Language for a discussion of ineffability).

While these responses by no means exhaust the debate, we may stop here by way of preliminary remarks about theories of knowledge in Indian philosophy. Finally, given that the theory of knowledge is the common ground of Indian philosophy and that every school attempts to advance its own position on each aspect of the matter, it would be best if our exploration were organized around the issues, rather than around each school.

The framework of Indian epistemology

The consensus on the role and significance of alethic knowledge means that philosophers of otherwise widely divergent schools all relate to one another within a common framework of inquiry. Indeed, traditional Indian philosophy can be delineated by reference to this framework.

The first feature of this framework of inquiry is that knowledge is a matter of cognition (*jñana*) that is veridical (*prama*) – that is, both true (somehow capturing the way things really are) and valid (arrived at non-accidentally). A cognition is, minimally, a particular state of awareness distinct from all others; and it can occur through different modes, such as seeing (or touching, tasting, hearing, smelling), thinking or remembering. There may even be extraordinary cognitions like clairvoyance or divine experience. Veridicality is the quality of not only being true but arrived at in some appropriate way (there is too much debate on veridicality to say more than this here). Veridicality naturally rules out error. I am in error when I claim that this is Kala, if it is her twin Priya that I see. But a veridical cognition also rules out truths arrived at accidentally. I may correctly say that I see Priya, but if I did not know that she had a twin and if I had previously seen one or the other without ever knowing that there were two of them, then I do not actually know that this is Priya (for I would claim to see her even if it were Kala in front of me). In order to *know* that I see Priya, I must not only know that she is one of twins, but also be able to distinguish between her and Kala. The Nyaya term for veridical cognition is *avyabhicara*, literally 'not wandering'; this can be translated technically as 'non-deviating' but has the literary meaning of 'not promiscuous'. The veridical cognition is one that is 'faithful' to its object, never losing track of it, whereas non-veridical ones are promiscuous in their indiscriminate choice of objects.

Knowledge (*pramanya*) gives content to – that is, goes into the making of – a veridical cognition. Technically, a cognition that is in error about the world is a non-veridical cognition (*apramajñana*). However, some schools consider only veridical cognitions to be cognitions at all, and treat erroneous ones (those that are not appropriately connected with what they are supposed to be about) as 'miscognitions' (*ajñana*).

The second feature of this framework is that veridicality – however it is defined by the different schools – is attained through particular 'instruments' or 'means of knowledge' (*pramana*). In other words, for a cognition to count as knowledge, there must be some particular means that connects the cognition properly to what it is about. For knowledge that something is the case, the cognition must be appropriately tied to what is the case, and only some means will count as appropriate. All schools agree that one such means is perception, or the deliverances of the various senses. Most also allow inference, which is reasoning through general principle from what is already known to a novel conclusion. Almost all the Hindu schools also accept testimony, or information conveyed through language by an authoritative source – in particular, the testimony of the sacred texts. All these will be looked at below. Even when some means are agreed upon, they are defined differently by the various schools. Three other means of knowledge are accepted by some schools – comparison, non-apprehension and postulation – but we do not have the space here to treat them. For the moment, the point to note is that there is agreement that there are certain instruments which, functioning properly, yield knowledge.

Beyond this bare consensus on the framework, Indian philosophers agree on virtually nothing else; but this minimal agreement provides them with sufficient common ground to engage meaningfully with each other. Accepting that there is a need to have alethic knowledge, they develop different definitions of knowledge. Over 1500 years, the debate develops into a highly technical field, but we can give only some of the well-known definitions in order to get a sense of the field.

The most widespread definition, followed by Nyaya, Mimamsa, the Jain schools, and the Vedanta schools outside Advaita, is the 'correspondence' theory: knowledge is the cognitive state that has the quality of being like its object. Of course, one must clarify what 'like' is: obviously, the cognition of an elephant cannot be 15 feet high and weigh 3 tons! But this definition is intuitively appealing, since it captures our sense that to know that this is an elephant, one must have come to possess an understanding *of* that elephant. This leads into what becomes the standard explanation of the correspondence theory: knowledge is the awareness of a thing *as* that thing. For the awareness of elephant A (male, asymmetrical tusks and ragged ear, 20 feet to the right of me) to be knowledge of it, I cannot make do with a memory of an elephant I saw yesterday, or the pink one that I hallucinated the other day, or even the other one, B, to one side of A. My awareness must be of A as it is. (There is a kink here in the definition. Obviously, my awareness of the elephant is not wholly of the elephant as it is, since I have no knowledge of, say, its stomach contents. The Nyaya school argues that there is a complex relationship between the parts and the whole of a thing, such that to see what is strictly the front surface of the elephant should count as knowledge of the elephant. Of course, this sensible notion opens up various questions, such as how much of a whole we must see before we can be said to know it.) But even this formulation is not precise enough to exclude other accidental situations that might count as knowledge. Suppose I am seeing an exact projection (a hologram, say) of the elephant, which is just in front of the elephant itself. In that case my awareness is of the elephant as it is, but it is only accidentally so and should not count as knowledge; but the definition seems to allow it. To counter this objection, the definition is refined by Nyaya: knowledge is awareness born of an *experience* of the thing as it is. In the case of the projection, my experience was of the projection, not of the elephant behind it, and so should not count as knowledge.

Since most Indian Buddhist schools deny that the world is really as we experience it, they do not subscribe to the correspondence theory. However, they want to grant that, even if ultimately things are not as we normally experience them, we do nevertheless function in this world and are usually successful in our actions. We must therefore have some way of distinguishing between veridicality and error in ordinary experience. To do this, they offer a 'success' theory, in which knowledge is cognition that leads to successful practice. To the extent that my cognition is that it is an elephant when in fact it is only a projection, I will be unsuccessful in my attempt to feed it. If I feed an elephant, then my cognition of it as an elephant (which is something to be fed) counts as knowledge. The Hindu and Jain schools of course agree that successful practice should count as a test for knowledge, but the Buddhist schools alone say that knowledge itself amounts to nothing but successful practice. This gives them room to say that eventually cognitions about the world fail to be knowledge when they fail to be successful in quenching our desires. The knowledge that ultimately remains is the knowledge of the Buddha – which, if we have it, is successful in taking us to *nirvana*.

Advaita Vedanta also wants to grant some provisional acceptance to our ordinary experience, while claiming that eventually, when the self realizes that it is no different from the universal consciousness (*brahman*), all of that seeming knowledge is set aside as misleading. (Not wrong – it worked before realization, after all – but misleading, because we thought that that was all there was, when it was not.) The Advaitins therefore negatively define knowledge through a 'fallibilist' theory: it is cognition that has not been invalidated but always could be, and hence is fallible. If a claim to know that something is the case has not been contradicted, then we should count it as knowledge. Of course, this sets up the situation when all cognitions about the ordinary world are set aside upon realization of *brahman*-consciousness.

Each of these definitions faces objections and each improves in an attempt to counter them, but further study will carry us into ever more analytic developments.

Perception as the primary means of knowledge: some issues

It will be seen now that every aspect of the theory of knowledge is subject to debate and divergent interpretations. This is certainly the case with the various means of attaining knowledge. The one means that all are agreed on is perception. But there is very little agreement beyond that bare fact. There are many major issues regarding perception, but three are particularly important: its definition, its nature and its form. Let us look briefly at a few of the many definitions available.

The Nyaya definition of perceptual knowledge (that is, perception that is successful in yielding knowledge), which philosophers from some other schools accept, concentrates on the notion of contact (*sannikarsa*). The first, seemingly simple step is to require there to be contact between the object and a relevant sense organ. This primary contact is the function of the way each sense organ works; so 'contact' does not mean just the physical touching of the skin, it also applies to the way vision establishes contact between colour and eye, or audition between sound and ear. But already we can see that the simplicity of the definition is short-lived, for 'contact' has a technical meaning here. Other complexities soon pile up. Take the perceptual knowledge of seeing a red pot. The eyes must be in contact with various elements: the physical shape of the pot, the red of the pot, and even – since the knowledge is not just of a pot or just of a coloured pot, but also of a pot as being red-coloured – the 'universal' redness (that is, the feature of reality universal to all red things) of which the red pot is an instance. And that is only the contact between sense and object. There is another contact, according to Nyaya: that between the mind and the sense, which is missing in sleep, for example, or inattention. This contact requires further analysis in terms of the functioning of the mind. So there is much to unpack in this notion. In all this, Nyaya works with a robust realism: the things that we ordinarily experience are really there. (Even absences exist. For example, my knowing that there is no helicopter on my table is possible only because I have perceptual knowledge of the absence of a helicopter there; which, Nyaya argues, is possible only because I see the absence!)

A very different definition concentrates on the content of perception. The Yogacara Buddhists, especially Dinnaga and Dharmakirti, say that perception that yields knowledge is an unerring cognition that is free of any conceptual construction. Perception is a pure registering in the senses of things as they are, without any intervening idea of what those things are. This would be puzzling if we thought that they were talking about ordinary objects: how could there be perceptual *knowledge* of a cow without the idea of a cow? (Of course, one could have perception of a cow without having an idea of it, as when meeting it for the first time; but then, we cannot be said to have knowledge that it is a cow.) But the Yogacarins argue that all the things in ordinary experience – cows and pots and elephants and trees – are in fact concepts created in the mind out of pure, conception-free sensations. We can treat them as if we had knowledge of them, to the extent that there is practical success in dealing with them. But in reality, under all these constructions lies an infinite series of unique, unnameable, ineffable points of reality. We ordinarily interfere with our perceptual grasp of that reality, by imposing concepts on that reality; think of it as mentally moulding snowman shapes out of a whirling blankness of snowflakes. So all our apparent perceptions are in error, because they are given form by concepts. True perceptual knowledge is attained only when we free ourselves from concepts. (Of course, we desire only objects, and these are constructed; there is nothing to desire in pure reality, so to have true perception is also to move beyond objects and desires.)

The Jains define perceptual knowledge as that which is 'vivid' in its grasp of an object, contrasting its standard of clarity with both erroneous perceptions and other forms of knowledge. The Advaitins define it as 'immediate' cognition of an object, contrasting it with inference or testimony, which have intermediate states of awareness. These and other definitions are all given with an eye to supporting a particular school's metaphysics.

The next issue has already been touched upon in the Yogacara definition: the nature of perception as a means of knowledge. The extreme Yogacara argument is that perception is pure sensation free of all conceptuality (*kalpana*) – free of the construction of ideas and the giving of names to those ideas, such as to individual objects, classes of things, their qualities, and so on. Yogacarins say that conception-free perception alone provides knowledge of the real, because it grasps what there is, unimpeded by the creations of language; it is alethic but not discursive. At the other extreme is the theory of the linguistic philosopher Bhartrhari, who, it will be remembered from chapter 5 on Language, takes all reality to be the linguistic manifestation of *brahman*. For him, nothing is free of language, so all perception is conceptual, potentially discursive even when not so expressed.

Most other schools try to mediate between these views, generally considering perception itself to have two stages, a preconceptual stage of sensation and a conceptual awareness of *what* is sensed. The details, however, are a matter of debate. To give just one example: Advaita Vedanta takes conception-free perception to be an invariable, preliminary stage of grasping indeterminately that something exists (grasping it as a 'bare' object without identity). This is followed by the application of a concept to the sensed object, which is thereby identified. Vististadvaita Vedanta rejects this line of argument and claims that the only time perception is indeterminate or conception-free is in the special case when an object is first encountered and before an appropriate concept has been applied by the perceiver; once that type of object is known, every subsequent perception is always conception-loaded. Some of the most vigorous technical debates in this area are between Nyaya and Yogacara Buddhism – on whether the introduction of concepts into cognition is necessary for knowledge (as Nyaya argues) or whether it only results in error and a mere simulacrum of knowledge (as Yogacara maintains).

The third major issue with perceptual knowledge is over its 'form' (*akara*). Suppose it is granted that perceptual knowledge is knowledge that an object is such and such. It must be *about* that object, and the perception must therefore be directed *at* the object. (Recall how the perception being directed at the projection of the elephant meant that it could not be said to be knowledge of the elephant itself.) The question is: how does a perception get to be 'about' its object? There are two broad answers. One is that the perception is simply given its 'form' – its character *as* that object – by the object itself. The perception is a formless cognition, which is said to be about an object when that very object gives it its form. The second and opposing answer is that the perception gets to be about an object when the perception *itself* takes the form of the object, through having the correct *idea* of that object. The perception is a cognition with its own form; the cognition is about the object whose form it takes.

The first answer is given by the theory of 'no form', and tends to be held by those such as the Nyaya philosophers who believe in a real world that we normally experience. These realists obviously want knowledge to be about that world, and are therefore anxious that perception should yield knowledge through the direct role of the external objects that are perceived. A perceptual cognition is about a pot because there is a pot that structures or gives form to that cognition. The Yogacarins, who give the second answer, hold the 'form' theory. For them, the objects we normally take ourselves to perceive are really only mental constructs imposed on pure sensations; so objects are formed in cognition itself. It follows that, in that case, the form that the cognition takes determines which object it is about (namely, the object that has that particular form). The concept of a pot structures or gives form to a perceptual cognition, which therefore is counted as being a perception of a pot. Yet again, there are intermediate positions taken and specific nuances given by other schools, generating intricate debates. Suffice it to say that the primacy of perception makes it the focus of a good deal of philosophical thinking in classical India.

Other means of knowledge

Apart from the Lokayata school, which is sceptical of anything beyond what is available to the senses, all others accept inference (*anumana*) as a means of attaining knowledge. Inference is reasoning that is based on logical structures, and as such is examined in chapter 7 on Logic.

The Hindu schools also appeal to knowledge by testimony. The study of testimony as a means of knowledge mainly covers the structures and functions of language, which were examined in chapter 5. The significant point to note is that the Hindu schools that accept testimony as a means of attaining knowledge treat language primarily as an alethic tool – as one that will help us get at the truth. The word for testimony – *sabda* – literally means 'sound' and indirectly means all utterances. The concept thus encompasses both spoken and written utterances.

The aspect of testimony most relevant to the theory of knowledge is the examination of the conditions under which it can produce knowledge; after all, we can all imagine endless situations in which spoken and written words have misled us! These conditions are divided into two: the conditions required of the giver of testimony, and those required of the receiver (who thus gains knowledge). Philosophically, much more attention was given to the first condition, and we will look only at that.

The conditions on the side of the testimony giver are of two kinds. The first concerns the ideal requirements that render him an authority (*apta*): intellectual qualification or expertise, and the moral commitment to conveying knowledge. These are clear enough. The challenge lies with the second kind of testimony-giver conditions: those that enable the receiver to *know* that the giver has the authority to convey knowledge. Without knowing that the source of testimony is worthy, the receiver will never be sure of the worth of what it conveyed. If I do not know that the person telling me something new about Indian philosophy is actually a professor in the field, I may accidentally come to possess the truth, but I could not be said to know it (for the speaker may be a charlatan, unbeknownst to me). If I do not know that the person telling me something is actually not the professor he claims to be, then again, regardless of whether what he says is true or not, I cannot be said to have knowledge; my coming to hear and believe the truth would be accidental, because it comes from an unreliable source. The key distinction in these cases is between coming to believe in something that is true because what the person said really was the case, and actually having knowledge. It is possible to believe in something true without knowing it (that is, without it being knowledge); this happens when the means of knowledge have not been used properly. (Imagine that a five-year-old left a page of sums on a table, and a four-year-old scrawled some random numbers on the answers column, some of which turned out to be correct. The older child might well come to believe the truth that $3 + 3 = 6$, assuming that some adult with bad handwriting had put the answer in; but we would be hard-pressed to say that she had learnt – gained knowledge of – the answer, for the younger child could have equally well put down '6' against some other column, or some other number against this one.)

Everything comes down to being able to determine the reliability of the source of testimony. For this reason, the Buddhists maintain that there is no independent means of knowledge called testimony. In order to gain knowledge from utterances, we have to determine the standing of the source, and that means reasoning about and checking out that source. Why is the source reliable? Has that person (or text) any features that would lead us to conclude that they are reliable? Can anything be inferred from their success in other matters, or in their general conduct? And so on. The Buddhists then point out that such reasoning is nothing other than the use of perception and inference to conclude whether the testimony giver is authoritative and his testimony is reliable. In that case, testimony should be reduced to the first two means of knowledge, perception and inference.

In response, the Hindu schools make different sorts of appeal to the independence and irreducibility of testimony, focusing on the sacred texts. Nyaya says that the testimony of the sacred texts is separate from all other means because it is the word of God, the author of the texts. This shifts the burden of the argument onto proofs for the existence and nature of God. The Mimamsa philosophers take an ingenious course. They accept that testimony from givers is always subject to the doubts of inference and perception (incidentally, this is why neither the God of Nyaya nor the Buddha is a sound source, according to them, since we can always entertain doubts about who they are and how far we can trust them). But they go on to insist that this concession does not infect the one source that is free of the shortcomings of testimony givers – namely, the sacred Vedas. The Vedas – the supreme source of testimonial knowledge – are in fact authorless! They have no source, there is nobody human or divine who composed them. They are eternal linguistic manifestations of reality, a sort of blueprint of the universe, as it were, but already part of it themselves. They have existed as the universe has always existed (there is no God in Mimamsa), and they are reliable because, being an intrinsic, manifested part of the universe, they are always right about it. We cannot here even begin to explore the complexity of both the defence of and the attack on this highly original claim; but we can see how testimony is a vital source of knowledge for the Mimamsa school, although it shifts the burden of proof onto their astonishing claim for an authorless text.

While the other sources have some philosophical interest in themselves, they seldom appear to be able to stand alone as separate means of attaining knowledge, and we must press on to the last of the topics on knowledge in the Indian traditions: challenges to the very idea of knowledge. Scepticism about the claims of knowledge will tell us quite a lot about the conceptions of knowledge they attack. Let us see how scepticism functions in Indian philosophy.

The varieties of scepticism: Indian strategies

Scepticism determines the boundaries of knowledge. The strongest scepticism denies the possibility of knowledge altogether. In general, the stronger the scepticism, the more tightly it draws the boundaries of knowledge, thereby leaving fewer things that can be known. Weaker varieties of scepticism draw the boundaries more loosely, allowing more things that can be known. Seen that way, there is no one thing called scepticism, but a continuum of sceptical attitudes. Below we look at three positions that are thought of as sceptical, and examine what they imply for theories of knowledge.

Possibly the sceptical Indian thinker best known in world philosophy today is the founder of Madhyamaka Buddhist philosophy, Nagarjuna (we will see him in the light of his commentator Candrakirti). Like Zhuangzi in China, he remains endlessly interpretable. His position may be understood as claiming that we know – or more accurately that, if we follow him, we will come to know – that there is no knowledge. By knowledge, he means settled conclusions about the way the world is, arrived at through the means of knowledge (*pramana*). His immediate objective is to show that claims to know anything about the structure of reality fail, because every such claim actually leads to some unacceptable consequence (*prasanga*). He analyses claims that are important to anyone committed to *pramana*-based knowledge, identifies the core concepts involved, and offers refutations of them. Some of the important concepts involved are those of cause (the relationship between the nature of a thing and the effects of its functioning); proof (the relationship between a claim and the way it is established as true); perception (the relationship between a person's sense organ and the object that the person apprehends through that organ); movement (the relationship between the continuously shifting positions of an object across time); and desire (the relationship between the identification of something and a consequent set of feelings and thoughts directed to its acquisition).

In the case of each concept, Nagarjuna claims that we cannot actually depend upon that concept to attain knowledge. His general strategy is to present a problematic fourfold option or tetralemma (*catuskoti*) for any concept that is supposed to give us knowledge about a relationship (and all the concepts above are expressed as relationships). A knowledge-yielding concept must relate (i) to itself, (ii) to something else, (iii) to itself and something else, or (iv) to neither. For each concept, he attempts to show that it fails to do any of these things. In the end, no concept that is used to gain knowledge has content. Nagarjuna concludes that the claim to know is invalid. In effect, he makes the claim that we can know that there is no knowledge. This looks to be self-contradictory (very clearly so in the extended example of his analysis of the concept of proof given below). How can we know that we cannot know? (How can we prove that there is no proof?) If we know that, we know something, so we do know. On the other hand, if we cannot know, then we cannot know anything, including that we cannot know. Either way, Nagarjuna's claim collapses. Let us get a sense of how he actually goes about getting out of this difficult position, and then we can see why he puts himself in it in the first place.

Nagarjuna's critique of proof speaks directly to the very possibility of knowledge. As with all his specific deconstructions of concepts, his attack on proof is demanding and really requires much more space than we can give it here. His basic argument is that proof for a claim to know something requires the proper use of the means of knowledge in relation to the thing to be known (I will use an obvious example to illustrate his very abstract argument: sight with regard to knowledge of a table). But to establish that one knows an object, one must first establish that that means of knowing works. The concept of *pramana* must relate to itself first; but does it? If a means of knowing (for example, seeing) is proven to work through another means of knowing (touching, or testimony that seeing works), there is regress, for the second means would itself require proof … and so on. Alternatively, without proof, the means of knowledge cannot be shown to relate to its supposed object. How can we claim to know that there is a table because we see it, if we cannot know that we are actually seeing (rather than, say, hallucinating) and if, furthermore, we do not first know that seeing is a proper means of knowing anything?

We cannot give up on the project of first establishing that the means of knowledge work, for then we will never know that we can know. Can the means of knowledge operate on themselves? For example, might we not see that we see, and thereby know that we know through seeing? Might the means establish themselves by relating to themselves first, before relating to an object to be known? Nagarjuna argues that we only prove that a means of knowledge works by first checking *independently* that it works. We should prove that seeing gives knowledge by checking against things that we already know are seen clearly (like an optician's chart). But this is hopeless, because how could those things be known to be seen clearly, except through the use of the means of knowledge — precisely those means of knowledge that are to be established in the first place? Nagarjuna sarcastically says this is like a father producing a son who himself produces the father. So, if a means cannot relate to itself or to another (the object) — options (i) and (ii) of the tetralemma — neither can it relate to both (option (iii)). And if it relates to neither itself nor its object (option (iv)), it fails to provide knowledge.

It might be argued that Nagarjuna is asking for too much; it could be argued that it is sufficient for knowledge just for there to be *no disproof* of the means of knowledge. There is no need to prove them, just to work with them. We will see below how Sri Harsa, the Advaitin, uses this line of thought for his own ends. In any case, we must go back to our earlier question: is Nagarjuna not contradicting himself? Now, he has to make a claim, because he is a Buddhist, not just a sceptic. He wants to propagate the Buddha's teaching about attaining freedom from desire, not just argue against all comers merely for the sake of expressing doubt. He wants people to realize that they cannot make knowledge claims, only so that he can show them the way of the Buddha. Consequently, he cannot help expressing himself in an apparently contradictory way. But is he really contradicting himself?

There is indeed a specific claim that Nagarjuna wants to make about knowledge-yielding concepts like proof and the rest: they are empty (*sunya*). He wants to say that while they appear to work, upon analysis they reveal themselves as incapable of doing so. It is here that the contradiction looms: Nagarjuna is saying that we know that we do not know; but then, the concept of emptiness of concepts will not be empty! But the Madhyamaka philosophers argue that this objection misunderstands what emptiness means. After all, emptiness itself can be subjected to the tetralemma (just as proof was subjected to disproof above). What that means is that emptiness itself is empty. This is a paradox, but a fruitful one. The knowledge that we cannot know is a certain sort of knowledge: it undercuts itself. Upon knowing that (as we will if we follow Nagarjuna properly, according to Madhyamaka), we will have exhausted all our epistemology. The whole illusion that we know that things are such and such, which drove our desire for things, will vanish. When we know that there is nothing to know, we will also know that there is nothing to desire. This is scepticism directed at transformation of awareness, if we are to believe Madhyamaka.

A much less problematic strategy is followed by Jayarasi, who is generally associated with the sceptical and materialist Lokayata school, the only system that does not believe in any state beyond this life. Jayarasi takes on various concepts in the *pramana* theory as they developed in the five centuries after Nagarjuna, and follows roughly the same strategy as the latter, albeit in a more detailed way. His conclusion, however, is more whole-heartedly sceptical: we cannot know that there is knowledge. He is perfectly willing to cast doubt on everything. He makes no claim about what we can know, merely showing that any claim to know is subject to doubt. We are even free to doubt whether his arguments work or not; that does not worry him. What he wants is to stop people from thinking that they can somehow establish clearly that there are certain truths to be known and that conse-quently there are certain things they must do. Now, if his arguments are successful (and they certainly are searching), no certainty remains about knowledge, including knowledge that his own arguments are successful. But the difference between him and his knowledge-seeking opponents is that he is perfectly at ease with not knowing if he knows anything (including, possibly, whether his arguments work or not). It is sufficient for Jayarasi that his opponent is reduced to the very state of uncertainty that he himself has arrived at.

Following the teachings of the Lokayata school, we must just reconcile ourselves to ignorance and live without the anxiety that comes with the ultimately fruitless search for knowledge. We must, as it were, return to an ordinary, unphilosophical life, taking things as they come and not trying to find any deeper meaning. Another name for the Lokayata school is the Carvaka, which literally means the school committed to the (pursuit of the) agreeable. We can see why this is so: the implication of philo-sophical uncertainty is that one must stop asking questions and enjoy oneself, as there is nothing else to do. Philosophy is used to render philosophy redundant; the case for a life of ease is estab-lished with scrupulous analysis.

We may finally look at Sri Harsa, the Advaita dialectician, who is often seen as a sceptic. In a sense going back to Nagarjuna, he argues that no knowledge claim can ever be conclusively proved. This failure of proof can happen in two different ways. Sometimes, each side to a competing claim turns out to have problems of its own, so neither wins out and the issue is inconclusive. At other times, both claims appear to be true to the facts, and one cannot rationally choose between them. The issue is therefore undecided. Sri Harsa sets out to subject a variety of issues – the nature of perception, the structure of inference, the general framework of knowledge, and so on – to this critique, but studying them will again take us deep into technical philosophical analysis. Our aim should be to see what his scepticism is about, or indeed whether he is a sceptic at all.

Sri Harsa's basic claim is a subtle mix of the sceptical and the anti-sceptical. He is sceptical in that he doubts whether knowledge claims can be established beyond any doubt. In this, he is akin to Nagarjuna. How can objects be known without knowing that the means of knowledge work, and how can *that* be known without either regress (to other means of knowledge, *ad infinitum*) or circular reference to supposedly known objects (resulting in what the Indians call the fault of mutual dependence: objects established through means and vice versa)? By subjecting various theories about knowledge to criticism, he demonstrates scepticism over their ability to provide us with conclusive knowledge of the world. At the same time, he is anti-sceptical about a less rigorous grasp of the world. His opening argument is precisely that we can conduct the transactions of ordinary life (*vyavahara*) perfectly well – communicate, argue, undertake successful action – without conclusive proof that the means of knowledge provide us with knowledge. As he himself goes on to show, these means cannot be established; yet we carry on perfectly well doing all the things that are supposed to be possible only with conclusive knowledge. What does this imply? Sri Harsa argues that we must acknowledge that it is indeterminate (*anirvacaniya*) as to whether there is knowledge of the world or not. There is no proof that there is knowledge; but there is no disproof either, since our ordinary lives appear to be based on knowledge. We must be content with the *assumption* that we have knowledge, but like all assumptions, it is provisional. Let us simply take knowledge to be an assumption of knowledge, and we will be able to function normally in this world, without the anxious burden of trying to establish that we have conclusive knowledge in the first place.

Sri Harsa argues that knowledge claims are perennially fallible because, as an Advaitin, he wants to say that eventually everything that we take for granted about ordinary experience is transcended in our reattainment of *brahman* consciousness. He therefore wants to deny that knowledge is of the ultimate, without giving up on its ordinary workability.

Interestingly, the Nyaya philosophers who came after Sri Harsa accepted the weight of his criticisms, but they also came back with this defence of the means of knowledge: if the *pramana*s work in ordinary life, why deny that they provide knowledge? Why not simply redefine knowledge as that which we are supposed to know, so long as there is no disproof of our supposition? In short, they ask that we move from merely *assuming* knowledge (as Sri Harsa says we should) to *presuming* knowledge (so that we take ourselves to have non-conclusive knowledge of the world). This is because Nyaya believes that the world of ordinary experience is all the reality to be known. Where Sri Harsa would say that inconclusiveness points to the provisionality of knowledge before the realization of *brahman*, Nyaya, more sanguinely, would take it to indicate only that our knowledge of the world is subject to correction and improvement.

In this long history of Indian theories of knowledge, there is much scepticism about simple certainty but also much anti-scepticism about complete uncertainty. Let us now turn to the very different concerns of the Chinese tradition.

Know-how from knowing-that: the Confucian paradigm

Confucianism concentrates on the cultivation of a life of ritual precision, proper engagement with society, and the search for an ordered state. Its concerns exemplify the conception of knowledge as pragmatic – what to do and the techniques to do it. Bearing in mind the Confucian use of *dao* as the guiding way constructed out of the creative interpretation of traditional practice, we see the pragmatic notion of knowledge evident when Confucius remarks that both knowing (*zhi*) and ignorance are determined by *dao*. This *zhi* is often used in the same way as another character *zhi*, which stands for the very general quality of wisdom. The *zhi* character includes a component radical for 'mouth', showing that there is a definite discursive aspect to it. But even speech for Confucius is more important as performance (as we saw in chapter 5), rather than as the statement of semantic truths.

Sometimes, *zhi* is translated as 'realizing'. This is interesting, because 'realization' in Indian thought indicates a grasp that exceeds expression in language, an alethic knowing of truth that is not necessarily discursive. With Confucius, we must understand 'realize' in a performative rather than alethic way, as the bringing about of some state of affairs through action (realization as 'making real' rather than 'grasping the real'). It is striking that for Confucius, even knowing people brings with it a guiding know-how. When his pupil Fan Chi asks him what knowledge is, Confucius replies that it is to know others. He explains that knowing others is to promote the straight over the crooked, so that one can make the crooked straight. Knowing someone is to *do* something: to make them 'straight' – to make them come to adhere to appropriate virtues if they fail to have them; and if they already possess such virtues, emulate them as models and thus 'promote' the straight. Confucius is not blind to the fact that there is knowledge-that people are such and such. He is not advocating acting upon any old belief about someone; but he is interested in teaching only about the pragmatic knowledge of how to conduct oneself with regard to them.

For Confucius, the point in discussing knowledge is not to define it but to teach his pupils how to know *properly*. He then goes on to say that knowing is a matter of *treating* something as right (*shi*) or wrong (*fei*). Here, to 'treat' something in a certain way is to relate to it in a certain manner; this implies both how one thinks of it and how one acts towards it – the thinking/acting disjunction is absent in the holism of the Chinese tradition in general. Once again, Confucius clearly understands that knowledge refers to the way things are, but is more concerned with what to do about it.

His successor, Mencius, moves decisively away from any show of interest in discursive knowledge. For him, the activity of *shi/fei* is purely a matter of choosing a certain action (*shi*: this is right/this is it; or *fei*: this is wrong/this is not it) through the innate quality of the heart-mind (the physical heart, traditionally thought of the organ of both judgement and emotion). There need be no grasp of how things are in the world. The alethic conception of knowledge is completely absent.

The more nuanced position of Confucius serves to describe some later Confucians. Xunzi makes a powerful case for a conventionalist view of the right *dao*/way: it is what the sage-kings and the tradition have shown us and what the rulers interpret them to be. Consequently, standards (*fa*) are those developed by the conventions of the elite, and the relevant knowledge is of how to act so as to attain and maintain order.

In terms of his main concerns, Xunzi is thoroughly pragmatic. But a wonderful paradox emerges: the more he asserts that what is required is know-how for socially ordered behaviour, the more he distinguishes it from and gives it value over knowing-that such and such is the case. People may believe that there is a reason that rain comes after a raindance or that an eclipse ends after a ritual to save the moon, but there are no such reasons; there are no hidden wonders of which we do not know. The rituals are cultural conventions, and knowing how to have them conducted is what the elite (the exemplary persons) possess and put into practice. Xunzi here is well aware of the truth of the matter: he knows that there is no link between dance and rain or ritual and eclipse. Indeed, this discursive knowledge is evident in his elitist dismissal of the inability of the people to know about the world. But such grasp of alethic knowledge is meant only to emphasize pragmatic knowledge: the elite must know how to construct a culture in which the people are kept contented. Xunzi has to appeal to the way the world is, in order to say what must be done. There is clearly an awareness of alethic knowledge, but it is not theorized, for it is never the Confucian's aim to explore reality and its possible hidden structures. Not even a theory of pragmatic knowledge is worked out; rather, there is a filling in of the details of what such knowledge should amount to, what it will achieve, and how one should go about attaining it.

Theory for practice: Mohism and knowledge

The followers of Mozi, the Mohists, are unique in Chinese philosophy in attempting systematic definitions of knowledge, which then play a role in the subsequent body of their work. The Mohists' views never gained acceptance, and whatever we find about knowledge in their writings is interesting in itself rather than for any wider impact on Chinese philosophy.

The Mohists have four constituents of knowledge, which do not seem to exclude either alethic or pragmatic conceptions of it. The first is intelligence, the capacity by means of which one knows that one must know. The example is seeing something: upon seeing that something is the case, the Mohists claim, one knows that one knows something. While knowledge appears to be a skill – a capacity to do something – this notion does nevertheless seem to include an alethic aspect. The second constituent of knowledge is 'thinking' (*lu*), which is seeking without necessarily finding. The apt example here is peering: we may ask whether peering should be analysed as the failure of the person to register how things are (a failure to know-that) or as the act of unsuccessfully doing a search (a failure of know-how).

The third constituent is contact (*jie*): having come across a thing, one is able to describe it. This has to be seen as a statement of discursive and alethic knowledge. The final constituent is fascinating in its visual impact as much as for its applicability to both conceptions of knowledge. Knowledge is clarity (*ming*), the Mohists say, adding the heart radical (*xin*) to the existing 'know' *zhi* character to produce *ming*. Mozi himself had taken clarity to reside in the ability to discriminate (*bian*) between what to treat as right/'this is' (*shi*) or wrong/'not this' (*fei*) when seeking what would give most benefit and cause least harm to people. Discrimination is an intellectual quality of knowing one thing from another, but it also suggests knowledge of how to sort out what to do from what not to do. The Mohists say that clarity is that by which one's knowledge is made apparent through discourse (the use of language).

Perhaps it is best to see Mohism as briefly bringing together in China the two very different conceptions of knowledge, before this culturally atypical analysis disappeared from the scene for want of interest. The Mohist attention to explicit epistemology is also evident in their classification of the means and objects of knowledge. Coming to it after reading about the *pramana* system in India is to be struck by the extraordinary but missed parallels. The Mohists say that knowing is through hearing, explaining and personal experience. Hearing is receiving knowledge second-hand (that is, through testimony). An example of explaining is when one knows that a square will not rotate. This is clearly inferential reasoning (it would appear here to be established by reasoning alone, as in geometry, a topic of great interest to the Mohists). Finally, knowledge through experience is gained by having been a witness oneself, obviously through perceiving things. Although this classification is systematic, there is no further exploration of potential problems with and interpretations of each of these means; and that is of course a contrast with Indian philosophy.

There is also a listing of the objects of knowledge (where 'objects', like the Sanskrit *artha*, can mean both the things known and the purposes of knowing): names (what things are called), matters (things that are given names), relationship (the mating of name and matter) and acting (intention and performance). Without doubt, the Mohists conceive of knowledge as being a capability determined by matters (things and facts) of the world. While names are indeed conventional, they cannot avoid being fixed by the intrinsic nature (*gu*) of things. Storks cannot be classified with cows, for all that the meaning of 'cow' or even 'cattle' may be fixed by the social norms through which we liken a set of things to a name. Understanding the relationship between names and things, therefore, is a matter of both knowing how to use language and knowing the world. Finally, the fundamental Chinese preoccupation with pragmatic knowledge is clear: knowledge is a matter of having the right intention and the performative ability to act. Knowledge culminates in guiding action.

It is sensible, then, to take Mohism to adhere to the Chinese tradition of taking knowledge to be a guide through the world, even when it demonstrates a remarkable if subsequently neglected interest in systematic epistemology.

Know-how without knowing-that? Scepticism in Zhuangzi

The Daoist philosopher Zhuangzi, in appearing to question the possibility of knowledge, helps us get a clearer sense of what knowledge means in classical Chinese thought. He delights in undermining ordinary expectations, but this is to bring openness rather than doubt to his audience. The perfect example of joyful perversity is the celebrated butterfly dream. Zhuangzi says that he dreamt that he was a butterfly. Then he woke up. He asks: is this Zhuang, who dreamt he was a butterfly, or a butterfly which is dreaming that it is Zhuang? He is not here trying to raise the hyperbolic doubt as to whether we know we are dreaming or not; he notes that there must be some difference between the butterfly and himself. Neither is he suggesting that there can be experience without objects. Rather, he is drawing on an immediately accessible example and using it to present an attractive alternative perspective. The idea of a butterfly's dream of being Zhuangzi suggests that there can be a very different perspective on the same situation (different, that is, from Zhuangzi's dream of being a butterfly). This is not scepticism about the world, our senses or our knowledge, but an insistence that we cannot be sure what perspectives there are on any given situation. Best not to exclude other possible perspectives (like that of the butterfly), since we cannot adjudicate between them.

We will return to Zhuangzi's advocacy of a plurality of perspectives. But first, we must acknowledge that there is a way in which he does appear to be a sceptic, questioning whether knowledge is ever possible. The knowledge that he doubts is discursive, alethic knowledge, asserted through language. (The complex issue of non-discursive yet alethic knowledge that seems possible in Indian thought does not arise here.) He does not deny that language has its uses: talking is not like mere puffs of wind, he admits. Language has its uses in guidance and interaction. But when Confucians and Mohists move from living their *dao*/way to stating that they know that their way is right and other ways wrong, such speech obscures their *dao*s. It cannot be decided which claim to knowing that a way is right is to be admitted.

The crucial consideration behind this sceptical conclusion is that what is claimed to be right is right only within the perspective of that *dao*/way. What is right is what is successful (*cheng*), but what counts as success varies from the *dao*/way of one school to another. Therefore, what counts as right will vary from one school's vision of the *dao*/way to another. Now, it may be the case that one person with one knowledge claim will, through debate, convince another with a different claim to change his position. But that will only show that someone has been persuaded, not that they were wrong. The claim to know that one is right (*shi*) and another is wrong (*fei*) cannot be settled by the disputants alone. Yet if they go to someone else to have it settled, that will simply put the burden on that other person's claim to know-that a way is right...and so on. (Note here that Zhuangzi does not concede anything like the classical Indian presumption that winning a debate actually establishes something.)

Is Zhuangzi's argument self-defeating? Well, he is clearly not adopting the deeply sceptical stance – which, as we saw with Jayarasi in India, is not self-defeating – that we do not even know if we know anything. He is quite clearly claiming to know that there are specific problems with the claims of the Confucians and Mohists. Is he therefore claiming, more like Nagarjuna, to know that claims to know that something is right are never right? If so, what then of his own claim? Actually, he is saying something different, and it is not directly sceptical. He talks of a wise man and a master musician who sought to enlighten others. Their ways would have been successful (*cheng*) if others had been enlightened by them. But the wise man ended in the darkness of logical disputation and nothing was left of the musician except the strings of his lute. This happened because both became bogged down in discursive teaching. Zhuangzi's claim is that conveying discursive knowledge is never successful; it always fails the task of getting people to act correctly (which he presupposes, in the typically pragmatic Chinese way, to be the proper purpose of conveying knowledge). He is sceptical about the practical success of discursive knowledge rather than about knowledge itself. His position is not self-defeating, but it is not quite as radical as it may seem. By way of comparison, even the most cognition-oriented of Indian philosophers thought that discursive knowledge alone was insufficient for enlightened understanding; they all agreed that other virtues and skills must accompany it.

Zhuangzi does not deny that know-how is possible, since it was possession of it that made the wise man and the master musician originally approach perfection. Indeed, Zhuangzi's point here is the opposite of scepticism about knowledge: there is an infinite plurality of know-hows (knowledge of how to live *dao*s). This pluralism towards *dao*/ways does contain two critical qualifications. First, the skills that he acknowledges demonstrate many of the ways of living *spontaneously*. Consequently, the elaborate rituals of Confucian ways and the heavy-handed calculations of Mohists are not equally valuable *dao*s, since they lack spontaneity. Second, since claims to exclusivity always fail, to the extent that Confucians and Mohists each seek to establish their own way to the exclusion of others, they are bound to fail. There is undeniably a plurality of ways under heaven (*tian*); a plurality of *dao*/ways is natural and is not exclusive, although not all *dao*/ways are equally valuable.

Let us, however, press the question further of whether, in accepting an endless plurality of skilful know-hows that reveal a plurality of *dao*/ways, Zhuangzi is not being amoral, relativistically denying that some ways are more valuable than others. If Cook Ding, the skilled butcher (see chapter 4), is the epitome of the natural Daoist, cannot a serial killer be one as well? It is notable that Zhuangzi's models are all benign; but he does not argue for the moral superiority of some ways over others, except indirectly, when criticizing the Confucians and Mohists. This may be a philosophical failure, but it may also be a conscious and clever decision. After all, if he did start saying that some ways were intrinsically or morally better than others, then he would self-contradictorily be indulging in claims to know that that is the case. So, if he does believe that people can be transformed to follow natural ways of living, then he can bring this about only by revealing his skill in his own *dao*/way; he can only *show* that there are some models of skill worth following and others not. This is how he can demonstrate that the *dao*/ways of Confucianism and Mohism, because of their artificiality, are not as valuable for living as is his, natural *dao*/way. There is no scepticism about pragmatic knowledge here. Indeed, that is why he did do something: he wrote the book the way he did. Zhuangzi's *dao* was to write the *Zhuangzi*.

The triumph of know-how: Neo-Confucianism

Neither the robust epistemology of the Mohists nor the searching criticisms of Zhuangzi were ever philosophically refuted by Confucianism; when it re-emerged after some centuries of Buddhist domination as what is now called Neo-Confucianism, it simply went on to develop a more carefully articulated awareness of the importance of pragmatic knowledge.

The Cheng brothers, progenitors of Neo-Confucianism, bring attention to bear on the late classical Confucian idea of *ge wu*. This phrase originally meant 'the investigation of things', and as such indicated the need for alethic knowledge (even if it was merely the first step in the characteristic Confucian sequence of the development of integrity of intention, correction of the heart, improvement of the person, regulation of the family, ordering of the country, and harmony in the world). They redefine the phrase to mean something much more pragmatic, taking *ge* to mean 'arrive at' and *wu*, 'activities'. This shift is reinforced by Zhuxi, possibly the most influential of Neo-Confucians. He says *ge wu* is the moral knowledge of what to do. However, he retains something of the original notion, recommending that such knowledge should come out of a continued study of the world. Knowing that the world is such and such is part of coming to know how to act.

Wang Yangming, who integrates Buddhist ideas into Neo-Confucianism, decisively rejects the idea that knowledge that the world is a certain way can have any bearing on knowing how to act: ethical guidance (on what one *ought* to do) cannot be derived from the way the world *is*. This disillusionment (apparently brought about when he became ill 'investigating' the nature of bamboo, which is poisonous to human beings) leads him to go back to a Mencius-like conclusion: to settle upon correct action (*ge wu*) is nothing more than to settle upon doing good and removing evil. There is nothing more to knowledge than moral know-how, which derives from the innate qualities of the person as brought out through mental discipline. This is not exactly like Mencius, however, because Wang is impressed with the (originally Indian) Buddhist concept of a thinking mind with a distinct cognitive ability, and consequently holds that the bringing out of knowledge is a cognitive endeavour, a thinking-things-through in the mind. This would have been baffling to Mencius, for whom the innate goodness of the heart-mind (*xin*) is brought out in ritual action. But even then, real knowledge is, ultimately, pragmatic for Wang, just as it was for Mencius 18 centuries earlier.

It is only after contact with the West in the early modern period that discursive knowledge starts becoming important in Neo-Confucianism. Fang Yizhi, a late Chinese Neo-Confucian, attempts to redefine *wu* to include things in the world as objects of knowledge, on the basis that activities (the dominant understanding of *wu* in his time) are things too.

Another Neo-Confucian concept that highlights the lasting East Asian focus on pragmatic knowledge is 'practical learning' (*shi xue*; but better known for its place in Japanese Neo-Confucianism through the Japanese *jitsugaku*, where it is better translated as 'real learning'). Again, it is Zhuxi who invigorates the concept, contrasting it with discursive knowledge – namely, the useless textual studies of ordinary Confucians and the impractical if lofty doctrines of the Buddhists. By contrast, practical learning is knowledge of how to conduct human relationships in a proper pattern. Although Neo-Confucians have internal debates over the precise content of practical learning, they generally agree that it has two dimensions: the inner dimension concerns self-cultivation and one's conduct towards others, and the outer concerns the socio-political ordering of the country. In all this, the focus on knowledge as the possession of skilful, guiding action is very clear. Interest in pragmatic knowledge is evident in such thinkers as the Japanese Neo-Confucian Kumazawa Banzan, whose experience as an administrator influences him to think of knowledge as practical learning, being the ordering and ruling of states, explicitly distinguished from the mere academic study of political and ethical principles. Once more, though, the concept of discursive knowledge fights back, as in Ogyu Sorai, who declares that he seeks the Confucian way in word and fact (those classic objects of discursive knowledge). Coming at the dawn of Japanese modernity, he perhaps speaks for a new paradigm in which the traditional pursuit of guiding discourse (knowledge-how) is married – pragmatically – to a newly scientific study (seeking knowledge-that) of the world.

7

Logic

Logic is the (study of the) pattern of reasoning that relates a conclusion to initial premises. The brackets are significant, as there are two senses to the term 'logic'. Outside the brackets, we have logic as the actual pattern of reasoning that people employ. This involves the use of various connective elements, such as 'and', 'either…or', 'if', 'if so, then', 'all', 'some', and 'not', which bring expressions together. It is just possible that even to conceive of logic in this way is to impose a particular Western (or at least Indo-European) form on the thinking of other cultures, like China. But it is hard to see how the Chinese or any other peoples could engage with the world without using most, if not all, of these and other elements, which connect the starting and end points of thinking. This chapter assumes that logic is present in most human beings and all cultures, as it is integral to the structure of our cognitive capacity and its evolutionarily successful engagement with the natural and social environment. We will therefore not spend time looking at the well-established evidence that Chinese philosophy, as seen in the classical philosophical texts, reveals evidence of 'logical' thinking, even in the relatively stringent sense of deliberately using the connective elements listed above in order to proceed from premises to conclusions. The matter is rather less debatable with regard to the Indian tradition, as it would take heroic self-deception to fail to see self-conscious and explicit logical theory in the texts.

If we include the bracketed phrase, however, we have a different matter: is logic as a philosophical discipline present in the Eastern traditions? Is there logical theory, as distinct from practice? As we will see, logical theory is a core element of Indian philosophy, and we will look at the way it has given shape to debates in general. In the logic of the Buddhist thinkers, we also have a uniquely cross-cultural body of work, changing as it goes from India to China and Japan, but always striving for the same religious ends. By contrast, it is undeniable that logical theory is somewhat marginal in Chinese philosophy, with even Buddhist logic playing only a small part during the short Buddhist ascendancy. Nevertheless, the subculture of logical theory in ancient China is relevant for the inspiration it has given to contemporary thinkers.

While it has not been possible to compare Eastern and Western thought in this book, one point has to be made in relation to logic. The Western tradition since Aristotle has taken logic to be focused on the pattern of reasoning regardless of meaning and content, striving to expose the bare features of thought. Logic is supposed to be about structures of reasons just as they are, regardless of who has them; it is potentially independent of human thinking. Logic is seen as a discipline separate from other areas such as epistemology (the theory of knowledge) and rhetoric (the study of the effective use of language). Although Indian logical theory, like its Western counterpart, is elaborate and well developed, it uses logic primarily to attain knowledge of the world, through debate and persuasion. Even the most abstract issues are still tied to the *pramana* system (see chapter 6 on Knowledge). Indeed, logical theory is most naturally found within the ambit of inference (*anumana*), one of the means of attaining knowledge. Logic here is very much to do with the actual thoughts and cognitions people have, and how they are used in the pursuit of knowledge. Logical theory in China is even more focused on pragmatic concerns, as we shall see below.

Logic as a means of knowledge: the basic features of inference in Indian philosophy

Indian logical theory starts with the tradition of debate (*vada*), in which the aim is to persuade someone who does not share your view that you are right (while, of course, he tries to do the same). Early texts such as the Buddhist *Kathavattu* systematically use logical patterns, while not explicitly giving a logical theory. In a medical treatise, the physician Caraka distinguishes between good/amicable and bad/hostile debates, and includes the explicit notion that a good debate should give a demonstration (*sthapana*) of the thesis (*pratijna*) if it is to be accepted, and outlines the way in which such a demonstration should proceed.

Already, then, there is a recognition that, if a debate is to be resolved successfully, there must be a pattern to the reasoning which establishes one side of that debate. The establishment of one side of the debate requires recognition of that most fundamental of logical rules, the law of non-contradiction: when two statements are such that one is the negation of the other, if one is true, the other must be false; they cannot both be true. The grammarian Patanjali defines contradiction (*vipratisedha*) as 'mutual prohibition'. The two sides to a debate cannot both be correct. (A later Nyaya definition, by Udayana, is precise on this: where two claims are mutually opposed, they cannot both occur with the same truth-value – both be true or both be false.) In debate, then, each denies the truth of the other, but only one is true. The energies of the Indian philosophers are consequently directed towards developing a model of argument in which establishment of one of two mutually opposed views as true can be brought about.

The *Nyaya Sutra* of Gautama (and the commentary by Vatsyayana) sets about explicating a model which, if followed, conclusively settles the issue in favour of one's thesis. The argument, says Gautama, must be in the form of an inference, an idealized movement from claiming something to establishing it. (He also widens the discussion to include the criteria for good and bad arguments, which we cannot go into here.) The idealization is important. While the logic takes concrete form only in actual cognitions and thoughts, it has a generalizable structure, such that it can be used in the cognitions of anyone who masters it. Given that anyone can potentially have any of the cognitions in the example below (that is, the logical content of the cognitions is repeatable in whoever has them), Indian logic combines abstract structures of reasoning with the rich mental process of actually using those structures in thoughts.

The following example of an inference (time-honoured or hackneyed, depending on your point of view) is simple, but helpful in bringing out the challenge of understanding the underlying logic of even apparently simple inferences. The claim or *thesis* is, 'There is (an unseen) fire on the hill.' The Nyaya account holds that this is the first stage of a fivefold argument. The second stage is the giving of the *reason* for the thesis: 'For there is smoke (that can be seen).' This is followed by an *example*, which brings out the underlying principle that is being evoked: 'As in the kitchen hearth (which shows that where there is smoke, there is fire).' Then, the *application*: 'This is like that.' Finally, the thesis is restated, but now it functions as the *conclusion*: 'There is fire on the hill.' Other schools argued that this was too elaborate and that the first three stages were sufficient. In a strong reiteration that logic has the rhetorical purpose of persuading others, Nyaya philosophers insist on keeping the last two stages when making inferences for others (they eventually acknowledge that the simpler version might do for oneself).

This structure (let us now keep to the first three stages, as they become widely accepted in Indian philosophy) shows how Indian logic is primarily concerned with seeking new knowledge through reasoning, rather than with analysing the features of reasoning as such. The interaction between deduction and induction in the inference stages described above demonstrates the epistemological nature of Indian logic. Inferences seek to prove a claim and do so by moving through premises to a conclusion. Most certain is a conclusion that cannot but follow from the reasoning preceding it, namely its premises. If, given that the premises are true, the conclusion has to be true (is necessarily true), then there is a guarantee that we know the truth of the conclusion. One way of looking at it (as in the classical Western tradition) is that logic is that pattern of inference that will hold, regardless of the exact content of what is being inferred. In order to do this, the pattern must consist of sequences of reasoning – premises – that do not need further proof; they must be evident straightaway, so that we can reason with them alone. At least some premises must be axioms – self-evidently true – and that will mean that if a conclusion follows, it must necessarily follow. This is the notion of *deduction*. Commonsense reasoning, of course, is seldom deductive. In fact, debates occur precisely because premises are not self-evident, or at least the conclusion does not necessarily follow from them. In gaining new knowledge (whether through inquiry for oneself or in debate with another), the Indian philosophers seek to arrive at a conclusion that extrapolates from and amplifies what is already known. In these cases, there is a generalization beyond the truths of the premises to a conclusion. This is the notion of *induction*.

The deductive side of the inferential pattern is seen in the fact that, (premise:) *if* where there is smoke there is fire, (conclusion:) *then* it *deductively* follows that there is fire on the hill where there is smoke. We do not go beyond what is available in the premise to reach our conclusion. The underlying logic is self-evident: if *A*, then *B*; here is *A*, therefore *B*. But there is a logical catch. How do we come to hold the premise 'if *A*, then *B*' in the first place? In this particular case, how do we come to hold that where there is smoke, there is fire? Here, the Indian system arrives at the implicit rule (where there is smoke, there is fire) by acknowledging that it is calling upon experience of the world, in this case, the kitchen hearth in which smoke and fire are seen. Must it follow, from the truth that the hearth has fire and smoke, that where there is smoke, there is fire? Obviously not; there may be a case of smoke without fire, for all we know, somewhere in the universe. The reasoning here is inductive, extrapolating from known cases such as the hearth (and, we may assume, others) to a general conclusion about smoke and fire. With this induction made, the deduction, about that particular hill with smoke having a fire, can follow. Indian logic combines the necessary certainty of deduction with the unavoidable need for induction.

The Buddhist logician Dinnaga saw clearly the need to tie together the various elements of the inference. He says that the 'mark' or 'sign' (*linga*) of the inference must fulfil three conditions in order to establish the property to be inferred. Take the inference that there is an (unseen) fire on the hill, because of the (seen) smoke. The sign is that on the basis of which an inference is made, for example, smoke. The 'property to be established' (*sadhya*) in the inference is fire. First, the sign must be found in the 'location' (*paksa*) under consideration – the hill where the fire (the property to be established) is supposed to be present. This is a minimal condition of relevance, as there will be no argument over a location without the sign (smoke) being seen: if a smokeless fire is seen, it will be self-evident and require no inference, and if hidden, it would escape all notice. Second, the sign must be found in a 'similar location' (*sa-paksa*); similarity is determined by the presence of both the sign and the property to be established. The example is the kitchen hearth, which has both smoke and fire. Thirdly, the sign must *not* be found in a 'dissimilar location' (*vi-paksa*) – in a location in which the property to be established is not found. The standard example is a lake. A lake is a dissimilar location in that being water, by definition, it can have no fire. Where there is no fire, there must be no smoke; and such is the case with the lake. The inference is therefore licensed.

What is the purpose of this triple condition for a proper inference? Take the false inference, 'There is (unseen) smoke on the hill, because there is (seen) fire.' Here, the sign is the fire, the property to be established is smoke. The first condition is satisfied: the fire is on the hill where the smoke is supposed to be. The second condition is met too: a hearth is a similar location, in that it has both the sign and the property to be established. But take a dissimilar location – one in which there is no smoke (the property to be established), as might be the case with a high-grade fuel. Obviously, the sign, fire, can be found, when the fuel is set alight. So the third condition is violated: there can be fire without smoke. The inference is therefore not licensed.

This might, however, lead to a worry: why use Dinnaga's second condition? Will not the first and the third suffice? All we need is the case at hand, and the dissimilar case, which will disprove a wrong hypothesis. Why do we need another condition, which will merely confirm a hypothesis? The answer is that the logic of the inference is directed towards the purpose of gaining knowledge through certainty. To do that, we must recognize that we have a general idea in the first place that relates the presence of smoke to fire; without first having the rule, 'where there is smoke, there is fire', would we argue that the hill on which we can see smoke has an unseen fire? Furthermore, would we not check that rule, at the very least to increase our certainty, at the time we make our present inference? To back up our inference we must point to an instance of a place where there is smoke and fire. It is true that a lake, where there can be no fire, shows that without fire there is no smoke; but that is not enough, because we also need to point to an instance in which the fire and the smoke are actually present together, just as the rule states.

To draw upon a modern example to drive home the strangeness of relying on the lake alone as an example for our inference, it would be like someone pointing to a white shoe to confirm the claim that all ravens are black! To say that all ravens are black (so it might be argued) is also to say that if a thing is not black, it cannot be a raven. In other words, a white thing by definition is not a raven. Anything white – like a white shoe – thus proves the claim that all ravens are black. (This at least sounds paradoxical, whether or not it is.) All three conditions are therefore needed, because logic is not just pure reasoning but is also aimed at the attainment of new knowledge, and so must direct our attention to things as they actually are in the world. Nyaya calls this the joint method of 'positive and negative examples' (*anvaya-vyatireka*), and from this point on there is broad agreement in Indian thought on the nature of inference.

The underlying idea here is that we must identify the way in which the property to be inferred and the sign that licenses the inference are intimately related. The Indians call this relationship 'pervasion' (*vyapti*). Dharmakirti, who develops Dinnaga's theories, points out that such pervasion alone can license inference. There have to be metaphysical connections in the world, the discovery of which will allow us to infer something beyond what we now see. If we can isolate the way in which the sign and the property to be inferred are invariably related in the world, then, by picking out the sign, we can conclude with certainty that the property to be inferred is indeed present. Dharmakirti gives a neat twofold classification of pervasion: by identity or by causality. Pervasion by identity holds when two terms (the sign and the inferable property) refer to the same thing. From knowing that something is a pine, we can infer that it is a tree, as a thing cannot be a pine without also being a tree. Psychiatric diagnoses, for example, are based on principles of human psychology, because they rely on the identity between the specific patient and human beings in general (imagine the problem of trying to diagnose the condition of an intelligent alien, who would have an entirely different set of psychological linkages, expressions, reactions, and so on). The second type of pervasion, which is due to causality, is normally illustrated by the case of smoke and fire, where the inference is licensed because smoke is caused by fire, and an effect is invariably linked with its cause.

Fire, by virtue of being its cause, pervades smoke; so if there is smoke, there is fire present. (Note that the converse does not hold: as smoke does not pervade fire, fire can exist without smoke.)

Nyaya philosophers criticize this classification, pointing out that it is inadequate, and fails to explain how such inferences as tomorrow's sunrise from today's are licensed. One powerful and very general Nyaya idea of pervasion is that it is 'natural' (*svabhavika*), without accidental features (*upadhi*). For *B* to pervade *A*, such that one can infer *B* from the presence of *A* through knowing that *A* would not occur without the occurrence of *B*, the connection between them should not be accidental. Suppose I see a crow perched on your house when I visit; I cannot infer from that that your house is the one with a crow on it, and use that fact to give someone else directions to your house. The presence of the crow (*A*) does not pervade the location of your house (*B*), as it was an accident that it was sitting there (unless, of course, it was your pet!). Obviously, accidental connections vitiate the inference process, because the connection is not really there as we think it is, and our inference therefore goes wrong. You might infer from your observing a silence between me and my wife that our marriage was on the rocks, but if an accidental feature such as my having a sore throat explained it, your inference would be mistaken. Later Nyaya logic spends a considerable amount of energy on developing highly technical definitions of 'accidental feature' and 'pervasion', in order to eliminate the conditions under which wrong inferences are made.

However, the fact is that, in India as in the West, any attempt to use logic to gain knowledge of the world is always subject to the worry about induction. Might there not be smoke somewhere in the universe that was not from a fire (although we might then call it something else)? Might the sun not rise tomorrow even if we have seen it do so throughout all history? Might this psychiatric patient not have neural pathways that do not obey any of the processes hitherto known to science? And so on. The Indian attempt to tighten up the definition of pervasion, like the development of formal logical apparatus in modern logic, never entirely dispels the uncertainty that reality might not obey any logic that we devise. One strand of Buddhist logical theory is always directed at understanding the limits of logic in the face of reality; we will look at that attempt in the last section of this chapter.

Logic for ethics: the multiple conditionalities of Jainism

We now turn to a very different use to which a theory of logic is put: fostering harmony. Jainism approaches the confrontations and disagreements of classical India in a way that is both metaphysically complex and ethically novel. The Jains believe that Mahavira taught them non-violence, a gentle disengagement from the desires of the world, and the creation of tolerance and social integration. In pursuing these ends, they look at the world and ask two questions. First, what is reality like, such that fundamental and irreducibly conflicting views about it are possible? They reject three possibilities: the sceptical, that conflicting views show we can never really understand reality; the relativistic, that there are simply different views, each acceptable in itself and with no bearing on any other; and the absolutist, that eventually all but one view will turn out to be wrong. They claim, instead, that what explains the irreducible diversity of conflicting views is that reality itself is realizable in multiple ways.

The second question they ask themselves is what should be done in a world with such conflicting diversity. The answer is that some way of integrating the conflicting diversity of views should be developed, so that the nature of reality is understood by everyone. Such understanding can then lead to non-violent accommodation of difference.

The Jains maintain that there must be a way of thinking that not only reconciles differences but also acknowledges that many different views are correct with regard to a multiplex reality (that is, a reality that is genuinely manifold, not merely complex). This way of thinking turns on a logic of assertion that contains many values and seems to violate a principle of consistency. The principle apparently violated by Jain logic is that a statement (that something is the case; call it p) and its denial (*not-p*) are exclusive; you cannot hold both. In the case of a conflict of views, between those who hold that p (the Nyaya school, say, which maintains that a pot exists metaphysically as a real entity) and those who hold that *not-p* (the Yogacara Buddhists, who deny that the pot is a real entity), the Jains want to say that the two views are not exclusive, although that appears to violate the logic of non-contradiction. The Jains want to say that both statements hold true of reality. Indeed, for any statement, there is a sevenfold schema to explain how it can be used and understood. Each statement is qualified by the word *syat*, which literally means 'somehow', and points to some condition under which each version of the statement is true and by virtue of which it escapes the charge of violating the law of non–contradiction.

For a statement p (the pot is a metaphysically real entity), let us see what the sevenfold schema is:

(1) Somehow, (it is true that) p.
(2) Somehow, (it is true that) *not-p*.
(3) Somehow, p and somehow, *not-p*.
(4) Somehow, inexpressibly p.
(5) Somehow, p and inexpressibly p [i.e., 1 and 4].
(6) Somehow, *not-p* and inexpressibly p [2 and 4].
(7) Somehow, p and somehow, *not-p*, and inexpressibly
   p [3 and 4].

The first member of the schema, (1), holds that somehow, the pot is a metaphysically real entity. The Jains point out that this statement cannot be made without any conditions or qualifications. One can only say that the pot is metaphysically real provided one has adopted the view that objects of ordinary perception should count as real in an account of the structure of the world; in other words, the statement p is true under the condition of the Nyaya metaphysical theory. In the same way, (2), the denial of the Nyaya view, also only holds 'somehow': namely, under the condition of the Yogacara metaphysical theory, in which objects of ordinary experience are analysed or deconstructed down to a combination of sensations and mental constructions, rather than left as independent objects in an external world (for more on the Nyaya and Yogacara positions, see chapter 1). What the Jains are saying is that assertion and denial of the real nature of the pot are not to be made in an unqualified manner. Each claim holds only in a certain way, with respect to certain parameters; and the important point is that the parameters of (1) do not coincide with those of (2). The Nyaya and Yogacara philosophers should recognize that what they state is subject to the limitations of their own, unqualified world-view. The real challenges for Jainism, however, come with the next two members of the schema. Member (3) appears to be a simple contradiction. A contradiction occurs when one asserts both that p and that *not-p*. If the Jains are saying this, then there is no point in listening to them, because anything can be said if contradiction is allowed. Non-contradiction is a basic logical rule. (Try running a coherent conversation while constantly contradicting yourself, and see what happens.) If the Jains were simply saying that p and *not-p* are true, they would be contradicting themselves; but they are not. If we look carefully at (3), what they are saying is 'somehow p, and some(other)how *not-p*'. There are two different somehows, and each points to a different condition. Under some condition (let us call this somehow$_1$), p; under another condition (somehow$_2$), *not-p*. The Jains are simply bringing (1) and (2) together to indicate the situation in which both Nyaya and Yogacara views of the pot are put forward. They first point to the holding of one view, and then point to the holding of the other.

There is an even more complicated situation indicated by (4). The Jains may, under (3), *successively* point to the condition under which *p* is asserted and then the condition under which *not-p* is asserted; but the fact is that both *p* and *not-p* – both assertion and denial – are *simultaneously* held. How can that be captured in their sevenfold schema? Only by being described as inexpressible, the Jains acknowledge; and that is what (4) says. The multiplex nature of reality is such that, at a level where incompatible and irreducibly conflicting truths hold of it, nothing else can be said of it. (Note: nothing *else* – nothing further – can be said of it; what *can* be said is precisely what has been said in (4).) This is not to assert nothing. One thing *can* be asserted about a reality that is simultaneously realizable in a multiplicity of conflicting ways: that is, that *nothing* can be asserted of it as a whole! One can assert all the things that are asserted of it only within the perspective of each; and that is what the sevenfold schema does with each assertion. Reality contains the truth of *p* from within the Nyaya way of looking at it, and the truth of *not-p* from within the Yogacara way; but that it contains them both cannot be stated without contradiction, for each statement is always made from within a particular viewpoint of reality. The Jain viewpoint acknowledges this by stating that this nature of reality is inexpressible.

The other members of the schema are simply combinations of the earlier ones for the sake of completing the sequence. The controversial claims are (3) and (4). This doctrine of conditionality (*syad-vada*) is a unique way of proposing a metaphysics and an ethics, via a theory of multiple logical values that lies beyond mere assertion and denial. The metaphysics is summed up as the doctrine of *multiplex* reality, literally 'non–onesidedness' (*anekanta-vada*). The Jain recommendation is that the debaters, like the Nyaya and Yogacara philosophers, should come to terms with the fact that reality cannot be seen in any one exclusive way. Any one way captures only one side or aspect of reality. Each side exists and is true, but the astonishing thing about reality is that different, incompatible truths hold of it!

One may ask the Jain: but are you not claiming to ascend to some superior viewpoint, from which you can 'see' all these different truths? Is that not what your doctrine of conditionality implies? And if you do that, by synthesizing other views, are you not being an absolutist yourself, reserving ultimate correctness for your own view? In response, the Jain invokes another doctrine, that of circumscribed viewpoints or perspectives (*naya*): she acknowledges that each view is always partial; we cannot see reality as a whole, and our specific claims – about the nature of objects, self, knowledge, society, and so on – are always subject to the limitation of the conditions under which our viewpoint operates. So, in a sense, anything the Jain says is subject to her own doctrine. The doctrine of conditionality does integrate partial views, by patiently giving space for each assertion and its denial, since *every* view is subject to the sevenfold schema. Jains are therefore not being absolutists, since they acknowledge that their own views are as limited by perspective as anyone else's. Consequently, their own theories are subject to this schema! This ingenious application of a logic on itself allows the Jains to teach everyone this lesson: always acknowledge that every view and its opposite is limited in the face of reality, and thereby accommodate yourself to others.

The passing wonder of paradox: early Chinese logic

As mentioned in the introduction to this chapter, there is little need to go back to the basic and prejudiced question of whether Chinese philosophy is logical; it certainly is. Sometimes, the arguments can be restated in terms of formal Western logic, but in any case arguments use patterns of reasoning, however informal, that are immediately observable. For example, take the familiar argument form in Western logic known as *modus tollens*: if *p* ('this is a square'), then *q* ('it has four equal sides'); it is the case that *not-q* ('it does not have four equal sides'); therefore it is the case that *not-p* ('it is not a square'). Even a Confucian such as Mencius, always cautious about the misleading nature of language and analysis, demonstrates his grasp of logical patterns. There are no talented men (i.e., *not-p*), he comments; if there were talented men, then he would be bound to know them (if *p*, then *q*). (Here, 'there are talented men' = *p*; 'Mencius knows all talented men' = *q*.) It is implied that it is the case that Mencius knows none (*not-q*); hence the conclusion that there are no talented men (not-*p*).

At the same time, something quite deep in the dominant Confucian paradigm of philosophy as a practical influence is evident in another instance. In the *Analects*, there is a story of Confucius accepting an invitation to visit a rebel leader. His companion points out that Confucius himself has said that if one is a gentleman, then one enters only the presence of a good person (i.e., if *p*, then *q*). The rebel is not a good person (*not-q*). So Confucius (a gentleman) should not enter his presence (*not-p*). We should note straightaway that, even if there is a logical structure here, it is expressed in terms of ethical conduct. Tellingly, Confucius does not deny the logic; he admits that he had indeed given that advice. But, he proceeds rhetorically, has it not been said that 'hard indeed is that which can withstand grinding, white indeed is that which can withstand black dye'? The practical goal of influencing a potentially powerful ruler is greater than obeying the logic of his (Confucius's) own teaching. It is not that logical arguments are not understood; it is that they are to be put in perspective within larger, practical concerns.

The earliest explicit uses of logic are presented as entertainment, but without any attempt to present a systematic logical theory. The contexts almost always concern paradoxes, and the two most notable proponents are Hui Shi, whose work is found only in that of his friend Zhuangzi, and Gongsun Long, especially in his 'White Horse Dialogue'. A paradox is a situation generated by two statements or two sections of a statement where it appears that it is reasonable to assert each statement or section as true, but when put together, they contradict each other. The statement of the paradox is thus logically equivalent to its negation. (Technically, its truth-value is indeterminate.)

Hui Shi introduces concepts into Chinese thought that do not appear to have any practical bearing but do have interesting theoretical consequences. His core idea is expressed in a pair of definitions: the perfectly large is that which has nothing outside it, and the perfectly small is that which has nothing within it. With these ideas, he grasps the possibility that we can talk about what is limitless in terms of limits; and that generates paradox.

The striking thing about his work is that it stands on its own, without influencing the surrounding and subsequent philosophical culture. One example will show the contrasting situation in classical India. From his definitions, Hui Shi generates the following paradox: the perfectly small, which has no dimensions, cannot be accumulated, yet its size is a thousand measures. The perfectly small is, by definition, partless – it has nothing within it. But having nothing within it means that it is without dimensions, and without dimensions it cannot be added up. Yet the perfectly small is that into which things of size and dimension are ultimately reduced, so it *must* be the basic building block of the largest of things (which are of 'a thousand measures'). This is the paradox of the perfectly small. But nothing is made of this intriguing argument; it is simply presented as a teasing thought in the middle of profound explorations of the *dao*/way by Zhuangzi. We do not know what Hui Shi intended to convey by means of this paradox, but it does not engage the attention of anyone in subsequent Chinese philosophy.

By contrast, the paradox of the perfectly small or the logical atom (*anu*) plays a significant role in Indian philosophy. On the one side are Nyaya and certain Buddhist realist metaphysicians, who say that the world of ordinary objects is composed of ever smaller entities, ultimately going down to partless things (Nyaya disagrees with the Buddhist realists on the relationship between these atoms and ordinary objects). This is presented as the result of logical analysis – things must be composed of other things, until one gets to things that have no further composition. Vasubandhu, the Yogacara Buddhist who rejects the concept that there are real objects external to the mind, attacks this atomism (his critique is adapted by the Advaita school). He argues that the partless, dimensionless, perfectly small atom is an incoherent idea. For an object to be formed by logical atoms, the atoms must come together. But if they are to create size, each atom must be in partial contact with the others. However, this implies that each atom has parts! If there is no partial contact, there must be either no contact – in which case no object will be formed; or only whole contact – in which case no increase in size will be possible. The apparent paradox of the infinitely small becomes a *reductio ad absurdum* of that concept, put to metaphysical use within a much larger debate.

Returning to Hui Shi, we see him provide other paradoxes. One example is that the centre of the world is up north of Yen and down south of Yueh. By this, he appears to be indicating that if the world is infinite, its centre is everywhere, its circumference nowhere. The mathematical possibilities of this elusive statement are not pursued. Yet another paradoxical statement is important only because it appears to feed through into Zhuangzi's Daoist idea of having plural viewpoints on the same thing: the sun at its zenith is in decline, a thing alive is dying. Hui Shi presents this as a paradox arising from the infinite divisibility of time. The zenith of the sun is part of its setting, the moment of death is already a part of life. But thus rephrased, the paradoxical nature of these statements is dissolved. What is left is the use to which Zhuangzi puts it, namely, the idea that there are different ways of looking at the same *dao*/way, with no exclusive claim made of that *dao*/way, whether it is the way of the sun or the way of life.

A far more detailed example of the way paradox might have sharpened logical conception in ancient China is Gongsun Long's

White Horse paradox. From its context, it appears to have been intended as entertainment and was perhaps put forward in a flippant manner. Nothing substantial results from his casual exploration of logical concepts, and he remains an isolated example of argumentative skill, possibly limited by the absence of the paraphernalia of logical theory in his culture. Gongsun Long's opponent asks him if it is admissible that 'a white horse is not a horse', as he, Gongsun Long, is supposed to have claimed. Gongsun Long subtly reworks this to say that his claim is that 'white horse' is not (the same as) 'horse'. But, while 'a white horse is not a horse' simply is not true, the claim that 'white horse' is not the same as 'horse' is arguably true, or at any rate defensible. Very simply, the one phrase is not the same as the other. But this is not paradoxical any more. Gongsun Long has put quotation marks around what were referential terms, but of course, this is not picked up in speech, and so would initially have slipped past his audience. (In anachronistic terms, we might ask him to draw quotation marks with the fingers of each hand when he talks of 'horse' and 'white horse', in the manner made familiar in American sitcoms! But then, his audience would not have been so puzzled by the further stages of his apparent paradox.) But our explanation draws on many centuries and cultures of knowledge about quotation and other linguistic devices; and while his audience would eventually have seen through it too, one must assume that at that time it would have had the impact of a refined joke.

Gongsun Long makes a series of moves in which he explores the ways in which the concept of 'horse' is different from the concept of 'white horse'. Most of these involve nuanced ways of showing that the one concept cannot do the work of the other. The key to his argument is that even his opponent must acknowledge the difference. If the difference were not acknowledged, 'looking for a horse' on its own should mean 'looking for a brown horse', which is not true, since one could be looking for a white or some other horse. So 'looking for horse' does not do the same work as 'looking for white horse'; the combination of 'white' and 'horse' is not the same as just 'horse'. Although it cannot be said that one can have a white horse without having a horse (that would indeed be absurd), that is not what Gongsun Long means at all. 'Horse' picks out all horses – white, black or brown; 'white' is needed to pick out 'white horse' and exclude 'brown horse' and 'black horse'. That which rejects something is not the same as that which does not. Hence his conclusion that 'white horse', because it excludes things that 'horse' does not exclude (namely, brown and black horses), is different from the latter.

There are incipient notions here – of exclusion and inclusion, of the uses of the predication of qualities to objects, and of different modes of logical reasoning. But they are developed for an essentially frivolous purpose, and it has taken contemporary scholars to go back and rescue the white horse from its cultural cul-de-sac. (Incidentally, this paradox never arises in India, where an early distinction is made between the function of 'qualities' that attach to objects, and the substances that are the 'qualificands' to which qualities attach. The concept 'horse', since it only refers to the qualificand substance, is an incomplete concept, when it comes to picking out the horse with the quality of being white; the complete concept is 'white horse', a substance with quality. So the apparent difference between 'horse' and 'white horse' need not be explored, because the former is simply an incomplete concept when compared to the latter.)

The Mohist practical logic of names

It is generally accepted that the only place where systematic logical analysis is found in Chinese philosophy is the collected works of the Later Mohists. But this is not to say that they present a theory of logic comparable to the theories of Indian philosophy or Aristotle's work in ancient Greece. Rather, they engage in a form of systematic analysis that reveals awareness of several concepts in logic. Their primary concern is with the relationship between names and objects (discussed in chapters 5 and 6). In striving to make names constant with regard to objects, the Mohists develop the notion of discrimination or analysis (*bian*). Logic is theorized as a means of attaining alethic knowledge of reality in India; with Mohism, it emerges from the quest for pragmatic knowledge of how to make society stable through constancy of name usage.

That logical procedures have great pragmatic significance is evident from the Mohist declaration of the purposes of analysis. It clarifies what is correct and what is wrong in rulership; it allows for discernment of the patterns by which names are applied to objects; and it settles what is good and what is harmful in actions.

How can analysis achieve such aims? The Mohists say that the key logical concept is the assessment of contradictory claims, leading to the acceptance of the claim that alone 'fits the facts' (*dang*). In Mohism, then, logical tools are used with a clear sense of their practical value. The Mohists give as an example of contradictories the rival claims that 'this is an ox' and 'this is not an ox'; both cannot fit the facts simultaneously. Their faith that reasoning will lead to a useful conclusion is shown in their assertion that, if both claims cannot fit the facts, then necessarily one of them must fit the facts while the other must not. They believe that the logic of deciding between contradictories will lead to knowledge of what to do. Mohism defines contradictories (*fan*) as statements that cannot both be regarded as inadmissible at the same time. The example is very general: either something is an ox or it is not an ox; it cannot be neither. Ultimately, therefore, every claim can be settled, since either it or its opposite is true.

Such a view of contradictories, as applying to all disputed statements, means that Mohism trusts in eventual pragmatic settlement. This is in contrast to the Daoist claim that sometimes both opponents can be wrong (and therefore both statements inadmissible), even though, *if* one side were correct, then the other would have to be wrong. The Daoist view, though lacking an explicit logical theory, in effect plays with the concept of contraries found in Western logic: contraries are statements that can both be wrong, even though, if one were true, the other would be false. The Mohists reject this conceptual possibility. According to them, when both sides are wrong, it is merely a failure of analysis (*bian*), a failure to engage properly in dispute, as when one person calls an animal an ox and the other calls it a horse, but it is neither. This response shows that the Mohist simply rejects potential logical categories if they do not help in practice.

Most Mohist analysis, such as the categorization of names as 'unrestricted' (e.g., having to call every object a 'thing'), 'classifying' (e.g., 'horse', which has to be used if communication is to be possible) and 'private' (e.g., 'Wang', which stays confined to the person concerned), is not obviously about logical structures. But some logical practices, such as quantification and substitution, have great potential, even if they are not presented in self-conscious theory.

Quantification is the logical practice of using words like 'all' and 'some' to indicate the scope of objects to which a category is applied: for instance, 'all humans are mortal' (logically expressed as 'for all beings, if a being is human then it is mortal'); or 'some humans are greedy' ('there are some beings that are both human and greedy'). The Mohists are seeking to respond to the objection that their doctrine of universal care, or loving all people, would be impossible if there were countless numbers of people. They define 'all' as 'none not being included' (taking 'none' as an undefined and obvious term; not something that would have looked obvious in classical Indian thought!). Their opponents argue that what is countless cannot be exhausted, so if there are countless numbers of people, they cannot *all* be loved (they cannot be exhaustively loved). The Mohists disagree; even if they are countless, something can be done for everyone. Resorting to the idea of 'all' as a mass term applying to the totality of people, they argue that if people are not countless, obviously they can be exhaustively loved; but even if they are countless, since 'all' can be loved (as a totality), in that case, too, they can be loved exhaustively. The Mohists then go on to say that their opponents themselves, in asking if all can be loved or cared for, are already using 'all' in the Mohist way, applicable to the totality of humanity without counting people individually. Although the real innovation in this argument is semantic (the meaning of 'all'), nevertheless the logical operator 'all' is also used ingeniously by the Mohists.

Similarly, with substitution, the Mohists reject out of hand the White Horse paradox. Appealing to practical considerations, they say that to ride a white horse is to ride a horse. But underneath this is the beginning of the distinction between a thing and its properties (what the Indians called the qualificand and its qualifiers): something is the case, they say, only when a thing (classified as 'horse') is combined with a 'such and such' ('white').

Arguably, the Mohist emphasis on ethics and pragmatic knowledge is not only characteristic of Chinese philosophy, but also has a major impact on subsequent thinking in the dominant traditions. However, their specific method of using logical categories in clarifying their decisions on how to act did not win favour amongst other schools. When it came to social order and self-cultivation, the Confucians mostly found this insistence on analysis, which was open to anyone who was properly trained, a social challenge to their aesthetic reliance on the model activity of cultivated, elite gentlemen. And the Daoists considered any attempt to get a constant society to be doomed to failure, and although they drew on paradox and contradiction for their own free-flowing purposes, they condemned these logical strategies as precisely the cause of an artificial estrangement from natural ways of living. For any further Chinese interest in logic as the pattern of rationality, we must look to the Buddhists, whose specific use of logic for the transformation of awareness spans different Eastern traditions.

Logic for transformation: Buddhist patterns across Asia

Early in the history of Buddhist philosophical analysis, the Madhyamaka Buddhist Nagarjuna argues that debate can be purely destructive (*vitanda*) and does not need to put forward a positive view. This is a challenge to the Nyaya view that proper debate (*vada*) must be between two views, with the aim of establishing one and refuting the other. The Nyaya position is not convenient for the Madhyamaka philosophers, since their strategy is to criticize every other school in order to show that all views are 'empty' (*sunya*) and that all entities (*bhavas*) are interdependent and conditional. Madhyamaka uses a method of deconstruction (*prasanga*), in which the premises of each thesis (*pratijna*) on offer are reduced to the clinching absurdity of contradiction (an example of this, in the critique of the concept of proof, is given in chapter 6).

The aim of *prasanga* is to make a series of refutations of competing positions, thereby demonstrating that neither side has a sustainable position. From a refutation of all views, emptiness emerges. Nagarjuna sets out to provide disproofs of several key concepts on which rival views are held, such as reality ('suchness' in Buddhist parlance), causality and so on. Finally, he turns to the concept of emptiness itself. For him, emptiness is not a position, but an outcome indicated by the deconstruction of all positions. Nagarjuna develops this demanding idea by arguing that one may not say that there is emptiness, or that there is non-emptiness, or both, or neither. These are all positions, and holding any of them is to fail to realize the emptiness of emptiness.

A statement such as this suggests that the emptiness that Nagarjuna wants us to realize is something essentially anti-logical. Is he not, at the very least, rejecting the law of the excluded middle, which holds that a statement is either true or false, and no value in between? A mystical interpretation would suggest that he wants us to break out of the chains of logic, so that some sort of transcendent realization can be had. But some reflection will show that Nagarjuna is using that keystone of logic, the law of non-contradiction, to jolt us into thinking anew what emptiness means. Nagarjuna is taking us through logic, not out of it, towards emptiness.

An example familiar from modern Western philosophy of logic can be embroidered to illustrate this way of understanding him. Take the statement 'the present king of France is bald'. The apparent negation of this would be 'the present king of France is not bald'. But in fact the latter is not a negation of the former; 'the present king of France' is an empty description, there being nobody to fit it. Another way of looking at it would be to say that only by presupposing that there is a present king of France would one of the statements have to be true. As it is, when there is no present king of France, either the two statements are contraries (where if one were true, the other would be false, but both can be false), or there is no truth to be attached to either of them. Now, Nagarjuna is in the position of the person who understands that there is no king of France (the concept is 'empty'), but all the opposing philosophers think there is one, whatever their differences over whether he is bald or not. They keep telling him that he cannot simply maintain that the king is neither bald nor hairy! They miss the point. Nagarjuna is trying to get them to see that while they can make coherent remarks about such a king (for instance, have arguments about whether he would need a wig or not), the whole of their debate is empty, because the concept in question is empty. However, to the extent that he has to be involved in undermining their beliefs about the king's baldness, he himself engages in the empty talk of asking what could possibly make the king's hair grow, or why nobody has seen his head, or some such intelligible but empty question. This is a rough analogy, of course, but it imperfectly points to Nagarjuna's goal, which, as he acknowledges, is to establish that all things lack intrinsic nature even while this very statement of his lacks it. Far from disrupting logical analysis, he uses logical analysis to disrupt our deeper assumptions about what that analysis means and to what it applies.

Although the sequence and purport of Nagarjuna's deconstruction was accepted by the Madhyamaka school, a disagreement arose over how his ultimate aim – training people in preparation for eventual, liberating insight – could best be accomplished. The Tibetan tradition gives an account of the debate, and once more we see the centrality of logical concepts for Buddhist practice.

The split in Madhyamaka is between two subschools, one committed to pure deconstruction (*prasangika*) and another to the possibility of independent assertion (*svatantrika*). The former, exemplified by Buddhapalita and Candrakirti, adheres to Nagarjuna's basics. The philosophers of this subschool take the Madhyamaka strategy for demonstrating emptiness and the limits of thought to lie in the destructive refutation of each and every philosophical position or thesis on offer. When all theses have been refuted, the intellect exhausts its capacity for desire-sustaining construction, and the person is freed into emptiness, in which life is lived out without desire. The key consideration here is that all theses must be refuted, and nothing else done. This is because, they argue, when one thesis is negated through deconstruction of its claims to coherence, its contradictory is implicitly affirmed. When you negate *A*, you are committed to the assertion of *not-A*; that, after all, is what Nyaya and other schools mean by the *vada* style of debate, in which one side is refuted so that the other side can be affirmed. But Madhyamaka cannot afford that, since all views have to be negated. Therefore, once a thesis has been refuted, one must refute the counterthesis (the thesis contradicting the original thesis), even if nobody actually holds it, to ensure that it is not imputed to Madhyamaka. Refuting one thesis and its implied counterthesis after another, the Madhyamaka philosopher eventually eliminates all claims for intrinsic, non-empty nature.

Despite the apparent success of the argument that Nagarjuna does not need to do more than deconstruct all views, Bhavaviveka, the exponent of the subschool of independent assertion, maintains that there is an inherent weakness in pure deconstruction. Refutation of a thesis does not necessarily direct the defeated opponent towards what the Madhyamaka philosopher wants. Even a comprehensive series of deconstructive refutations will only accomplish the end of defeating opponents; it will never teach them what emptiness is all about. Bhavaviveka thinks that the purely deconstructionist subschool makes a leap of faith from refutation to insight. For how will the refuted opponent know what Madhyamaka seeks to convey? To attain the insight that Madhyamaka seeks, argument in support of its position is required, not just argument against others. Naturally, refutation of explicitly asserted theses by various opponents has to be undertaken; but then one must move on to give examples in support of the Madhyamaka inference of emptiness. In short, the Madhyamaka position has to be established independently and positively. Only then can refuted opponents know how to direct themselves towards the understanding of emptiness. Bhavaviveka now has to face the question of the pure deconstructionists: how can one avoid getting bogged down in implicit commitment to the counterthesis of any refuted thesis?

It is in answer to this that Bhavaviveka draws on a logical thought with a long provenance in India, made especially potent by the Yogacara logician Dinnaga: there is a form of negation that does not commit one to the counterthesis of the thesis negated. In order to see what Bhavaviveka is trying to do, we must go back through the centuries and make sense of this concept.

In ancient Indian grammar, as well as in the Mimamsa theory of action according to sacred injunctions, a distinction is made between two different sorts of injunctions that prohibit certain ritual actions. In one category, there is the following type of instruction: 'Not at ritual *A* shall mantra *y* be chanted.' The other type is a negative injunction: 'At ritual A mantra y shall not be chanted.' Both prohibit the chanting of mantra y at ritual A. The former, nonetheless, implicitly affirms something, which is that mantra y *is* to be chanted, but at some other ritual or all other rituals. (This is quite clear when the situation divides into just two possible states: telling a student negatively 'you have not failed' carries a commitment to some *other* state of affairs, namely, her having passed.) This is committed negation (*paryudasa pratisedha*). In contrast, the second form of negation implies nothing about where mantra y is to be chanted, or if it is to be chanted at all. This is commitment-free negation (*prasajya pratisedha*).

Dinnaga draws upon this distinction for his ingenious theory of how concepts name apparently external things, in spite of the fact that his metaphysics commits him to the denial of all external things. In his theory of exclusion (*apoha*, covered in chapter 6), Dinnaga says that concepts pick out their objects or delimit them through exclusion alone. The concept 'cow' is simply the exclusion of non-cows. So too with every other concept: when using a concept, one simply leaves out all others. At no point is one committed to there being real objects to refer to in the world. The obvious objection is that, by the rule of double negation, something that is not a non-cow is simply a cow. The *apoha* theory, however, insists that that rule operates only with committed negation, where negating one thing commits one to its contradictory. Commitment-free negation, on the other hand, is denial *simpliciter*. When one talks of non-cow, there is no implicit reference to cow, only a denial of non-cows. So, to talk of 'cow' as 'not non-cow' is not to commit oneself covertly to a thing like a cow, but merely to say that at that point one is not talking of anything else. In this way, concepts identify without commitment to real things.

Bhavaviveka is impressed by this use of negation in epistemology. With the use of commitment-free negation, a thesis refuted is not a counterthesis supported. Refutation is just refutation. The Madhyamaka philosopher can refute a position without being saddled with its opposite. He is then free to go on to argue positively for his own view.

Underlying the intra-Madhyamaka debate is the common Buddhist technique of using logic as a method for transforming awareness. Even with Dinnaga, it is a way of showing people how their ordinary use of ideas is possible within an extraordinary view of the world. (He does this, of course, to bring people to a detachment from the world of objects; with the realization that objects are not real, the desire for them will vanish.)

The dual concept of negation also made its way into Chinese Buddhism, which was mainly influenced by Yogacara, through the *Nyayapravesa*, a short manual by Sankarasvamin on Dinnaga's logic. It was translated into the Chinese by Xuanzang (and further clarified by his pupil Guiji). They introduce Dinnaga's definition of negation by exclusion through the Chinese concept of 'blocking' or 'keeping out' (*zhe*) what 'is not'/is wrong (*fei*). So, the ancient Chinese notion of negation, which is an ethical concept of holding that something is not to be done or is not to be taken as correct, is married to the logical operator 'not', introduced from Indian thought. Guiji then proceeds to say that a thesis can be established in one of two ways. One is 'pure negation', as in 'The "I" does not exist', in which the 'I' is simply denied without being categorized as a non-existent. This is straight out of Dinnaga. The other way of establishing a thesis is through the method of 'negation and affirmation', as when one says 'the Buddha-nature is eternal', thereby indirectly negating non-eternality. This is an intriguing variation on the Indian Buddhist use of different forms of negation.

Chinese Buddhist logic (*yin ming*) was caught in a context all of its own. Whereas the Indian Buddhists had argued against other schools and amongst their own well-established subschools, the Chinese Buddhists had only this one logic text to work on and nobody to argue with on common terms. Chinese Buddhist logic found no engagement with Confucianism or Daoism, and concentrated for a few centuries on internally developing the classical distinctions of Indian logic through native Chinese concepts. A good example is the distinction between substance/qualificand and attribute/quality, the absence of which we saw played a role in the ancient White Horse paradox. In some cases, there was development on the Sanskrit original. For example, Xuanzang appears to improve on Dinnaga's three conditions for inference by introducing precision through quantification (the Mohist discussion of which was mentioned above). Where the original goes 'the inferential sign must be found in the location', Xuanzang phrases it as 'at least *some* sign must be found…'. The original 'the sign must be found in a similar location' becomes '*all* signs must be found…'; and 'the sign must not be found in a dissimilar location' is worded as '*no* sign must be found…'. Sadly, the circumstances were such that this breakthrough found no sustained interest in Chinese philosophy. In any case, the use of logic to establish Yogacara idealism, while faithfully re-creating standard Indian arguments, simply did not fit into the largely ametaphysical framework of Chinese philosophy, and Chinese Buddhism itself gradually became more integrated into larger Chinese philosophical concerns.

We see, then, that Buddhist logic deserves to be seen in a category of its own because of its particular use in training awareness for the attainment of enlightenment. Far from being anti-logical, when Buddhism uses logic, it does so with precision and rigour, but with the explicit end of liberation in mind.

In the last case we shall consider, however, which concerns Koan Zen, it is not clear whether anti-logical procedures are indeed important for the attainment of enlightenment. The Rinzai subschool of Japanese Zen Buddhism, in particular, employs *koan*s in spiritual training. A *koan* is a puzzle (*kongan*), a statement that is meant to engage the student's mind in a way that the teacher judges appropriate. Many clearly do not make sense at first reading: 'What is the sound of one hand clapping?' is a celebrated example from the cluster of *koan*s known as the One Hand ('What is the form of the one hand?' is another). Others are stories that have only a superficial semantic sense, where their apparent meaningfulness immediately gives way to bewilderment: the monk asked the master, 'what are you thinking?' The master said, 'I think of not-thinking.' 'How can one think of not-thinking?' The master replied, 'Not-thinking.'

It is clear that the initial impact of a *koan* depends on its not making sense. It arrests the mind by challenging logic. Its role in helping a student towards meditative facility and spiritual insight at this stage appears to lie in focusing the mind, like any puzzle does. What happens next is that the baffled student keeps thinking about it until a semblance of intelligibility emerges, and an apparent solution presents itself. However, this solution is deceptive, as further probing shows it to be irrelevant, incomplete, incoherent or in some other way problematic, and the student is off again...

The uncertainty about *koan*s is over what happens next. The anti-logic view is that the constant failure of solutions eventually exhausts the mind's capacity to seek and rest on logic and language. With the exhaustion of cognitive resources, and without the support of logic and language, a person's ordinary awareness breaks down, allowing it to be transformed into free consciousness, which is enlightenment. *Koan*s are without logic, and because logic is part of the unliberated life, it is by seeing past it that one is liberated.

By contrast, the logic-oriented view of *koan*s, famously articulated by the Zen philosopher Dogen, is that language and logic themselves liberate, since liberation requires discernment, and discernment comes through language and logic. The paradox of language and logic – indeed, of analysis as a whole – is that, while enlightenment transcends it, it takes awareness of the power of language and logic to achieve that enlightenment. Dogen uses a variety of lexical strategies to release what he sees as the hidden meaning of *koan*s. In the case of the non-thinking monk, for example, he plays with the questions and answers, rearranging the words, so that 'I think of not-thinking' becomes 'thinking is not-thinking', and 'how can one think of not-thinking' becomes 'not-thinking is how thinking is'. This begins the process of radically revising expectations about these concepts. Ordinary thinking is presented as ultimately not-thinking. If thinking is meant to relate to reality, but thought is full of its own constructs, it does not attain the state of lucid and pure realization of buddha-nature (which is emptiness, the state of being free of the imaginary metaphysics of self, objects and desires). So thinking is never what it takes itself to be; it is, in relation to the realization of emptiness, actually not-thinking. Real thinking, on the other hand, being empty of ordinary thoughts, is therefore actually 'non-(ordinary) thinking' – it is the mental state that is free of ordinary thinking. Dogen's reworking of the *koan* leads to a sophisticated under-standing of Buddhist teaching. Again and again, he reads *koan*s through different interpretive devices, rearranging the words to tease out Buddhist meaning. He thereby demonstrates that *koan*s can be analysed logically; they are not meant to thwart analysis but promote it! Here, one can compare his approach to that of the Indian dialecticians, Buddhist and Hindu, who hold that analysis is central to transformation of consciousness.

But there is, nevertheless, something beyond this. Obviously, I have not undergone any spiritual transformation upon thinking my way through the *koan* above; so, surely, analysis does not suffice? This is always a problem for those who would preserve logic on the path to liberation. The proper response should be that there is no denying the need for many other virtues to accompany analysis. Working on a *koan* will involve austerity, calmness, other meditative techniques, perhaps even the culti-vation of skills, from martial arts to flower-arrangement (*ikebana* arose out of practical *koan*s given to women practitioners in early

Zen). The intellectual answer will not suffice. Zen masters exhort students not to be contented with the obvious if clever answers to the *koan* of the One Hand (either by saying 'silence' or by showing a hand to enact silence). They may have to wear out many meditation cushions, seeking insight....

All that can be said of insight is that, when it comes, one feels 'this is it!'; but the content of awareness when that happens is only for the person who has it. Given that that is the end-point of the *koan*'s work, it is easy to see that it would be tempting for practitioners to give up on logical analysis, claiming that they have gone past it! That is always the problem with making logic do more than its analytic work: one never knows exactly when to stop.

Glossary of Names and Schools

The following is an alphabetical ordering of the principal names and schools in the history of philosophy in India, China and Japan. The aim is to indicate the rough historical period of the thinkers mentioned in this book and their place in the tradition, and hence to give a basic orientation to the reader and to avoid the need to constantly repeat the dates and historical period of philosophers. Although the dates of some figures are known with great precision, not only are others datable only to within a century, there are basic questions about the very existence of the authors of certain bodies of texts. Frequently, a single name has come to be associated with a text which is very likely to have been composed by several people over a period of time. It seems best to approximate dates to a century, just to provide a broad temporal bearing; and also to attribute the date to the named figure with whom a text is associated, regardless of whether we know him to be a historical figure or not. All dates refer to the Common Era (CE), unless otherwise indicated.

China
Cheng brothers (11th cent), Chenghao and Chengi, followers of Zhou Duni, who carry forward early Neo-Confucian philosophy.

Confucius (6th–5th cent BCE) (Kongzi), generally taken as the baseline in Chinese philosophy, although some works pre-date him. He is said to have founded the school of Ru (*Ru-jia*), although it is generally called Confucianism. His teachings are recorded in the *Analects* (*Lun You*), but other hands contributed to the version as we have it.

Fazang (7th–8th cent), an important exponent of the Huayen Buddhist school.

Gongsun Long (4th–3rd cent BCE), associated with the school of Logic. At least two chapters, including the famous 'White Horse Dialogue', are certainly his, within a collection called *Gongsun Longzi*.

Han Feizi (3rd cent BCE), the only attributed author in a collection of texts on statecraft classified under the school of Law, or Legalism.

Heshang Gong (4th cent), author of a commentary on the *Laozi*, belonging to the school of Neo-Daoism.

Huang-Lao school (3rd–2nd cent BCE), a school which brought together Legalism and the mystical statecraft of Laozi.

Huayen (5th–8th cent), a Chinese school of Buddhism, based on the interpretation of the Flower Garland text, translated from Sanskrit. It shows some influence of Daoism; Fazang (7th cent) is its most influential thinker.

Hui Shi (late 4th cent BCE), a figure associated with the School of Logic (the *Ming-jia*), but found only in the stories of his friend Zhuangzi.

Laozi (a supposed contemporary of Confucius), the legendary figure to whom the *Laozi* or *Daode Jing*, the first major work of Daoism, is attributed. The date of this work appears to be 4th cent BCE; the text itself is in many fragments.

Legalism (*Fa-jia*), a school, dominant especially in the 3rd century BCE, whose rigid support for a totalitarian implementation of obedience to the state was decisively rejected in the establishment of Confucianism as state doctrine in the 2nd cent BCE. Han Feizi is the only named thinker associated with this school.

Logic, School of (the *Ming-jia*) (4th–3rd cent BCE), the name given to a small number of ancient Chinese thinkers who tackled topics in logic such as paradoxes; Gongsun Long's White Horse paradox is the best-known work of these thinkers.

Mencius (4th cent BCE) (Mengzi), an early follower of Confucius, whose discussions and sayings are recorded in a book that bears his name. He subsequently became almost as influential in the interpretation of Confucianism as Confucius himself.

Mohist school or the **Neo- or Later Mohists** (4th–3rd cent BCE), a group of anonymous followers of Mozi. Their collective work is called the *Mohist Canons*, preserved as part of the *Mozi*. Mohism did not survive the establishment of the Confucian hegemony in the 2nd century BCE.

Mozi (5th cent BCE), a self-made thinker from the artisan classes and founder of the Mohist school (*Mo-jia*). His own arguments are recorded along with those of his immediate followers in the *Mozi*.

Neo-Confucianism, the name given to reinterpretations of Confucianism after the mid-9th century, when the Tang dynasty started persecuting Buddhism, so leading to its loss of dominance in China. Its followers call it the Learning of Nature and Principle (*xinglixue*).

Qan Buddhism, an important school of Chinese Buddhism, which spread to Japan as Zen.

Wang Bi (3rd cent), author of an influential commentary on the *Laozi*, belonging to the school of Neo-Daoism.

Xuanzang (7th cent), the first philosopher to attempt to explain Indian Buddhist logic (*yin ming*) in Chinese terms.

Xunzi (3rd cent BCE), a Confucian whose reading held sway over theories of rulership in China for a while.

Wang Yangming (15th–16th cent), the principal thinker behind the move of Confucianism towards an assimilation of Buddhist idealism.

Yong Jia (10th cent), a proponent of Qan Buddhism who argues for a unitary mind free of the constraints of the world.

Zhangzai (11th cent), originator of many new themes in Neo-Confucianism.

Zhou Duni (10th–11th cent), the first major Neo-Confucian thinker.

Zhuangzi (late 4th cent BCE), the author of some sections of the composite work called the *Zhuangzi* and the subject of anonymous stories in other sections. He is one of the two earliest and most influential figures in Daoist philosophy (the other being Laozi).

Zhuxi (12th cent), an extremely dominant influence on Neo-Confucianism, thought of as the second Confucius.

Zongmi (9th cent), a philosopher of both Huayen and Qan Buddhism, uniquely a patriarch (formally appointed leader) of the religious traditions of both these schools.

Japan

Dogen (13th cent), the most important philosopher of Zen Buddhism, especially in his work, the *Shobogenzo*.

Honen (12th cent), the founder of Japanese Pure Land Buddhism.

Kumazawa Banzan (17th cent), a Neo-Confucian interpreter of Japanese philosophy in response to the challenge of European culture.

Nakae Toju (17th cent), the first to introduce Neo-Confucianism to Japanese philosophy.

Nichiren (13th cent), a follower of the Pure Land Buddhist doctrine; his particular interest was the Japanese translation of the Indian Buddhist text, the *Lotus Sutra*.

Ogyu Sorai (17th–18th cent), a Neo-Confucian who makes a determined effort to go back to the wisdom of classical China as a response to the challenge of European culture.

Pure Land Buddhism, a Japanese tradition, founded by Honen.

Zen Buddhism, from the 12th century onwards, an influential Japanese form of Buddhism, with several subschools; it had an impact on aspects of culture ranging from tea ceremonies to martial arts.

India

Schools are given separate entries only if no author from them is named in this book.

Abhidharma (4th cent BCE–1st cent CE), the name given to the earliest collection of Buddhist philosophy, written in demotic Pali and Prakrit, rather than the high Sanskrit of the brahmins/Hindu thinkers.

Advaita Vedanta, founded by Sankara in the 8th century, the earliest systematic interpretation of the ancient Upanisads; it is represented both by a series of commentaries and sub-commentaries on Sankara, and by various independent works.

Aranyakas, see Vedas.

Bhagavad Gita (2nd cent BCE), the Song of the Lord, a composition supposed to report the teachings of Krishna, God incarnate. It succinctly presents the dominant philosophical themes of that time as they become evident in the later tradition.

Bhartrhari (6th–7th cent), a grammarian who, though independent, invokes themes from Vedanta philosophy.

Bhavaviveka (7th cent), a commentator on Nagarjuna's Madhyamaka Buddhist philosophy, especially well-known in later Tibetan Buddhism.

Brahmanas, see Vedas.

Buddha (the Enlightened One) (6th–5th cent BCE), the founder of Buddhism, whose name before his enlightenment was Prince Gautama Siddhartha.

Buddhapalita (6th cent), a commentator of the Madhyamaka school.

Candrakirti (7th cent), the most authoritative commentator on Nagarjuna's Madhyamaka Buddhist philosophy.

Dharma Sutras (4th–1st cent BCE), a collection of texts on law and social order, five or six of which are highly influential.

Dharmakirti (7th cent), responsible for developing the early ideas of Dinnaga within Yogacara Buddhism.

Dinnaga (6th cent), a Yogacara Buddhist who developed new directions in Indian logic and language; he is usually called a Buddhist Logician.

Dvaita (Dualism) **Vedanta,** the last of the three major Vedanta schools, founded by Madhva in the 13th century; its theology is associated with a religious sect that continues to this day.

Gautama (3rd–1st cent BCE), the traditional name for the author of the first text of the Nyaya school, the *Nyaya Sutra*.

Jaimini (3rd–1st cent BCE), the traditional name for the author of the first text of the Mimamsa school, the *Mimamsa Sutra*.

Jainism, the religion founded by Mahavira, and the key contributor to Indian philosophy that is neither Hindu nor Buddhist.

Jayarasi Bhatta (7th cent), an independent and sceptical thinker who associates himself with the materialistic Lokayata school.

Kamalasila (7th–8th cent), a student of Santaraksita, who joined him in the enterprise of synthesizing Yogacara and Madhyamaka Buddhist philosophies, which he introduced to Tibet.

Kautalya (3rd cent BCE), the author of the single most important work on political science in ancient India, the *Artha Sastra.*

Kumarila (7th–8th cent), the founder of a subschool of Mimamsa philosophy.

Lokayata, the lone ancient Indian school that is strictly materialistic, denying anything beyond the physical world. Apart from a book by Jayarasi Bhatta, its ideas are known mostly from critiques in the works of other schools.

Madhva (13th cent), the founder of Dvaita Vedanta, the last of the three major Vedanta schools.

Madhyamaka, a Buddhist school, normally taken to be founded by Nagarjuna (1st cent). The school flourished in India for nearly a thousand years, and some variants of it became influential in Tibet from the 7th century.

Mahabharata (4th cent BCE–2nd cent CE), a poetic composition, the longest single work of literature in the world and one of the so-called 'Indian epics' (the other being a somewhat shorter poetic narrative, the *Ramayana*). It is often used as a source for examples in Hindu ethics and philosophy of religion.

Mahavira (6th–5th cent BCE), known as Vardhammana, the founder of Jainism; so called from his title Jina, or conqueror (of the conditions of life).

Mahayana, one of the main forms of Buddhism (distinguished from the Theravada), which developed around the 1st cent BCE with the aim of widening the social and ethical bases of Buddhism from what it believed to be the narrow and strict definition of Buddhism given by the earlier Theravada. The majority of Indian and all Tibetan, Chinese and Japanese Buddhist philosophers are Mahayana.

Manu Smrti (2nd cent BCE), a significant text on social order and personal duty, considered separate from the *Dharma Sutra* texts, although it deals with the same issues.

Mimamsa, the School of Exegesis, so called because it is committed to the close interpretation of the sacred Hindu texts. It is based on the root text of Jaimini's *Mimamsa Sutra* (c. 2nd–1st cent BCE); in the 7th century it splits into two major schools, founded by Kumarila and Prabhakara.

Nagarjuna (1st–2nd cent), the founder of the Madhyamaka Buddhist school.

Nyaya, usually called the School of Logic (although it in fact treats all the major issues in Indian philosophy) and based on the root text, Gautama's *Nyaya Sutra* (3rd–1st cent BCE). It had become synthesized with the Vaisesika school by the 9th century.

Panini (5th–4th cent BCE), responsible, in his *Astadhyayi*, for the first systematic study of grammar, which subsequently has a major influence on Indian philosophy.

Patanjali (3rd cent BCE), a commentator on Panini's grammar.

Prabhakara (7th–8th cent), the founder of a subschool of Mimamsa philosophy.

Ramanuja (11th–12th cent), the founder of the Visistadvaita (Qualified Non-dualism) Vedanta school and the most significant systematic theologian of Hinduism; the religious sect associated with his lineage still flourishes.

Sankara (8th–9th cent), the founder of the Advaita (non-Dualist) Vedanta school; his works have made him possibly the most influential of all Hindu philosophers.

Sankhya, one of the schools of Hindu philosophy, the first text of which is the now-lost *Sankhya Sutra* of Kapila (3rd–1st cent BCE).

Santaraksita (7th–8th cent), responsible for synthesizing Yogacara and Madhyamaka Buddhist philosophies.

Sautrantika, a school of the early Buddhist tradition of Theravada.

Siddhasena (6th cent CE), a Jain philosopher, author of the *Sanmatitirka*, and one of the most influential Jain philosophers.

Theravada, the Doctrine of the Elders, the form of Buddhism that takes its orientation from the Buddhist texts that contain the earliest record of the teachings of the Buddha. It was the first systematically organized sect in Buddhism, and is the dominant form in contemporary Southeast Asia.

Udayana (11th cent), a Nyaya philosopher associated with developing the school into its 'new' phase.

Upanisads (11th–3rd cent BCE), the first compositions in India with explicitly philosophical themes; although there are many, between 10 and 14 major ones command later commentarial attention.

Vacaspati (10th cent), an encyclopedic thinker, author of commentaries on almost all the Hindu schools, but especially famed for his work on the schools of Advaita and Nyaya.

Vaibhasika, a school of the early Buddhist tradition of Theravada.

Vaisesika, one of the traditional Hindu schools, dominant in the 5th and 6th centuries, eventually assimilated into Nyaya.

Vasubandhu (5th cent), an influential early thinker of the Yogacara Buddhist school.

Vatsyayana (5th cent), the author of the commentary *Nyaya Bhasya*, which is on the first text of the Nyaya school, the *Nyaya Sutra* of Gautama.

Vedanta, the general name for all the Hindu schools that rely upon the root text of Badarayana's *Vedanta Sutra* (2nd–1st cent BCE), which is itself a summary of the teachings of the Upanisads; the name means either the end or the summation of the Vedas. Advaita, Visistadvaita and Dvaita are the three main Vedanta schools, but there are also several less influential systems.

Vedas, Brahmanas and Aranyakas (15th–9th cent BCE), four works which, together with their appended texts, form the roots of Indian philosophy. Although they themselves are not recognizably given to philosophy, seminal concepts found in them, as well as their status as the sacred fount of all knowledge in later Hinduism, make them the starting-point for Indian philosophy.

Yoga (3rd to 2nd cent BCE), a traditional Indian school based on the *Yoga Sutra* of Patanjali (a semi-historical figure distinct from the philosopher of grammar). It was assimilated first into the Sankhya school and then taken up by virtually all other Hindu and Buddhist schools for its techniques.

Yogacara, a Buddhist school, extant from about the 2nd century but established on a philosophical footing by Vasubandhu in the 5th century; it is also called Vijnanavada (Doctrine of Mind) and Cittamatra (Consciousness-Only). The Yogacara thinkers Dinnaga (6th cent), Dharmakirti (7th cent) and their commentators are often called the Buddhist Logicians for their pioneering work on logic. This school dominates the subsequent Buddhist tradition in Tibet from the 7th century.

Further Reading

General

Deutsch, Eliot and Ron Bontekoe (eds), *A Companion to World Philosophies* (Oxford: Blackwell, 1997). A good collection of essays by experts, written in a systematic and accessible manner and also including Islamic and other philosophical traditions.

Scharfstein, Ben-Ami, *A Comparative History of World Philosophy* (Albany: State University of New York Press, 1998). A massive but generally accessible work, focusing on specific thinkers from Western, Indian and Chinese traditions.

Smart, Ninian, *World Philosophies* (London: Routledge, 1999). A sweeping and entertaining (if necessarily superficial) read.

Chinese philosophy

Graham, Angus C., *Disputers of the Tao: philosophical argument in ancient China* (LaSalle, Ill.: Open Court, 1989). The most authoritative study of classical Chinese philosophy; lets the texts speak through extensive translation accompanied by mostly non-technical analysis.

Hall, David L. and Roger T. Ames, *Thinking through Confucius* (New York: State University of New York Press, 1987). An influential and entertaining study of the contemporary relevance of Confucius.

Hansen, Chad, *A Daoist Theory of Chinese Thought: a philosophical interpretation* (Oxford: Oxford University Press, 1992). A magisterial and highly original analysis of classical Chinese philosophy.

Harbsmeier, Christoph, 'Language and Logic', in Joseph Needham (ed), *Science and Civilisation in China*, vol 7 (Cambridge: Cambridge University Press, 1998). A scholarly and detailed survey, accessible to the non-specialist.

Schwartz, Benjamin, *The World of Thought in Ancient China* (Cambridge, Mass.: Harvard University Press, 1985). A relatively accessible and fluently written interpretation of classical Chinese philosophy.

Buddhist philosophy

Conze, Edward, *Buddhism: its essence and development* (Oxford: B. Cassier, 1951). Several reprints exist of a dated but still classic treatment for the general reader.

McGovern, William M., *Introduction to Mahayana Buddhism: with special reference to Chinese and Japanese phases* (Columbia: South Asia Books, 1997). A clear and systematic account.

Warder, A. K., *Indian Buddhism* (Delhi: Motilal Benarsidass, 2nd edition, 1980; and other editions). Competent and clear introduction by a significant scholar of the early 20th century.

Williams, Paul, *Buddhist Thought: a complete guide to the Indian tradition* (New York: Routledge, 2000). A sound introduction.

Indian philosophy

Ganeri, Jonardon (ed), *The Collected Essays of Bimal Krishna Matilal* (Delhi: Oxford University Press, 2002). Covering some of the work of a great interpreter of Indian philosophy, it includes both technical and more popular essays.

Krishna, Daya, *Indian Philosophy: a counterperspective* (Delhi: Oxford University Press, 1991). A provocative and accessible reading of the tradition.

Matilal, Bimal K. (J. Ganeri and H. Tiwari, eds), *The Character of Logic in India* (Albany: State University of New York Press, 1998). An excellent and concise book for the non-specialist.

Mohanty, Jitendranath, *Classical Indian philosophy* (Lanham, Md.: Rowman & Littlefield Publishers, 2000). A succinct yet sophisticated introduction for the general reader by a leading philosopher.

Index